197

THE Goddess REVIVAL

AÍDA BESANÇON SPENCER

WITH

DONNA F. G. HAILSON

CATHERINE CLARK KROEGER

& WILLIAM DAVID SPENCER

Baker Books

A Division of Baker Book House Co
Grand Rapids, Michigan 49516

© 1995 by Aida Besançon Spencer, Donna F. G. Hailson, Catherine Clark Kroeger, and William David Spencer

Published by Baker Books
a division of Baker Book House Company
P.O. Box 6287, Grand Rapids, MI 49516-6287

Printed in the United States of America

Library of Congress Cataloging-in-Publication Data

The goddess revival / Aida Besançon Spencer . . . [et al.].
p. cm.
Includes bibliographical references and index.
ISBN 0-8010-8385-0
1. Goddess religion—Controversial literature. 2. Apologetics.
3. Evangelicalism. I. Spencer, Aida Besançon.
BL473.5.G62 1995
239'.9—dc20   94-41977

CONTENTS

Portraits in the Dawn

The Painter of the morning is a kin to the wind
and deftly paints a portrait in the dawn.
Chameleon leaves of autumn in the springtime of their change
shatter night to frozen sunbeams on the lawn.
    Take a breath; it is past.
    Colors dying, fading fast.
    Crystals melting in the grass,
    Death's the image in their glass.
Ink's blotting out the portrait in the dawn.

The tree of earth's a mother giving shelter to her brood.
A bough of clouds can shield a world away.
Passing time has marked her life in cycled growing rings
of endless day and night and day and night and day.
    Ah, rip the gauze blind from your eyes!
    Watch her sway with tired sighs.
    See that sleep is drawing nigh.
    Even great sequoias die.
Ink's blotting out the portrait in the dawn.

If you must sing, here is a funeral dirge
to the helpless gods as they return.
If you must write, here is a eulogy.
Dedicate it to the emptiness you learn.

You called the dawn another name and not so long ago,
seeing chariots not brushes in the sky.
Not sunflakes but tears were the crystals on your lawn.
Not a painting but a chessboard was the sky.
    God and goddess ruled your fate,
    by capricious love and hate,
    in your spell and song and play,
    so the Great God turned away.
Ink's blotting out the portrait in the dawn.

The morning is a cushion set upon the bench of earth.
Its embroidery depicts God's acts of love.
We rest upon God's footrest in the household that is grace.
As God's Spirit fills the universe above,
    god and goddess bend the knee,
    and confess their fealty,
    to the great Divinity,
    to whom lasting praises be,
etched out in the portrait of the dawn.

a song by William David Spencer, ©1967, 1993

PREFACE

*T*he whole idea of this book began with the Northeast Evangelical Theological Society executive team. In February of 1990 they designed a conference on neopaganism. Dr. Mark Shaw, professor of the Seminary of the East, asked if I would give a plenary talk on the New Feminism. What should biblical feminists think of such a movement? Can evangelical feminism be saved from this type of secular feminism? When I asked him what raised these questions to his mind, he mentioned Kathleen Hirsch's *Boston Globe Magazine* article on "Feminism's New Face."[1] He kindly sent me the article (which I still have). When I presented my thoughts at the conference, Rev. H. Malcolm Newton, then studying at Harvard Divinity School, (now president of International Black Evangelicals United) asked if I would present the same talk there in October. That same year I was asked to present a talk for the Institute of Biblical Research National's November meeting in Kansas City. When I asked IBR member Dr. Edwin Yamauchi, professor of history at Miami University in Ohio, for an idea, he was intrigued by this same topic: "God as Mother, Not Mother as God: A Biblical Feminist Response to the 'New Feminism.'" At that presentation Baker editor Allan Fisher was present. He asked me to develop the talk into a book. By that time, I had had the article published by *Priscilla Papers*.[2] When we were all completing our first drafts of the book in November 1993 already the influence of goddess spirituality was affecting many churches, well publicized by the World Council of Churches' conference on "Re-Imagining . . . God, Community, and the Church."[3]

Sometimes an author gets inspiration for a book and seeks out publishers until after a lengthy siege one publisher succumbs. This book is not one of those. This book came from requests. My only qualifications for preparing it were love of God, concern for the church and especially for women's participation in it, specializing in biblical interpretation, and, hopefully, some well-balanced wisdom. I am professor of New Testament at Gordon-Conwell Theological Seminary in South Hamilton, Massachusetts. I have written *Beyond the Curse: Women Called to Ministry,* now published by Hendrickson in Peabody. I have studied biblical style (*Paul's Literary Style*), as well as other topics. Goddess feminism is so broad with so many challenges to the church, I asked a team of experts to work with me.

I asked my husband, the Rev. Dr. William David Spencer, adjunct professor of theology at Gordon-Conwell Theological Seminary, who for years had been interested in the Rastafari cult (some of whom worship Emperor Haile Selassie I of Ethiopia), to write a chapter on the male deities now being worshiped (chapter 2). He now is completing the manuscript *Dread Jesus,* a book on Rastafarion Christology. His specialty is the theological analysis of popular culture. Everyone mentions female deities. But, what about male deities?

I have also asked the Rev. Donna F. G. Hailson, a former Gordon-Conwell student, now a pastor and founder of Evangel Ministries, working on a doctorate contrasting the new age, Goddess revival, and Christianity, to write a chapter giving a broad overview of Goddess spirituality (chapter 1). Whenever people have a question on the New Age or cults in our area, they are told to contact Donna.

Since so many deities now being lauded were originally worshiped during Bible times, I also asked Dr. Catherine Clark Kroeger, adjunct associate professor of Classical and Ministry Studies at Gordon-Conwell, and co-author of *I Suffer Not a Woman* (Baker), to write a chapter from the perspective of the first century (chapter 3). What were these deities really like? Specialists on the Greco-Roman world, Greek, and women are very few.

I could then be free to analyze from a biblical perspective the writings on goddess feminism.

I thought I had my team ready. God, though, sent me two more workers. A new parishioner in our church, I discovered, had been seduced by witchcraft for some years, a witchcraft that highlighted the goddess. Now she is a devout and strong Christian. I asked Lupe

Rosalez to give me a brief account of what enticed her (appendix A). Her coworker, Peter King, had helped her leave the coven. Could he share how he helped her (appendix B)?

Therefore, I have an exceptional team on this project: practical and experiential, and thoughtful, analytical, and scholarly.

Even though each writer is ultimately responsible for every chapter, Bill and I have read the whole manuscript and made suggestions. Wendy O'Brien eagerly served as a research assistant for Donna Hailson, as well as read an early version of the manuscript. Lawyer Betsy Cunningham has also read the manuscript.

I tried to approach this topic with grace and truth. I hope you, too, will approach this book and this movement with both of these key godly qualities.

Other people also were part of our team. Faculty secretary, Heidi Hudson, is always fantastic. She received the news of typing this book with enthusiasm. She is an efficient, hard-working, and positive typist. Thanks Heidi! Although Goddard Library at Gordon-Conwell had a number of the books I needed, I still had to order many books through interlibrary loan. I am deeply appreciative of Meredith M. Kline, Goddard Library assistant for technical services and interlibrary loan, and Norman Anderson, Goddard head librarian, for all their help in obtaining books. Several publishers were also kind enough to mail me some books: Harper and Row, Paulist, InterVarsity, Abingdon, Continuum, Word, Fortress, and Eerdmans.

My hope is that this work is glorifying to God and a service to the church and to many.

Aída Besançon Spencer

CONTRIBUTORS

Aída Besançon Spencer

Ph.D. in New Testament Studies from Southern Baptist Theological Seminary.

Since 1970 she has been studying the role of women in the church, from a biblical perspective. She has authored *Beyond the Curse: Women Called to Ministry* (Hendrickson), as well as *Paul's Literary Style* in the Evangelical Theological Society Monograph Series. She co-authored with William *Joy through the Night: Biblical Resources for Suffering People* (InterVarsity), *2 Corinthians*, Bible Study Commentary (Zondervan), and *The Prayer Life of Jesus* (University Press of America), as well as many articles.

She is professor of New Testament at Gordon-Conwell Theological Seminary and pastor of organization with the Pilgrim Church of Beverly, Massachusetts.

Donna F. G. Hailson

M. Div. from Gordon-Conwell Theological Seminary.

She is pursuing a Ph.D. in Religious Studies (cult research) through the University of Stirling, Scotland. She is researching the many threads of the New Age movement, especially contrasting Christianity with Goddess Revival and the New Age movement.

She is pastor of the First Baptist Church of Hampton, New Hampshire, and founder and president of the Massachusetts-based Turning Point. With the latter, she serves as a lecturer and consultant on

11

cults and the occult. She works with therapists who are counseling individuals who have come out of these backgrounds; teaches in the churches; advises pastors; and ministers one-on-one to present and former cult adherents and occult practitioners.

Her ministry has been profiled during an internationally-telecast Billy Graham Crusade and, for that evangelist's organization, she created a film on ministering to those caught up in the occult.

Catherine Clark Kroeger

Ph.D. in Classical Ava Studies at University of Minnesota.

She is one of very few scholars whose research blends archaeology and ancient texts, a classicist, and New Testament scholar whose graduate work centered on women in ancient religions. She is adjunct associate professor of Classical and Ministry Studies at Gordon-Conwell Theological Seminary and President of Christians for Biblical Equality, as well as author of many articles and *I Suffer Not a Woman* (Baker), an in-depth study of 1 Timothy 2:12–15.

William David Spencer

Th.D. in Theology and Literature at Boston University.

He has researched cultic thought for 27 years, and is a specialist in West Indian theology. His specialties are theology, biblical theology, and popular culture. He has written the well received "Practical Male Afterword" in *Beyond the Curse* as well as many articles, some of which are on biblical feminism, and several books: the groundbreaking *Mysterium and Mystery* (Southern Illinois), *2 Corinthians, Prayer Life of Jesus,* and *Joy Through the Night.* He is pastor of encouragement at Pilgrim Church in Beverly, Massachusetts, and an adjunct professor of Theology at Gordon-Conwell Theological Seminary.

INTRODUCTION

A small muscle becomes a small home. And in this home lives a small being, no windows, no sky, and the door is never open. But the small being is most likely happy floating in a small, warm sea of nutrients, as long as no pollutants enter. Far away can be heard a gentle voice, and a regular pulsating beat creates a musical background. Sometimes the sea would turn bright red. Comfortable and soothed, the child feels. But every once in a while the walls press in and press out until one moment when these walls press so hard that the door opens and the child feels itself rejected and ejected from this all sufficient womb. Some children slide out backwards content to let the waters and the pressure take them where they will. But others want to see and jerkily come out on their chins with their eyes wide open. Now, for the first time, they will see the sky, if the sky is dark. They will breathe the air of a new, larger womb. They will see the face and the body of the gentle voice and beating heart. But they will continue to feel and touch, too. Many babies will be placed on their mother's chest and rest peacefully on that recognized heart beat. When they are held by the arms of their loving father, they recognize his voice too, and are happy and at peace.[1]

Birth is a synecdoche of ways to perceive life. A synecdoche is a part representing a whole. The sense of having one's total world all around one is the sense of immanence. The mother is experienced first as this all-encompassing presence in the womb.[2] Thus, for many people immanence and mother, or feminine, are associated with each other. The appreciation of percussion may also be associated with immanence, because the heart beats may have been felt by the fetus. Close relationships may also be associated with immanence too, for who could be closer than a mother and an embryo, yet, ironically, strangers too? Similarly, Jürgen Moltmann wisely perceives that we know so little about the Holy Spirit because the Spirit is too close, not because the Spirit is so far away from us.[3] As Jesus says, we can not see the wind but we can only hear and feel its effects (John 3:8). The leaves move. The trees may shake. Our skin may feel cool. But we can not see the wind itself. Similarly, the child and the mother are very close to each other, but they only perceive each others' effects. Bill and Aída remember at five months in the womb, Bill hearing a thump and Aída feeling a quiver from Steve's kick. Yet neither the parents nor the child saw each other face to face.

For other people, that departure from the womb becomes a historical truth that must be hidden, ignored, and repressed. That first sense of otherness, identity, separateness from the womb becomes the first step toward transcendence. God is other, we are others. God is above all, beyond all, separate from all. Relationships should be distant. Music should be ethereal, arrhythmic. God becomes the Father who is distant, cold, impersonal, unmoving, wholly different.

Those are the two archetypes. Some people are continually moving back (to the womb), others are continually moving away (to the sky). Like two runners racing in opposite directions, each calls the other lost, directionless, misguided, heretical. In the religious fields, we end up with two opposing senses of spirituality.

Do we become more "spiritual" if we learn about God through the everyday events, things, people, and life around us? Or do we become more "spiritual" if we learn about God by casting out these everyday phenomena so that we might take an inward sense-less journey? Charles Williams calls these the Way of Affirmation of Images and the Way of Rejection of Images. Creation as a symbolic image can reveal aspects of God's nature. The heavens and the firmament witness that God discloses Godself in all things. As Mary McDermott Shideler summarizes: "Human love manifests divine love; particular beauties exhibit ultimate beauty."[4] "This also is Thou." This is the way of the artist and the poet. Images are their means to intellectual and emotional experience.

Creation as a symbolic image can also conceal aspects of God's nature. Shideler explains: "the flesh hinders the spirit; sensed beauty hides ultimate beauty; human love veils the divine love. All images, even the holiest, conceal God, not because they are evil but because they are finite. . . . The Way of Rejection of Images makes way for the One who, in some place or state or mode of being, is in Himself: unimaged, absolute, and wholly other." "Neither is this Thou." This is the way of the ascetic, the celibate, the mystic.[5]

Truth, however, needs both aspects. James Fowler calls this the "Conjunctive" stage of faith, a stage of maturity when one realizes what appears to be opposites are in reality necessary corollaries. This stage of faith: "sees both (or the many) sides of an issue simultaneously. Conjunctive faith suspects that things are organically related to each other; it attends to the pattern of interrelatedness in things, trying to avoid force-fitting to its own prior mind set."[6]

May not our whole life be understood as a womb preparing us for heaven—the beyond? And even in the womb is not complete knowledge limited by not having a face to face encounter of two separate beings?

Only God knows us both in the womb and out. Our earth with its watery firmament may seem but an immense womb to God, yet God allows us to be free and other. As King David so eloquently wrote, God formed our inward parts, knit us together in our mother's womb, God knows us right well, our frame was not hidden from God when we were being made in secret, intricately wrought in the depths of the earth. God beheld our unformed substance. But when we awoke, we were still with God (Ps. 139:13–18).

That is the point of this book. God is the God of gods and goddesses because God is an immanent and a transcendent God.

If the two runners keep dashing off in opposite directions, both will get off track entirely. Both may reach a goal, but not the goal of truth. What we want to explore is that truth about God. Who is God? Who is *not* God?

We will begin the first two chapters by exploring and explaining current interests in female and male deities. Who are the ancient deities that are now prominent in the United States and in other parts of the world? How can postscientific people go about promoting such deities, even, for some, worshiping them? What is the appeal? In what way are these ancient deities part of the women's and men's movements? And why have they become a part?

Then we will continue by comparing the contemporary descriptions of these deities with ancient descriptions. Are we all being told the truth? What historical information do we have? What were the results of ancient worship? Was the ancient appeal similar to today's?

Chapters 1, 2, and 3 mainly describe and briefly analyze the worship of gods and goddesses: female and male as god. Chapters 4, 5, 6, 7, and 8 are an extended analysis, an apologetic, an appeal, a call. Who is God? How is God unique? Why is God neither a male nor female god? How is God both transcendent and immanent? How may God be known? What is the place of general revelation, knowledge of God through creation, as a means of knowing God? How should we watch out for idolatry? What is idolatry? What is the appeal of Christianity for feminists and "masculinists"? What is the charge the church needs to hear?

The appendices should also be helpful resources. Appendix A includes a testimony of someone brought up in the church who was then attracted to witchcraft, but later left it. Appendix B is written by a Christian who helped her leave witchcraft. Appendix C is a summary of key references to "Father" in the Bible. Appendix D is an eight-part Bible study on the nature of God and on ministering to witches that can be used in churches. I highlighted key issues raised by this movement. The bibliography is in two parts. The first part lists a number of books and articles that critique goddess spirituality. The second part lists all the references quoted. The final index should help readers find all the key references they need.

In 1985 I published an in-depth biblical defense of women in ministry called *Beyond the Curse: Women Called to Ministry*. I am not repeating that information, except in brief summary where necessary. This book also interprets the Bible at face value: history is treated as history, and metaphor as metaphor. Many fine books and articles have been written to support the historical reliability and consistency of the Old and New Testaments. The challenge, as I understand it, from goddess spirituality is not to the Bible's reliability but to the Bible's message itself and the God revealed within the Bible's pages.

Nevertheless, since translation can be a factor hindering the Bible's message, if not otherwise indicated, all Bible translations are by the author of that chapter or from the New Revised Standard Version.

We, like children, have a limited view of our world. Children are even one of Jesus' images for himself (Luke 9:48). Yet the world God has created is good and to be enjoyed. This book has been written with dual perspectives: humility and enjoyment, transcendence and immanence, criticism and appreciation, truth and love. May our readers receive it with the same attitudes.

GOD AS FEMALE

*I*n December of 1991, I visited Glastonbury Abbey in England. Those who revere the goddess, in this part of the British Isles, believe that their deity is revealed in the landscape and that the abbey, built for the worship of the "male god," has supplanted the goddess's rightful place of honor.

I was, therefore, not surprised by a carnation and a note that I found at the foot of a cast iron cross on the altar of St. Joseph's Chapel (also known as the Lady Chapel). The note read: "In honour of the Goddess—and with love and prayers for greater acknowledgment of and reverence for the feminine in 'God.'" I felt compelled to leave an answer and so appended to the note:

> Dear One, We are all created in the image of God but Jesus, not the goddess, died on the cross for our sins and rose from the grave and ascended into heaven. And only through Jesus do we have eternal life.

This exchange points to the existence of a growing phenomenon: a growing challenge to the church of Jesus Christ. All around the world, women and men—many feeling disenfranchised within Christian circles or disillusioned by the liberalism within much of the church, many simply seeking answers to the world's ecological crisis and/or remedies for their own vacuous spiritual states—are turning to paganism in its many expressions: witchcraft, earth-centered worship, worship of the pre-Christian god/dess in his/her many forms.

We will focus, in this chapter, on the modern revelations of the goddess. In the next chapter we will focus on the modern revelations of the god.

Books, with titles like *Mother Earth Spirituality, When God Was a Woman, The Feminine Face of God, The Book of the Goddess, Womanspirit Rising,* and *Beyond God the Father* are selling off of bookstore shelves. Interest in related pagan paraphernalia is also on the upsurge. The following is just a sampling of items available, by catalogue or on site, from one company based in Salem, Massachusetts:

- A medicine woman talisman inspired by the petroglyphs of North America. The piece of jewelry is meant to bring the wearer into harmony with the visible and invisible worlds.
- An angelic goddess pendant, symbol of the force of light.
- A stoneage Willendorf goddess, a reproduction of the oldest sculpture of the female form yet uncovered—said to represent the abundance and stability of Mother Earth.
- Sculpted representations of the Egyptian Cat Goddess, symbol of fertility and female sexual power; a Rune fey; Athena, Goddess of Wisdom, and Shelob, Queen of the Middle Earth.
- Feminist Tarot Cards.
- Taped music including one cassette with the title *Enchantress, Songs of the Old Religion.*
- Hundreds of books and periodicals on the many faces of the goddess.

Today, one can tap into an intricate network of pagans to find festivals, workshops, films, art exhibitions, covens, and circles of friends all determined to revive the "old ways." There is a National Alliance of Pantheists, a Witches League for Public Awareness, a Pagan Parenting Network.

In Salem, Massachusetts (often called the "Witch City" because of its association with the witch hysteria of 1692 and its promotion of witchcraft today), the local religious leaders association has welcomed a witch to its number. This high priest of the Rosarian Order of Wicca, whose coven is called the Black Rose, now regularly meets with Catholic and Protestant ministers and a Jewish rabbi at the Immaculate Conception Catholic Church to plan activities and discuss issues of faith.[1]

In Walnut Creek, California, the Contra Costa Pagan Association was, at this writing, contemplating the opening of a school if movement toward the granting of tuition vouchers for private education is successful.[2]

And in Jonesboro, Arkansas, "about 60 self-described witches and pagans from several states marched . . . to denounce intolerance and promote religious freedom."[3]

According to Beth Wolfensberger, in an article written for *Boston Magazine,* modern Paganism has taken root, is holding strong, and is moving into its second generation in the United States: "Children are being raised Pagan, with Pagan rituals that correspond to christening and confirmation. By the time they are grown, schools for training Pagan clergy, now being established, will have stood or failed the test of time. Unitarians have long admitted Pagans to their seminaries." She continues: "The EarthSpirit Community, a national Pagan organization with 3,000 members, is headquartered at a home in Medford (Massachusetts). The Covenant of Unitarian Universalist Pagans (CUUPS), recognized as an affiliate organization of the Unitarian Universalist Association, is based in Cambridge (Massachusetts)."[4]

No accurate head count of Pagans exists but nearly every urban area in the United States has a Pagan community.[5]

Much of the interest in earth-centered, god/dess worship has arisen as a result of a freshly-empowered feminist spirituality, a repackaged witchcraft, and a concern for the environment. Unfortunately, Judaeo-Christianity is perceived—with its emphasis on the biblical mandate to "subdue" the earth—as to blame for the world's ecological crisis and the oppression of women.

Faced with—what many see as—an inequitable present and a bleak future, some are looking back to the early history of humanity for answers for today. Archaeologist Marija Gimbutas has been key in reviving praise for supposed prepatriarchal civilization in which, she claims, matristic, goddess-worshiping cultures held nature in higher esteem and thus lived in greater harmony with the environment. Some scholars may challenge her conclusions on the existence of a goddess religion in Neolithic Europe with its roots in the Paleolithic, but, for our purposes here, we do not need to argue the point.[6] Suffice it to say, her work—along with that of others—has been influential enough to spark a trend.

Joseph Campbell, writing in the foreword to Gimbutas' *The Language of the Goddess,* asserts, "One cannot but feel that in the appearance of this volume at just this turn of the century there is an evident relevance to the universally recognized need in our time for a general transformation of consciousness. The message here is of an actual age of harmony and peace in accord with the creative energies of nature which for a spell of some four thousand prehistoric years anteceded the five thousand of what James Joyce has termed the 'nightmare' (of contending tribal and national interests) from which it is now certainly time for this planet to wake."[7]

Author Elinor W. Gadon concurs: "In the late twentieth century there is a growing awareness that we are doomed as a species and planet unless we have a radical change of consciousness. The reemergence of the Goddess is becoming the symbol and metaphor for this transformation . . . (and) has led to a new earth-based spirituality."[8]

Woman of Power, which identifies itself as "a magazine of feminism, spirituality and politics," offers—in its "Statement of Philosophy"—this blueprint for change:

> Woman's spirituality is a world-wide awakening of womanpower whose vision is the transformation of our selves and our societies. The ancient spiritual voice of woman now speaks its long-hidden wisdom and becomes an active force for the conscious evolution of our world.
>
> This emerging voice speaks of . . .
>
> - the recognition of the interconnectedness of all life
> - the awareness that everything has consciousness and is sacred
> - the re-membering of our selves as sacred beings, and the loving of our psyches, bodies, and emotions
> - the empowerment of women and all oppressed peoples
> - the creation of world peace, social justice, and environmental harmony
> - the activation of spiritual and psychic powers
> - the honoring of woman's divinity
> - reverence for the earth, and the celebration of her seasons and cycles, and those of our lives[9]

And so, everything old is new again. In the United States, the revival of pagan, pre-Christian religions moves to embrace a blend of Native American, Greek, Norse, Roman, Celtic, and other Cre-ation-centered spiritualities. Pagans choose their own pantheon according to their needs, recreating God/dess to suit one's mood and personal interest. This neo-paganism is the newest trend under the umbrella movement that is new age theology, and yet, at the same time, many goddess worshipers have balked at jumping into the new age soup, seeing within that concoction a patriarchal attitude rival-ing that which they have found within Christianity. Z. Budapest, in "A Witch's Manifesto," claims that, though the new age movement grew from the spirit's hunger, it was not "politically informed," and so "ended up male-identified and male-dominated. The new white-gurus, the self-help boys, market spirituality like a precious middle-class commodity, and help themselves to witchcraft's wisdom for the information, rituals and chants—then cut out the Goddess and turn the wisdom into self-help exercises. Most women who support these sanitized versions of witchcraft never know they are partaking of their own gelded culture for a high fee. The personal is political."[10]

And so, the battle is on between the gurus and the goddesses.

In the following pages, we will examine paganism, witchcraft, the rise of interest in Gaia and the "Gaia Hypothesis," other manifesta-tions of the goddess, and the stepped-up devotion (within Catholic circles) to Mary, mother of Jesus, which is being played out in a deeper form of Mariolatry (worship). We will explore the founda-tions linking these systems of thought and will close with a word to Christians.

▼ Paganism Defined

Margot Adler, in *Drawing Down the Moon*, notes that the word "*pagan* comes from the Latin *paganus*, which means a country dweller. . . . Similarly, *heathen* originally meant a person who lived on the heaths." She asserts: "Negative associations with these words are the end result of centuries of political struggles during which the major prophetic religions, notably Christianity, won a victory over the older polytheistic religions. . . . Pagan had become a derogatory term in Rome by the third century."

Adler notes that pagans or neo-pagans "consider themselves part of a religious movement that antedates Christianity and monothe-ism. By *pagan* they usually mean the pre-Christian nature religions of the West, and their own attempts to revive them or to recreate them in new forms. The modern Pagan resurgence includes the feminist goddess-worshipers, new religions based on the visions of science-fiction writers, attempts to revive ancient European religions—Norse, Greek, Roman, Celtic—and the surviving tribal religions. The Pagan movement does *not* include the Eastern religious groups. It includes neither Satanists nor Christians."

Further, she writes: "Most Neo-Pagans sense an aliveness and 'presence' in nature. They are usually polytheists or animists or pantheists, or two or three of these things at once. They share the goal of living in harmony with nature and they tend to view humanity's 'advancement' and separation from nature as the prime source of alienation. They see *ritual* as a tool to end that alienation. . . . They gravitate to ancient symbols and ancient myths, to the old polytheistic religions of the Greeks, the Egyptians, the Celts, and the Sumerians."[11]

Paganism is, at its heart, a religion of pantheism and immanence. Pantheism (from the Greek *pan*—"all inclusive" and *theos* "God") asserts that god/dess is all and all comprises the god/dess. Immanence may be defined as the god/dess's activity within nature, within human beings.

Carl G. Jung, a self-avowed occultist, one of the pioneers of psychoanalysis and a key individual that both neo-pagans and new agers cite as foundational, provided these concepts of God with a psychological base with his introduction of the "collective unconscious" and the "archetype." He also saw this aliveness in nature. Moreover, Jung's thesis is that: "In addition to our immediate consciousness, which is of a thoroughly personal nature and which we believe to be the only empirical psyche (even if we tack on the personal unconscious as an appendix), there exists a second psychic system of a collective, universal, and impersonal nature which is identical in all individuals. This collective unconscious does not develop individually but is inherited. It consists of preexistent forms, the archetypes, which can only become conscious secondarily and which give definite form to certain psychic contents."[12]

Jung developed the sense of archetypes as patterns of instinctual behavior that expressed themselves through dreams, fantasies, and mythological symbols. Gods and goddesses are, thus, in his system of thought, merely archetypal patterns.

The witch, Starhawk, explains: "The Goddess can be seen as the symbol, the normative image of immanence. She represents the divine embodied in nature, in human beings, in the flesh. The Goddess is not one image but many—a constellation of forms and associations—earth, air, fire, water, moon and star, sun, flower and seed, willow and apple, black, red, white, Maiden, Mother and Crone." She adds: "The Goddess has many names: Isis, Ceridwen, Astarte, Miriam, Oshun, White Buffalo Woman, Kuan Yin, Diana, Amaterasu, Ishtar, Changing Woman, Yemaya. . . . And She has many aspects: Maiden, Mother, Crone, moon, earth, tree, star, flame, Goddess of the cauldron, Goddess of the hearth, Healer, spider, Lady of the Wild Things. And the God who is Her male aspect or, we could say, the other pole of that once-unbroken unity, also has many names: Pan, Dionysos, Osiris, Dumuzi, Baal, Lugh, Coyote, Alegba . . . and He too has many aspects: child, dancer, father, sower of seeds, Horned God, Hunter, Dying God, Healer, Green Man, sun, tree, standing stone."[13]

And so, today, the goddess (in archetypal or personal form) is worshiped. And included under the pagan/neo-pagan umbrella of devotees are those who would identify themselves as witches, practitioners of the Craft, or initiates of the religion Wicca.

▼ Witchcraft

Adler says that Witches/Wiccans "consider themselves priests and priestesses of an ancient European shamanistic nature religion that worships a goddess who is related to the ancient Mother Goddess in her three aspects of Maiden, Mother and Crone. Many Craft traditions also worship a god, related to the ancient horned lord of animals, the god of the hunt, the god of death and lord of the forests. . . . The word *Witchcraft* comes from the Old English *wicce* and *wicca,* referring to female and male practitioners, respectively. Many Witches have said that these two words derive from the root 'wit' or wisdom. Others . . . have said the word derives from the Indo-European roots 'wic' and 'weik,' meaning to bend or to turn. According to this view, a Witch would be a woman (or man) skilled in the craft of shaping, bending and changing reality."[14]

Starhawk, whose book *The Spiral Dance,* offers an overview of the reemergence of Witchcraft as a goddess-worshiping religion, delineates the three core principles of Goddess religion as "immanence, interconnection and community. Immanence means that the Goddess, the Gods, are embodied, that we are each a manifestation of the living being of earth, that nature, culture and life in all their diversity are sacred. . . . Interconnection is the understanding that all being is interrelated, that we are linked with all of the cosmos as parts of one living organism. What affects one of us affects us all. . . . And Goddess religion is lived in community. Its primary focus is not individual salvation or enlightenment or enrichment but the growth and transformation that comes through intimate interactions and common struggles. . . . Community is personal. . . . But in a time of global communications, catastrophes, and potential violence, community must also be seen as reaching out to include all the earth."[15]

Laurie Cabot, who is known as the "Official Witch of Massachusetts" (so designated by one-time governor Michael Dukakis), echoes, in her *Power of the Witch,* a similar theology: the witches' belief in their "oneness with the source of all life, the Great Mother," and their position as "co-creators of the universe"; the interconnectedness of nature; the agreement with "the philosopher Thales, who told the ancient Greeks, 'All things are filled with gods'"; the desire to develop psychic ability and the push to access hidden knowledge. And since "religion is about creation," Cabot writes, "religion should be about the earth."[16]

As we have already noted, the goddess with her bipolar mate is alive within paganism. This goddess is seen as the Triple Goddess with the aspects of maiden (virgin), mother, and crone. More specifically,

> the virgin, or new moon, is Artemis/Diana, the huntress, the wild and free young woman who belongs to no man. The mother, or full moon, is the matron, the nurturer at her peak of fecundity and sexuality; she is Selene, Demeter, Ishtar, Isis, Queen Maeve. The crone, or waning and dark moon, is the old woman past menopause, the hag, the Wise Woman, the keeper of the mysteries of death, the destroyer to whom all life must return in death. In this aspect, she is frequently represented as Hecate, a triple goddess in herself, and sometimes as Kali.
>
> God is usually the Horned God (even 'Old Hornie') after pagan deities such as Pan and Cernunnos. He is lord of nature, the fertilizer of life, the Sun to the Goddess's Moon, the sacrificial king of pagan

rites whose blood and dismembered body are scattered upon the fields to ensure the continuing fecundity of the land. While God is considered co-equal to Goddess, he is given far less attention in rituals and writings.[17]

In its various incarnations, then, we have in the pagan and Wiccan religions of the Earth, systems that elevate nature to living consciousness, declare its Oneness with humanity, and pull it altogether as an idea—a goddess.

▼ Gaia and the Gaia Hypothesis

Some steam has been fed into the pagan revival by modern science, which has come with its tithe to Mother Earth. Two individuals are particularly responsible: British atmospheric scientist James Lovelock and American microbiologist Lynn Margulis. They have postulated—in their "Gaia Hypothesis"—that the planet Earth is a living creature, "that the Earth's climate and surface environment are controlled by the plants, animals, and microorganisms that inhabit it. That taken as a whole, the planet behaves not as an inanimate sphere of rock and soil . . . but more as a biological superorganism—a planetary body—that adjusts and regulates itself."[18]

The name Gaia (also Gaea, Ge) refers to the Greek goddess of the Earth, goddess of marriage and goddess of death and what lies thereafter. She is the first-born of Chaos and mother of the Titans, cyclopes, furies, giants, and tree nymphs, mother of Uranus (god of the sky), Ourea (god of the mountains) and Pontos (god of the sea).[19]

Lovelock introduced the Gaia hypothesis to the general public in 1979 through his work *Gaia: A New Look at Life on Earth* and, while it and other writings of Lovelock and Margulis have sparked much scientific debate, the scholarly attention has also lent an air of validity to the spiritual descendants of the theory.

Lovelock and Margulis, however, appear to differ on the spiritual aspects of Gaia. While Margulis has not appeared to embrace the Gaian religion, according to Tal Brooke, of the California-based Spiritual Counterfeits Project, Lovelock "has a statue of Gaia in his garden at Cornwall and is a member of Lindisfarne, the New Age group headquartered at the Episcopal Cathedral of Saint John the Divine in New York City (and) Lovelock cautiously revealed his deeper convictions in a recent interview in *Orion Nature Quarterly:* 'Gaia is Mother

Earth. Gaia is immortal. She is the eternal source of life. She is surely a virgin. She does not need to reproduce herself as she is immortal. She is certainly the mother of us all, including Jesus.'"[20] Lovelock attributes to Mother Earth (Gaia) sentience and willfullness.

Stuart Chevre explains: "Feminist and ecologically based spiritualities (witchcraft, goddess worship, ecofeminism, paganism and other earth worship groups) have become strong supporters of the mystical, quasi-religious Gaia. Earth spirituality, in particular, is quickly becoming equated with Gaia worship to the applause of most New Age leaders."[21]

Counted among these is David Spangler, who has been associated with the Scottish Findhorn Community. He explains:

> Accepting Gaia simply as a "return to the Goddess" or jumping on the bandwagon of a new planetary animism, without thinking through the implications of just what Gaia might mean in our culture, can lead to sentimentality rather than spirituality. If Gaia is an important spiritual idea for our time then we must remember that a spiritual idea is not something that we think about but something that inhabits and shapes us. It is like a strand of DNA, organizing and energizing our lives. . . . It is incarnational in a profound way. . . . It becomes part of the foundation and architecture of our lives. Being a new icon for worship is not enough. Invoking the spirit of Gaia is insufficient unless we understand just how we in turn are shaped and participated in by it.[22]

Lovelock and others have called for the development of a new theology more compatible with contemporary views of reality as now offered by the sciences. But this new theology is really just a return to the old paganism.[23]

According to individuals like Matthew Fox, theology should be creation-centered rather than redemption-centered. Fox, an ordained Dominican priest for 27 years, was dismissed from the order in March 1993 because he had persisted in preaching a new age gospel. In April 1994, he joined the Episcopal Church. This founding director of the Institute in Culture and Creation Spirituality at Holy Names College in Oakland, California, and author of many books, calls for a theology of the panentheistic "Cosmic Christ," God being *in* all and all in God. He rejects fall/redemption theology in favor of creation-centered theology and speaks of an evolving God:

"Mary, the mother of Jesus, teaches us that not only is God mother, but God is also child. And we are to be the mothers of God. . . . To birth wisdom or to birth compassion is to birth God. Here lies the deepest of all meanings behind cosmogenesis, the unfolding birth of the cosmos, and here we, as co-creators with God, have so significant a role to play. . . . To suggest that Mary and ourselves birth God is to suggest that God can be a baby, a child, a new creation. It is to suggest that in some sense God is not born yet. And that is indeed the case . . . humanity is responsible for the birthing and the nurturing of God." Fox finally announces that "To recover our divinity and the doctrine of our deification and divinization is itself salvific."[24]

Fox's "divinity located only within deified Creation and within man's deified unconscious is essentially paganism," concludes Margaret Brearley, Senior Research Fellow at the Centre for Judaism and Jewish-Christian Relations, Selly Oak Colleges.[25]

To grasp better the impact of creation-centered, goddess worship today, one needs to look to the manifestations of the phenomenon in popular culture.

On Ted Turner's superstation WTBS, comedienne Whoopi Goldberg provides the voice of Gaia in a cartoon entitled, "Captain Planet." The plot line? Gaia has chosen five children and given them the power to use earth, water, wind, fire, and psychic telepathy to fight against evil polluters of the earth. In a circle—reminiscent of Wiccan ritual—they combine and project their powers to summon Captain Planet who announces that he is their powers combined and magnified.

Otter and Morning Glory G'Zell, of *Green Egg Magazine,* describe themselves as priest and priestess of Gaia. Rather unlikely places (such as the Boston Museum of Science) sell books and magazines focusing on Gaia. A group of women have come together on an island in the Pacific Northwest, now called Gaia Island. Here, one meets such artists as Diane Snow Austin, whose song "The Goddess Walks Again" has a rousing pop hit style.

In 1989, at the Goddess Festival in New York City (held at the New York City Open Center), Gaia received her share of praise from everyone from Merlin Stone, author of *When God Was a Woman,* to Olympia Dukakis, Academy Award-winning actress.[26] According to Rusty Unger: "Dukakis became involved with Goddess worship when she acted in *The Trojan Women* in 1982. . . . Now Dukakis develops improvisational theatre pieces based on Goddess myths. Her most recent is called *Voices of Earth.* "[27]

But Gaia is not the only goddess experiencing a popular revival.

▼ Other Goddesses

Greek and Roman

As we have already noted, the mother goddess among the Greeks—the primordial goddess, the earth goddess—is Gaia. Before Hera (Goddess of Marriage equivalent to the Roman Juno); Aphrodite (Goddess of Love and Beauty—the Roman Venus); Athena (Goddess of Wisdom and Handicrafts—the Roman Minerva); Artemis (Goddess of the Hunt and Moon—the Roman Diana); Hestia (Virgin Goddess of the Hearth—the Roman Vesta); Hecate (Goddess of the Crossroads, a personification of the wise witch); Persephone (Queen of the Underworld—the Roman Proserpina) and Demeter (Goddess of Grain/Agriculture—the Roman Ceres)—there was Gaia (the Roman Cybele, Magna Mater).

Writers like Jean Shinoda Bolen have suggested that one or more of these cultural archetypes are active within women today. Knowledge of these "goddess patterns," she says, provides individuals with a means of understanding themselves and their relationships. She asserts: "Goddess patterns help account for differences in personality; they contribute information about the potential for psychological difficulties and psychiatric symptoms. And they indicate the ways a woman in a particular goddess pattern can grow." Her book (*Goddesses in Everywoman*) describes "a new psychological perspective on women—provided by the Greek goddesses—that have stayed alive in human imagination for three thousand years."[28]

Egyptian

C. J. Bleeker, in his chapter in *The Book of the Goddess Past and Present,* offers an overview of the Egyptian goddesses: Nut, goddess of the sky, partner of Geb, the earth god. Ma-a-t, goddess of truth, righteousness, social order, and cosmic order; Buto, in the shape of a vulture, connected with northern Egypt; Nechbet, in the shape of a snake, connected with southern Egypt, and, also, Sachmet, Bastet,

Neith of Sais, Nephthys. But the two who surpassed them all were Isis and Hathor.

Isis, daughter of Geb and Nut, sister-wife of Osiris, mother of Horus—mother goddess, is identified with other mother goddesses like the Greek Demeter and the Anatolian Cybele. Hathor, goddess of love and joy, is a sky goddess, a cow goddess, protector of infants, consoler of the dead.[29]

Today, the ankh, ancient Egyptian symbol of eternal life, is worn; people wear their names spelled out in hieroglyphics in cartouche pendants; the pyramid—in various forms—is sat under and contemplated over. And Isis, especially, is receiving great attention in Wiccan circles and in cults that bear her name.

Native American

Ake Hultkrantz, in his chapter on "The Religion of the Goddess in North America" in *The Book of the Goddess Past and Present,* says there are three important traits of the goddess in North America:

First, the goddess is characteristically the patron of women, a religious symbol of the qualities of womanhood in a bilateral hunting-and-collecting society. She is often the partner of the male supreme being, and is occasionally depicted as his spouse. Particularly in agrarian cultures the goddess is the professional guardian, inventor, and, except in the Southwest, main agent of agricultural work. Second, the goddess in her capacity as birth goddess may, through her sexual union with the sky father, give impetus to the idea of creation through emanation. She may even stand out as a kind of supreme being, sometimes usurping the role of, or merging with, the male supreme being. This may explain the occurrence of bisexual gods in North America, like the Zuni Indian Awinowalona. Third, as Mother Earth and fertility divinity the goddess is intimately associated with the germinating underground powers. Within the agricultural system she is linked to the idea of a subterranean realm of the dead, often gloomy in comparison to the rather superterrestrial afterworld of hunting peoples.[30]

According to Paula Gunn Allen, author of *Grandmothers of the Light: A Medicine Woman's Sourcebook,* the goddesses in native cultures had been in varying states of decline for a varying number of years. But the Navajo, she says: "have been the earliest to signal the Goddess's return, . . . The goddesses the Navajo have claimed are the multiple goddesses of the Pueblo—the Anasazi as they are called, the elders. These supernaturals include Thinking Woman, also known as Spider Woman; Nau'ts'ity and Ic'sts'ity, or Iyatiky; and the Little War Twins, Masewe and Oyoyowe. In the Navajo pantheon these beings become Spider Woman, goddess of weaving, . . . and Changing Woman and White Shell Woman, along with their sons Monster Slayer and Child of Water." This pantheon of goddesses and supernatural brothers is not unique to the Southwest, Gunn says. "They form the center and foundations of the gynocentric universe throughout the Americas" with counterparts found throughout the other native cultures.[31]

The Shoshoni Indians of Wyoming speak of both male and female deities. Within the culture, belief exists in a powerful Mother Earth whom the Shoshoni think is identical with the earth itself: "She is particularly hailed in two religious ceremonies, the sun dance and the peyote cult."[32]

The Dakota Sioux have as one of their heroines the Buffalo Calf Woman, mistress of the buffalo, related to Mother Earth. The Shawnee speak of the Grandmother; the Iroquois and Hopi of the Corn Goddess and the Huichol Indians of Jalisco and Nayarit in Mexico. They "believe in a whole universe of goddesses that enclose their daily lives. . . . The great goddess of the Huichol, the earth goddess, is known in many forms": Great-Grandmother Nakawe (who is depicted surrounded by snakes); Mother Urinanaka (Mother Earth after the sun and the rains, ready for the planting of the maize), and Mother Utuanaka (ready to bear the maize). Along with the several earth mothers are the rain mothers and corn mothers. There is also the Eskimo Sea Woman (goddess of sea fauna and the sea itself), who is known by many names: "In the Far West she is called Nulirahak, 'the great woman,' and west of Hudson Bay Nuliajuk, 'the dear wife.' Her name on Baffinland is Sedna, 'the woman of the depth of the sea.'"[33]

Native American spirituality is experiencing a revival not only interiorly but throughout the Americas. Many individuals who are seeking a reconnection with Mother Earth have embraced the culture's philosophy, symbols and rites. This is evidenced in the proliferation of interest in earth prayers and ceremonies, sweat lodges, the telling of the ancient tales, kachina dolls, and other spirit symbols (fetishes), medicine bags, Native American art, jewelry, music, crystals, medicine cards, shamanism, and the visions of Black Elk.

New book titles seem to hit the shelves each week: *Mother Earth Spirituality, Wisdom of the Elders, Birth of a Modern Shaman, The Sorceror's Crossing* (Yaqui Indian spirituality harkening back to the earlier work of Carlos Castaneda), *Indian Herbology of North America.*

Celtic

R. J. Stewart explains in *Celtic Gods, Celtic Goddesses:* "the fundamental root of the Celtic goddess imagery and worship is this: the goddess is an embodiment of the forces of the sacred land. This sacred land may be a region or locality of specific topographical location, it may be the territory of a family or tribe, and in higher forms it may be the planet, the solar system or a pattern of stars. . . ."[34]

Kathy Jones notes:

> The Goddess in ancient Britain was the One and the Many. She was the Creatrix, Continuer and Destroyer of all life. She was the Matrix, the Great Mother, the Weaver of the Web. All souls were born from Her sacred Womb, lived for a span upon Her Body the Earth and then returned to Her Tomb/Womb at death. She was the Maiden, Mother and Crone; the Virgin, the Lover and the Whore. The Grail of Innocence, the Chalice of Love and the Cauldron of Wisdom were all in Her keeping, reflecting Her Triple nature. She was the Three and the Nine Sisters, Ladies, Faerie Queens and Hags.
>
> In Ireland She was Domnu, Danu, Anu, Ana, Banba, Eriu, Fotla, Babh, Kessair, Kersair, Kele, Artha, Brigit, Grainme, Macha, Morrigu, and Sheila na Gig. In Wales She was Bloudeuwedd, Arainhod, Mona, Rhiannon, Gwenhwyfer and Kerridwen. In Scotland She was the Cailleach, Bera, Brigit, Cale, Carline, Scota and Mag Moullach. In England She was the White Lady, Ana, Dana, Amma, Annis, Artha, Alba, Graine, Ker, Madron, Modron, Mab, Morg-Ana, the Great Queen Rigantona (later Epona), Guinevere, Vivienne, the Lady of the Lake, Elaine and Nimue.[35]

R. J. Stewart notes that the culture has also traditionally honored warrior goddesses, horse goddesses, goddesses of beauty, longing, and joy (as neo-pagans do today).

Norse

Frigg and Freyja are the primary female deities. The former is called the goddess of the sky and the latter, goddess of love, beauty, and endless rebirth. The Norse pantheon consists primarily of two tribes of deities: the Aesir and the Vanir, which—at one time—warred against one another. The Aesir consist of Odin (ruler of the world, husband of Frigg, Iord, and Ring), Thor, Balder, Freyr, Tyr, Bragi, Hodr, Heimdall, Vithar, Vali, Ullr, Ve, and Forseti. The Vanir include Njord, Skadi, Freyr, and Freyja (leader of the Valkeyries).

Carolyne Larrington asserts that "the taint of Nazism has proved hard for Germanic myth to shake off . . . Odinn/Wotan and Sigurdr/Siegfried remain icons of Aryan purity to white supremacists; in Oxford recently a group of Odinn-worshippers picketed a theatre in which a black singer played Wotan in Wagner's *Ring*. Revivals of Norse cult tend to be associated with extreme right-wing, masculinist and racist elements. . . . The strong woman—Valkyrie, shield maid, or Gudrun Osvifrsdottir, has been an empowering and positive image for Scandinavian women."[36]

▼ Mary, Mother of Jesus

The Bible speaks of the virgin Mary, as the mother of Jesus, as the most blessed of all women, having been chosen by God to bear the Savior. Every Catholic schoolchild is taught that Mary is not God. Only Jesus is Savior. According to official Roman Catholic teaching, Mary, like other perfected saints, can intercede with God for believers on earth. She can be "venerated," but not "adored." Adoration is for God alone. However, some Catholics "on an emotional, imaginative, and experiential level experience the love of God in the symbol of Mary, and thus they experience Mary as a symbol of God."[37] Herein is the setting for the cult of Mary, which has elevated her to the roles of coredemptrix and comediatrix with Christ Jesus. These latter roles exceed the biblical image of Mary.[38]

Many of the Catholic attitudes toward Mary have come down from apparitions of "the Lady." John J. Delaney and others chronicled eight of these in the book *A Woman Clothed with the Sun.* In 1531, one entity, who appeared in a vision at Guadalupe, said, "I am the ever-virgin Mary, mother of the true God." Four centuries later, another entity, claiming to be Mary, said, "I am the Mother of God, the Queen of Heaven." According to Delaney, "Our Lady" has characteristically appeared near water, as a young and beautiful woman clothed in white, accompanied by brilliant light. Many of the apparitions were witnessed under adverse conditions by the simplest of people, "the poorest, humblest, most unlearned and illiterate," those "whose minds were uncluttered."[39]

In Catherine Laboure's 1830 vision of the "Virgin of the Globe" (what is better known today as "the Lady of the Miraculous Medal"), for example, the first phase of the apparition "is concerned with the doctrine which describes Mary as the Mediatrix of all graces. Briefly, this doctrine, which is not yet defined by the Church but which is considered certain by theologians, states that all prayers and petitions, whether addressed specifically to Mary, or to God and the saints, are presented to God by her, and all graces, whether answers to prayer or gifts unsought, pass through her hands to mankind. . . . this is the intercessory office of Our Lady. . . . Our Lady's part of Co-redemptress of the race."[40]

Delaney sees in each of these circumstances a positive. We can, as easily, see the negative. For those who hold a high view of scripture, the visions are troubling because they cannot be reconciled with the Word of God as revealed in the Holy Bible. The apostle Paul exclaims no one can condemn the Christian because: "Christ Jesus is the one having died, and all the more having been risen, who also is at God's right, who also intercedes in our behalf" (Rom. 8:34). The writer of Hebrews also concludes that Jesus is able "to save fully" "the ones approaching through him God, always living to intercede in their behalf" (Heb. 7:25). The Bible tells us to test the spirits to see whether they are of God and if a spirit counters biblical revelation we are to reject the counterfeit. As Elliot Miller and Kenneth R. Samples have asserted in *The Cult of the Virgin,* no biblical basis exists for a sharing of those roles that Jesus specifically claimed (in our discussion, redemptor and mediator): "There is no biblical basis for granting Mary such exalted titles as Queen of Heaven, Mother of the Church, and Queen of all Saints."[41]

This overexaltation of Mary borders on goddess worship. Sometimes Mary clearly becomes a goddess. Elizabeth Gould Davis, in *The First Sex,* writes: "the only reality in Christianity is Mary, the Female Principle, the ancient goddess reborn."[42]

Mariolatry robs Mary of her essential humanity and the respect due this exemplary human for her willing submission to the will of God and it robs her God, the one true God, of the worship that is due to God alone. Mary herself would abhor it.

▼ Conclusion

The links in the chain that are the goddess revival are these:

- creation-centeredness
- pantheism, polytheism
- a belief in humankind as cocreators with god/dess
- a belief in personal god/dess as archetype
- a belief in humankind as being part of the oneness that is god/dess
- an overemphasis on immanence as against transcendence
- a belief in the power of ritual to end alienation with god/dess
- a belief that the recovery of our sense of divinity equals salvation

I believe our history has been a history of pendulum swings: from the masculine to the feminine, from rationalism to romanticism, from secular humanism to cosmic humanism. Our western culture seems to function only in the extreme.

As the pendulum swings to the feminine, as it appears it *is* moving, the church will face a challenge that it must finally meet: how to affirm that both men and women are made in the image of God—without embracing in any way—a perception of God as some sort of androgynous oddity, as a god/dess, as an archetype or as one demifigure in a pantheon of gods and goddesses, or as a pantheistic, panentheistic oneness that encompasses each human being.

We must hold firm to the inspired, authoritative, infallible Word of God—translating as faithfully as possible (without altering a word in obeisance to the demands of modern culture)—for all that we need for our walk is there—the clear expression of:

- the triunity of the one God, the personal God, the eternal, nonslumbering, nonchanging, nonillusory God who created the world and is not contained by creation;
- the sinfulness of all human beings through the fall of Adam and Eve and individual choice;
- the only means of salvation—repentance from sin and acceptance of Christ Jesus as Savior and Lord;

- the partnership of men and women in the priesthood of all believers; the call upon the life of each redeemed one to share the gospel of Christ.

The answer is not in going back before the coming of Christ but in going forward with Christ.

GOD AS MALE

On a hot day last year I stood in the sweltering sun, pressed against police barricades by a six-deep crowd, craning my neck to see . . . the Sons of Orpheus, the energetic East Bay drum corps. My boyfriend Rob was clearly visible in the front line, wearing a shirt with shredded and beaded sleeves, a black bandanna, and streaks of paint running down his ruddy cheeks. He was playing a small Brazilian drum; every few steps he'd give a little skip-jump, obviously euphoric to be marching with his buddies . . .

"We're the new bra-burners," said (Bruce) Silverman (founder of the Sons of Orpheus) . . . "I never thought, I'm gonna be a part of the men's movement. I just wanted to start a group for men." He says that the formation of Sons was an example of *zeitgeist*—the spirit of the times.[1]

*M*arcy Sheiner's vivid description in Berkeley, California's *East Bay Express* does indeed capture the spirit of our times with our searches for our absent fathers, bands of male drummers, abortion decision rights for men, and male support groups.

A mere decade ago feminist statesperson Betty Friedan was complaining: "Until recently, the so-called 'men's liberation movement' has seemed a whiny imitation of 'women's lib,' or a withdrawal into 'separatism.' But new publications like *M.-gentle men for gender jus-*

tice (deliberately lower case) and *American Man* grope for new definitions at national conferences on 'Men and Masculinity' that go
beyond imitation of or reaction to 'women's lib,' and that go beyond
retreat into sulky separatism."[2] Ten years later that groping for "new
definitions" has exploded beyond sulking and whininess in Robert
Moore's and Douglas Gillette's *King, Warrior, Magician, Lover: Redis-
covering the Archetypes of the Mature Masculine* (1990), Robert Bly's *Iron
John* (1990), and Sam Keen's *Fire in the Belly: On Being a Man* (1991)
and in such organizations as MR, Inc. (Men's Rights, Inc.), initiat-
ing what has come to be called the new men's movement.

What many of us envision when we think of the modern men's
movement are accountants in loinclothes going 1940's-Hollywood-
native. But even a cursory look past the talking, bandu, and gumbe
drums into the reasonings behind these rituals shows us an attempt
is being made to recapture something profound about the nature of
masculinity that has been lost, for the modern male quest for identity is nothing new. It is age-old and global—as old and as extensive
as boys turning into men. Over the threshold of the twenty-first century it is expressing itself alongside of, and in some cases in opposition to, the modern male's love and concern for women. And it has
inspired in return attacks from forces as diverse as Christian and
pagan, for key leaders of the men's movement, while attempting to
provide counsel that is positive and wholistic, also issue calls to worship competing deities that reflect men. As drums have been used
to facilitate rites of passage, so male deities are being used today to
facilitate a male's passage from boyhood to manhood.

▼ The Men's Movement

Much of the current thinking of the new men's movement can
be summarized by the work of psychoanalyst Robert Moore and
mythologist Douglas Gillette, who extend Swiss psychiatrist/psy-
chologist Carl Jung's concept of the archetypal self to embrace four
categories: King—the ordering factor; Warrior—the decisive/pas-
sionate aspect; Magician—the knowing/technological factor; Lover—
the compassionate and the vital. Their book *King, Warrior, Magician,
Lover* and the preceding tape series emerged from years of counseling wherein Robert Moore discovered men had lost touch with their
masculinity. Fascinating is his view that patriarchy and reactive fem-

inist criticism have served unwittingly together as dual causes of this condition, both being attacks "on masculinity in its fullness as well as femininity in its fullness":

> What they were missing was an adequate connection to the deep and instinctual *masculine* energies, the potentials of mature masculinity. They were being blocked from connection to these potentials by patriarchy itself, and by the feminist critique upon what little masculinity they could still hold onto for themselves. And they were being blocked by the lack in their lives of any meaningful and transformative initiatory process by which they could have achieved a sense of manhood.[3]

The Men's Movement Has Some Wisdom

As a result, Moore and Gillette divide masculinity from patriarchy: "In our view, patriarchy is *not* the expression of deep and rooted masculinity, for truly deep and rooted masculinity is *not* abusive. Patriarchy is the expression of the *immature* masculine."[4] Patriarchy expresses what the authors call "Boy psychology," whose "sado-masochistic" characteristics are "abusive and violent acting-out behaviors against others, both men and women; passivity and weakness, the inability to act effectively and creatively in one's own life and to engender life and creativity in others (both men and women); and, often, an oscillation between the two—abuse/weakness, abuse/weakness."[5] This Boy psychology causes the immature to attack women and mature men, for it is a Peter Pan complex that fears growing and refuses to let others grow. But, "Man psychology is always the opposite. It is nurturing and generative, not wounding and destructive."[6] The book champions mature attitudes and practices, among which it numbers monogamy as a "product of a man's own deep rootedness and centeredness" and puts a premium on true humility.[7] As all three books listed above, it contains much wisdom about wholeness, as it attacks those who drag back down to mediocrity anyone who tries to achieve excellence, observing sagely "envy blocks creativity."[8]

Who could argue with such positive conclusions? One person who takes sharp opposition is the witch Starhawk who writes in *Dreaming in the Dark:*

Since Jung, most thinkers who explore mythology have looked at the Goddesses and Gods as *archetypes* that represent underlying structures of the human psyche. Archetypes are then organized into dualities—they tell us how to divide the world and its powers, how to divide our nature, into masculine and feminine, in spite of the fact that historically the aspects of Goddess and Gods overlap and are interchanged. She may be sun and He may be moon; She may be sky and He may be earth; both have roles to play in the drama of birth, growth, and death.

The concept of archetypes is itself a symptom of estrangement, derived from the Platonic notion that the world itself was not the real, but only a shadow, an imitation of perfect preexisting forms. To a Witch the world itself is what is real. The Goddess, the Gods, are not mere psychological entities, existing in the psyche as if the psyche were a cave removed from the world; they too are real—that is, they are ways of thinking-in-things about real forces, real experiences.[9]

Christians might initially welcome the positive aspects in Moore's/Gillette's work and fear the demonic behind Starhawk's "real forces." For example, she explains, "God who is Her (the Goddess') male aspect, or, we could say, the other pole of that once-unbroken unity, also has many names: Pan, Dionysos, Osiris, Dumuzi, Baal, Lugh, Coyote, Alegba . . . And He too has many aspects: child, dancer, father, sower of seeds, Horned God, Hunter, Dying God, Healer, Green Man, sun, tree, standing stone."[10] As a result, Christians might feel impelled in reaction to embrace Jung's work, thinking, "If the witches don't like it, I guess I should," especially in view of the fact that Robert Moore, along with Sam Keen, has a long-term identification with Christianity.

"Personally, I am a Christian," Moore told Bill McNabb, associate editor of *The (Wittenburg) Door,* Christianity's watch-dog journal:

Jesus Christ is a wonderful image of the positive king. There is incredible wisdom about the positive king in the Christian story. Conservative and evangelical Christians have much more of a feeling for the liberator king—the warrior Christ who is impatient with evil. I like to tease the liberals a bit and point out that when you get in touch with this warrior/king aspect that conservative Christians understand, then you realize there is a part of the human psyche that is not comfortable with injustice. There is a part of the human psyche—deep in our deepest being—that is indignant when children are addicted to drugs, that is indignant when young girls are sold into prostitution. One of the great visions Christians have to share is the vision of a morally serious God. The wonderful thing, by the way, about the king archetype is that it is inclusive in its care. The Good Shepherd in the Christian stories leaves *no one* out of his care. When a man gets in touch with that part of his psyche, he cannot walk the streets of our cities today without feeling the pain of the people of the city who are in pain.[11]

Historic Christianity Is Questioned

Yet, when a Christian, enthusiastically inspired by this quotation dives into Moore's/Gillette's *The King Within,* his head bashes the bottom of the pool with a sickening thud. No water of life fills such a view of Jesus as this one:

An odd thing happened shortly after the death of the Jewish prophet Jesus two thousand years ago. The early Christians transformed Jesus into the archetype of the King. Never having known the man, they vested in him the structures and dynamics of the King-Gods from their non-Hebraic heritages.

Many early Christians came from religious backgrounds that included the sacred-king traditions of ancient Egypt, Greece, and Rome, as well as Hermetic influences, the Mystery Religions, and the Persian religions of Zoroastrianism and Mithraism. The myths of these various faiths were replete with King-Gods, even where actual sacred kings were a thing of the distant past.

Jesus was soon considered a God incarnate, born of a mortal woman divinely impregnated. Like Osiris in the Egyptian myths, he had been slain by his evil brother, called Satan by the early Christians. Again like Osiris, Jesus Christ had then been resurrected and had become the ruler of the dead. After his sacrifice, Jesus did just what the ancient pharaohs had done, ascending into the heavens and becoming one with the high God. . . .

From a depth-psychological point of view, the Christological controversies of the first three centuries of our era stemmed from attempts by theologians to understand the proper relationship between the human Ego and the archetype of the King. We can see an unconscious depth psychology at work. Those who argued Jesus was a God and not a man were, like the ancient Egyptians, *identifying* the human Ego with the King energy. Those who argued he was a man, not a God, were, like the Hebrews, *distancing* the Ego from the archetype.

In the end most theologians compromised with theories of co-inherence between the human and the divine . . .

An excellent film to watch in light of these issues is Martin Scorsese's *The Last Temptation of Christ*. Irrespective of any cinematic value the piece might have, it gives an excellent record of these issues. The basis of the film is that the man Jesus doubts his divine kingship, while his followers want him to accept it. Jesus can't shrug off the King projections his disciples try to give him, but he doubts the origin of his inspiration, the nature of his calling, and the necessity of his sacrifice.[12]

Further, in *King, Warrior, Magician, Lover,* Moore and Gillette tell us the resurrection is also "mythic": "What is the end of the Hero? Almost universally, in legend and myth, he 'dies,' is transformed into a god, and translated into Heaven. We recall the story of Jesus' resurrection and ascension, or of Oedipus' final disappearance in a flash of light at Colonus, or Elijah's ascent into the sky in a fiery chariot."[13] The problem with Moore's and Gillette's work for Christians is the problem with all three prominent men's movement books. Since Moore and Gillette read the biblical accounts as mythical stories, despite witches' objections, they also adopt the prevalent pagan mythologies of our times in opposition to biblical revelation:

> It seems that in prepatriarchal times, the earth as Mother was seen as the primary source of fertility. But as patriarchal cultures rose to ascendancy, the emphasis shifted from the feminine as the source of fertility to the masculine . . . Our Jewish, Christian, and Moslem God today is never seen as being in creative partnership with a Goddess. He is viewed as male, and as the sole source of creativity and generativity. He is the sole source of fertility and blessing. Many of our modern beliefs come from the beliefs of the ancient patriarchies.[14]

Robert Moore and Douglas Gillette would have us believe, then, that our chapter's quest for male deities worshiped today should end at no other altar than the Judeo-Christian God's, and at that God's reflection in Islam. And, further, they would contend that the Judeo-Christian God is a patriarchal product, patriarchy, as we know from their work, being an immature state hostile to maturity.

In their perspective, God from Judaism to Christianity to Islam to each of their cults has been coopted by males to be pictured as a Great Ayatollah peering fiercely down, or as a Great Grandfather in the sky, watching earthly antics from his cloud-cushioned easy chair with a mug of ambrosia in his gnarled hand.

▼ Male as God

"How's it hanging, Death?" ask the quintessential teenagers Bill and Ted, whose first marauding antics through history for the trivial purpose of passing an exam in order to save the universe spoke so pithily about the values of North American pop culture. Out of respect they hesitate to repeat the question to God, but the Cecil B. DeMillish voice that thunders from the great white throne says it all.[15] The Judeo-Christian God in the popular mishandling of theology is currently viewed as a boisterous cosmic male who has rudely shoved over a gentle Goddess who got here first in order to call the shots in the universe. Sounds silly when one spells it out, of course, but take away the coded technical language and this is what is being touted.

The God of the Old Testament Is Viewed as Patriarchal

Sam Keen, for example, in *Fire in the Belly* agrees with this mythological view, adding a currently popular slant, "Feminists who argue that goddess-worship historically preceded the notion of God as father are certainly correct."[16] Espousing the nineteenth-century evolutionary concept of the development of theological thought, he continues, "But ever since God became Father, and men have considered themselves the lords over nature (and women), we have defined man as active and WOMAN as reactive." "We are self-conscious animals," he contends.[17]

For Keen, the Judeo-Christian God was "formerly a God of war and territory." According to his view, during the "early agricultural revolution" religion celebrated the fertile earth:

> If some of these ceremonies involved the bloody rites of animal and human sacrifice, it was only because blood, like seed, was thought to be a necessary investment to keep the cosmic mother regular and fertile . . . The historical facts of the matter are these. About 1700 B.C. warlike tribes of peoples called Aryans, who had mastered the use of iron and horses as weapons, swept from the north into Greece, India, and the Fertile Crescent. They brought with them a fierce loyalty to

a single, patriarchal God. In the story we are most familiar with, Yah-weh, God of the Hebrews, sanctified war.[18]

Keen portrays this popular view of a conflict between a new patri-archal deity and a previous matriarchal one as a kind of divine fam-ily squabble with human sexuality as the ultimate loser—a sort of history in genital perspective:

> Being a jealous God, He ordered His followers to worship no other deities . . . Yahweh, in the manner of oriental kings, thus dethroned and demeaned the Great Mother. Beelzebub (formerly god of the phallus) was proclaimed a devil . . . As a sign that the umbilical cord binding them to nature had been severed, they circumcised the phal-lus and sacrificed the foreskin to Yahweh. Sexuality, henceforth, was to be governed by tribal morality, by the law that came down from above rather than by the impulse that came up from below. Nature was not to be trusted. Nor were women. In effect, the Judeo-Christ-ian God cast the phallus and the vulva out of the sanctuary and reduced nature to a backdrop against which God's redemptive drama was being played out on the stage of history.[19]

According to Keen, sex was replaced by violence, the fierce, war-like Yahweh ordaining war as "an established social habit"—bang, bang, in effect, winning out over kiss, kiss. But, this was all necessary, Sam Keen decides, in order for us to have technology, for, "It took the notion of a God who transcended the order of nature, whose power created and controlled nature to provide the social sanction for the development of individualism. This God, who stands above the fatedness of nature, commands men to stand above nature and society and woman and take charge of his own destiny. Without the historical introduction of the notion of a transcendent God who ordered his subjects to name the animals and to have dominion over the earth, neither individualism nor empirical science and technology would have developed," since "life in the garden of the goddess was harmonious but the spirit of history called for man to stand up and take charge."[20]

What is one to do with such a cosmology? Instead of the Genesis picture of man and woman created and called together to worship the one God reflected in both creatures and till and nurture the ground together, Keen and his colleagues envision sexual dualism at war on earth and in heaven.

Finally, Robert Bly rounds out this consensus of viewing the God of Judaism and Christianity as a violent celestial patriarch by perceiving a "malignant Jehovah," "God, whether male or female, also has, it is said, two sides, and God will surely never come to live with a person who hasn't made space in the soul for the King, for the mentor, and for his own father's blessed and poisoned sides."[21]

Christian readers, coming to these books with high hopes, attracted by all the positive male virtues being sought, will recoil in confusion, wondering what "in heaven" is going on here? How can a supposed Christian like Chicago Theological Seminary professor Robert Moore posit, for example, the kind of reading he does of the Job and Eden accounts?

God, we are told by Moore, is deceived by Eden's "delusional nature" and Job's praises, wanting all creation to be good and Job to be sincere. Satan's role, as heavenly court jester in tempting Adam and Eve (whose "sin" is considered by the authors as Judaism's "slander against women") and in plaguing Job, is to expose "the hypocrisy in the whole thing": "God doesn't want to believe Satan, but he goes along with the plan, probably instinctively knowing that Satan is right." The result? "Only after Satan had exposed the evil in creation—and, by implication, in the Creator—could honesty and healing begin."[22]

People Create God in Their Image

Evil, dishonesty, hypocrisy in God? How can this be? What really is going on? What is happening here is that all three sets of authors have shared the vision of Joseph Campbell, who in *The Masks of Eternity* claimed, "Every god, every mythology, every religion is true in this sense: it is true as metaphorical of the human and cosmic mystery," and again, "I see a deity as representing an energy system, and part of the energy system is the human energy system with love, malice, hate, benevolence, compassion. And in Oriental thinking the god is the vehicle of the energy, not its source." All three sets of authors also agree with Campbell's assessment: "All of these symbols in mythology refer to you." This is a theological basin that can only empty into one conclusion: "You are God in your deepest identity. You are one with the transcendent."[23]

If our God is really simply a reflection of each of us, *no male* can escape worshiping a masculine deity, and *no female* can escape worshiping a feminine one. God is limited here by our genders. And if God reflects us, rather than we reflecting God, then one would read the biblical accounts as stories reflecting human frailty and all these interpretations would make perfect sense. However, if one considers Scripture as the divine revelation of the one true all-good God in whom is no shadow of turning, these interpretations are all far afield!

The God of the Bible Is above Gender

What exactly does Scripture teach us about the Judeo-Christian God? Is God really a reflection of our best and worst sides? Does Scripture present God as a Great, Violent, Masculine Potentate in the Sky who commissions His male child as emissary to earth simply to quiet His rebellious subjects? Even a cursory glance at the mission of Jesus Christ will seriously contradict such a conclusion.

That Jesus was born male is obvious, but Jesus' message was far beyond simply angling to have himself set up as an earthly king, simply another aspiring male deity like the Emperor Nero, the later Leonard Howell, Jim Jones, a god-for-a-day.[24] Commissioned by the Trinity, Jesus, God Incarnate, was working to achieve cosmic reconciliation. Therefore, Jesus continually pointed not to his maleness but to unity with the Triune God beyond gender.

The Judeo-Christian God, unlike the gods and goddesses of pagans new and old, exists above the limitations of gender. In fact, both genders, as we noted, were needed in creation to reflect the image of God, for God is not human and, further, despite the didactic anthropomorphically relational image "Father," neither male nor female.

Jesus' teaching style taught metaphorically, anthropomorphizing everything into parables, creating teaching word pictures for his hearers. None of us think the Rule of Heaven is a plant of mustard, that we are wise virgins with trimmed lamps, that God owns a vineyard and needs some day laborers. While our minds deal in analogy, not only with simile, but also with metaphor, in these and many other images in Jesus' teaching, why do we suddenly turn literal with the "Fatherhood" of God? Elijah mocked the truly literal anthropomorphic maleness of the god of the prophets of Baal.

"Maybe, he's in the john," he sneered, when Baal could not rain fire on the pagan sacrifice (1 Kings 18:27). Elijah knew the true nature of the one true God.

The "Glory of Israel is not a man or human who lies and repents," announces God in 1 Samuel 15:29. The general word for humanity (*adam*) employed here is made more sex specific when Numbers 23:19 proclaims, "God is not man *(ʾîš)*" and Hosea 11:9 repeats this fact, "I am God and not man *(ʾîš)*." The Hebrew word *ʾîš*, pronounced "ish," is the masculine form for "human," as opposed to the feminine form *(ʾiššâ)*, which is translated "woman." Lest we still remain unclear, in Deuteronomy 4:15–16 God cautions the Israelites that since God showed no form to them at Horeb, they must not carve an image of God as either male *(zākûr)* or female *(něqēbāh)*. Spiritual beings are not sex specific so that they do not marry or are given in marriage, explains Jesus in Mark 12:25. God is not human, God is not man, God is not male or female. That is why Genesis 1:27 specifies the *adam*, humanity, *is* comprised of male and female. Since God is the source of both, both are needed to reflect who God is. Moses, Samuel, Isaiah figured this out. Why cannot we?

Instead, many today look like the pagans of Lystra, bowing before Paul as the god Hermes and Barnabas as Zeus come to earth (Acts 14:11–12). They are looking for containable deities.

In the opening scene from Bruce Lee's kung fu classic "Enter the Dragon," a pupil is trying to follow the teaching of his master, who is pointing in analogy to the sky, by focusing intently on the master's pointing finger. He is rewarded with a slap on his pate. "Don't concentrate on the finger," growls the exasperated master, "or you will miss all the heavenly glory."[25]

Jesus was pointing us continually back through all the metaphors for his source—the vineyard owner, the farmer whose enemy sowed weeds among his crops, the woman with the lost coin, the shepherd with the lost sheep, the father of the prodigal son, his own heavenly "father" (not Joseph) whose business he was about—to the "Glory of Israel," the blessed Trinity with whom Christ as an obedient full person of the Godhead was united and for whom Christ was representative.

But, often, instead of with the full Source for both types of humanity (males and females), people end with a solely or predominantly male deity in a Jim Jones or a Zeus, or a Thor or Baal or a Pan, or a

Father Divine, or a David "Yahweh" Koresh of the Branch Davidi-
ans (who wrote before he allegedly murdered his small flock by fire,
"I AM your God and you will bow under my feet. Do you think you
have the power to stop my will?")[26] Any one of these is a second
class kind of pocket deity, what Queequeg kept in his cloak in *Moby
Dick*, pulling it out periodically to praise it when things went well or
berate it when things went bad. They find themselves worshiping
male and female deities like those fourteen-year-old Rakesh Shah
described to *Life Magazine*'s report on "Who is God?":

> There's lots of gods in Hindu. Goddesses too. It depends what you
> want to believe in because there are different stories for each one. I
> have pictures of 25 in my cabinet. Each one serves a different pur-
> pose. I have like a baseball pitching rotation. I do one one day, sec-
> ond one the next day, like that. I have four gods and two goddesses,
> but I left two of them out because I didn't think they were doing their
> job . . . My dad bought this lottery pen. It shoots out numbers like in
> the lottery; sometimes I have nothing to do, so I pray extras. I take
> out a number. The first god's like from one to five, second one, six to
> 10. Whichever number comes out, I pray to that god. The gods have
> different powers. . . . I'm going to make it into the major leagues some-
> day. But I wouldn't pray to God just to get to baseball. That's selfish-
> ness. You don't actually *need* to be a baseball player when you grow
> up. If I got into baseball, with all the media and things, I might for-
> get about God.[27]

Little Rakesh Shah, with his desire not to use his "God(s)" for
"selfishness," is actually more altruistic than the utilitarian men who
see anthropomorphized deity as only reflective of the human condition. But, the Christian has become a Christian because the Christian recognizes more in God than a mirror of fallen humanity: a completely all-loving heavenly parent. The authentically Christian male
does not project a philandering Zeus, an inebriated Bacchus, a bloodthirsty Odin, but seeks to honor a perfect Father of lights in whom
is no shadow of turning, no demonic, no dark side (James 1:17).[28]
Christian women reflect the powerfully defending God who shows
the protecting compassion of a woman with a nursing child (Isa.
49:15), who comforts us like a mother (*em*) comforts a child (Isa.
66:13), and calms us as at a mother's breast (Ps. 131:2). Neither
Christian males nor females worship a human reflection of a half-

God, half-devil. Christians honor a liberating, loving Parent—a personal source who loves in ways greater than we evil people do and knows how to give good gifts to children, who answers more quickly than our unjust judges do, and who gives graces to beloved children with open hand and no reserve. Against such a wholesome picture of God most presentations fall woefully short.

▼ Deities of the Men's Movement

When one cuts oneself off from the true revelation of the God of the universe, one is set adrift on a dangerous sea of deities who lurk like treacherous squalls just over the theological horizon. Where does one turn for worship? The places each of our authors under consideration would turn males for wholeness are hardly safe harbors.

Sam Keen, retaining his memory of the supragenderal God, wants to find this God again. He writes:

> Nearing the year 2000, both of these genderal theological metaphors have outlived their usefulness. I suggest that the time has come to cease using genderal metaphors for God or nature. It is more confusing than helpful to speak now of God as "Father" or the Earth as "Mother." We need to find metaphors that do not build a genderal claim of superiority into our way of theological thinking and spiritual practice.[29]

Wholesome as this may sound, Keen's call for linguistic wholeness does not end him in the center of biblical revelation. Instead, Sam Keen, in his practical application section, fully opts for adapting "Eastern religious practice," drawn from "Zen Buddhism and the more mystical forms of Hinduism" with "the martial arts—judo, kung fu, akido" as "meditations" to "discover our true identity and participate in the ultimate reality by consciously inspiring and expiring" and to "discover that atman (the human breath-spirit) is Brahman (the universal breath-spirit)."[30] If the Manichees and the macrobiotics ended by eating right in order to create the holy life, Sam Keen seems to end by breathing well: a sort of theology of aerobics. He concludes his book by upholding the ideal of Buddhism not Christianity. Only the otherworldliness of eastern religion can help him escape the masculine captivity of his view of God.[31]

Robert Bly, on the other hand, is in complete disagreement with Keen's end. For Robert Bly, the search for wholeness does not end "in the force field of an Asian guru." Yet, his quest does not take him through the entire revelation of Jesus, either, or to Jesus' heavenly Father, nor does it let him understand the full scope of the Judeo-Christian God, who contains the complete wellspring of what masculinity and femininity reflect in the image of humanity, nor does it let him understand the two self-revealed, ruling characteristics of God: grace and truth (Exod. 34:6). If his vision could see the God who lives and works in history, he would understand the "gentle Jesus"[32] he rejects, the love of God that exists in perfect harmony with the vital truth in Jesus that drove out the temple's money-changers, sparred verbally with the religious hypocrites, and warred for liberation against the demonic on behalf of captured humanity. He would see Jesus not as ancillary, but as the central archetype of *unfallen* humans, the goal of heaven, the harbinger of Eden reclaimed, restoring a birthright in place of the mess of substitute porridge served up by a shabby group of anthropomorphic ancient deities unworthy of Robert Bly's finest ideals.

But instead, Bly's search for an ideal, "pre-Christian" "Wild man" has him concluding that as "women have taken on the task of lifting Sophia and Kali up again . . . Our job is to lift up Dionysus, Hermes, and the Zeus energy."[33] He would have us reintroduce dead pagan deities to our self-images.

As psychotherapist, Robert Moore goes even a step further, counseling therapeutic *worship* of female and male deities, prescribing therapy to one counselee, for example, to seek "the Goddess in her many forms," directing one's "spiritual sense of the All-Mother, Mighty, toward the archetypal Great Mother."[34] If one sees the Judeo-Christian God as purely male—and a limited, evil cosmic male at that—of course, one is going to seek other gods for wholeness. And this Moore and Gillette do, commending another young man to overcome his timidity with women by praying to Eros, the Greek god of love: "Part of the prescription in his therapy was to read all he could about the Greek god of Love, Eros, especially the Cupid (Eros) and Psyche story, and then to pray to Eros to help him to feel sensual and attractive." The answer to this counselee's prayer was to encourage him to act like Eros, meeting a woman on a cruise who gave him the tribute Caligula wished, "You're as handsome as a god!"

and with whom he had sex, a year before they married. A tired procession of crystals, pyramids, incense, candles, and similar invocations to other gods and goddesses (as archetypal representations) are also recommended.[35]

Since Jesus' story is seen as merely one myth among many, and his heavenly Parent is rejected as a patriarchal vestige, these counselors seem to feel that a counselee does best to choose whatever mythic deity within whatever myth system seems best able to help one in one's current psychological dilemma and one prays to that. What we need is a celestial yellow pages with advertisements under "deities: self-help." The same sort of thinking must have been going on in ancient Corinth as countless temples lined the pathway up the acropolis and jostled for attention in the market place: so many divine snake oil sellers with a miracle cure for loneliness.

▼ Conclusion

The problem with this kind of syncretism, this mixing of beliefs, of course, is the problem with any view of simple theological unification, as the New Age movement, or the "many faces of God" position, and that is simply that we do not all worship the same God. One continuing male-oriented deity Christians decidedly do not worship, for example, is the Moslem god. Sheikh Ahmed Ibrahim, a dedicated thirty-eight-year-old father of a four-month-old baby, and a fervent believer, who was recently set free after spending eighteen years in an Israeli prison camp for terrorism understands: "I am ready to kill and be killed myself in fighting the jihad—the holy war—because it is Allah's wish. Allah is a vengeful God. Jihad is a struggle between Right and Wrong. Justice and Injustice. Readiness to fight for God is a sacred matter. Killing for the jihad is a holy deed."[36] Such a god indeed reflects our worst drives to violence.

When the true God is largely missing, a shabby array of male deities lurch and lounge again through their chronicles of violence, fornication, dissolution, and lust for human sacrifice. Such a summary sounds melodramatic until one reads the primary, legendary texts, on which our thinkers under consideration draw and then it sounds understated.

What witches, neo-pagans, these theorists of the men's movement, and similarly counseling psychologists of the present day are trying to recapture is what Robert Parker in the *Oxford History of the Classical World* notes as the appeal of anthropomorphic deities.

> Greek religion belongs to the class of ancient polytheisms: one can in very general terms compare the religions of Rome, of Egypt, of the ancient Indo-Iranians, and most of the religions of the ancient Near East. The gods of such a polytheism have each a defined sphere of influence. The balanced worshipper does not pick and choose between them but pays some respect to them all. To neglect one god (Aphrodite, for instance) is to reject an area of human experience.[37]

Human experience may be reflected in a pantheon of deities, but what unwanted baggage is freighted in as well with ancient pagan gods? Especially, as with Moore's/Gillette's suggestion, when one begins for the sake of therapy to pray to them? Robert Bly's dark side of deity will soon become a terrifying reality when we consider each deity cited, as we will in the next chapter, from the Dionysus behind Sam Keen's Dionysian view of Christianity to the Zeus of Robert Bly and the Eros of Moore/Gillette.

Essentially, in all three visions, God functions in inverse as a reflection of the image of humanity, not so much as a God reflected in us. For Robert Bly and his colleagues, stories of gods in mythology are "a good help" "because they give both the light and dark sides of manhood, the admirable and the dangerous. Their model is not a perfect man, nor an overly spiritual man."[38] As God literally functions as the image of "man," if humans are fallen, well, so does God contain a dark side. This reasoning is what leaves so many in the men's movement with a great thirst and nothing to drink from but the styrofoam cup of Zeus, ultimately unbiodegradable in a true theological environment, but served up in place of the new wine grail of Jesus Christ, which is a far better vessel for containing the clear, pure, primal edenic spring water for which all humanity has thirsted since Eden's locks clashed closed, and of which ambrosia, refreshing as it may appear, is but a secondary image.

Thus, instead of finding wholeness in Christ, and despite his own warnings against the damage caused by mythology, Robert Bly, for example, finds himself longing for the lessons of a pagan past: "When the Church and the culture as a whole dropped the gods who spoke for the divine element in male sexual energy—Pan, Dionysus, Hermes, the Wild Man—into oblivion, we as men lost a great deal."[39]

Here Robert Bly is not taking seriously enough his own warnings in *Iron John* about the full dangers of the paganism from which the world was so gladly freed by God's love in Christ. To romanticize a dark side of God is to romanticize what in history was a most grim and oppressive reality. In the next chapter we will explore the question: did men and women really lose a great deal when they dropped the pagan gods?

But, the truly good God in the true Jesus displays wholeness, an unfallen ideal alive in this world for both men and women in equal measure. Christ's full selfless, giving example of steadfast love and firm truth is the one on which we all should be modeling ourselves.

3

GOD/DESS OF THE PAST

urrently, to romanticize the cults of the goddesses, and of the gods as well, is fashionable. From a distance of nearly two thousand years, to view these deities with a kindly haze is possible. As Sheila D. Collins states, in those times "Poetry was not a mirror of life, for life *was* poetry; and ecstasy was found in the most usual of places," or as Laurie Cabot declares, "The Great Goddess and her priestesses were living examples of the integration of body, mind, and spirit" and "Goddess worshipers sang, danced, feasted, and discovered, as the Charge of the Goddess put it, that 'all acts of love and pleasure are my rituals.'"[1] But, some of the traditions as they were told in classical antiquity are rather a different matter. The goddesses were not necessarily benevolent in their actions or their demands.

Near Eastern goddesses were frequently served by sacred prostitutes who lived in the temples and offered worshipers a mystic union with the goddess herself. Their position was one of honor and power. Indeed, the cult prostitutes attached to the great temple of Aphrodite at Corinth were said by their prayers to have stopped the Persian fleet as it advanced upon mainland Greece. During the period of temple service, the woman—even if she was married—was considered a "virgin." Women in the cult of the Syrian Goddess would serve one day a year as a prostitute or else cut off their hair as a sacrifice. The temple of Mylitta in Babylonia was famed because all female devotees had to serve as sacred harlots once in their lives. The rich women would arrive at the temple in chariots or litters, the poor on foot. All must remain there until a man cast the required fee onto their laps. After the women had performed their service, they might return to their own homes—but the homelier ones sometimes had to wait a long time at the temple! The Egyptian goddess Isis, though ultimately demanding absolute chastity from her devotees, had herself served as a harlot in Tyre; and frequently the porches of her temple were used by street walkers to ply their trade.

Sexual sacrifices were not demanded of women only. Male devotees, in cults such as those of the Syrian Goddess, Cybele, and Artemis of Ephesus, castrated themselves in the service of the goddess. Especially in the cult of the Great Mother of the Gods, Cybele, these men were thereafter identified as women and served the goddess as "she priests." These officiants also practiced self-mutilation and cross dressing.

▼ Terrifying Aspects of Ancient Deities

The Babylonian Inana and Ishtar—closely related goddesses of love and war—were at times savagely destructive. Ishtar, descending to the netherworld, shouts: "I will smash the door, I will shatter the bolt, I will smash the doorpost, I will move the doors, I will raise up the dead, eating the living, so that the dead will outnumber the living," while the Ugaritic Anath declares: "My long hand will [smash] thy skull. I'll make thy gray hair flow [with blood], the gray hair of thy head with gore."[2] She slaughters both gods and mortals with equal viciousness. Her thirst for bloodshed is insatiable. Having "plunged knee-deep in knights' blood, hip-deep in the gore of heroes," she "proceeds to her house. Not sated with battling in the plain, with her fighting between the two towns, she pictures the chairs as heroes, pretending a table is warriors, and that the footstools are troops. Much battle she does" and at last she is "sated with battling in the house," and she returns the furniture to its original state.

In ancient text and modern tradition, the Hindu mistress of the universe and mother of all, the savagely destructive Kali, chewed up her own baby and swallowed it. Her four hands bear "a bloody sword, a noose or goad, a freshly severed head, and a cup made from half a human skull, filled with blood. From her neck hangs a garland of human or demon heads; newly cut human hands dangle from her waistband; and two dead infants form her earrings."[3] Formerly the recipient of human sacrifices, in each of which she was said to take a thousand years' delight, she must now be content with the blood of animal offerings.

In classical antiquity, Hera, queen of the Greek gods, was somewhat more restrained but equally vengeful and malignant. She dashed the young Hephaestus to the ground and thereby permanently crippled him. Dionysus was attacked by her when he was yet in the womb, while she delayed the births of other children begotten by her perpetually unfaithful husband, Zeus. She sent two serpents to destroy the infant Hercules and later visited him, as well an assortment of other gods and mortals, with madness, pain, and death. Hercules understands full well that he has been unjustly victimized by Hera:

> Let the noble wife of Zeus begin the dance, pounding with her feet Olympus' gleaming floors! For she accomplished what her heart desired, and hurled the greatest man of Hellas down in utter ruin. Who could offer prayers to such a goddess? Jealous of Zeus for a mortal woman's sake, she has destroyed Hellas' greatest friend, though he was guiltless (Euripides, *Heracles*, 1303–10, trans. W. Arrowsmith).

From the myths recorded by just one ancient author, Philip Slater has prepared an astonishing table of the deities who killed, or permanently maimed, their own parents and children. The list is a long one![4] The families of the gods were enormously disturbed.

In Christianity we follow a God who has willingly been sacrificed so that God's followers need never physically harm or sacrifice another living being. In Judaism and Christianity we believe in a God without form. Since much of the Western culture has been influenced by Judeo-Christian values, we have forgotten what societal effects the Greco-Roman gods had. In this chapter let us recall the violence in the Greco-Roman myths, the violence in the worshipers, and the pagan as well as Jewish and Christian complaints of the ancient gods and goddesses so that we can today understand exactly why "pagan" had become a derogatory term in Rome by the third century.[5]

60   *The Goddess Revival*

▼ Artemis, the Mistress of Death

Artemis was the patron deity of Ephesus; and her temple, the great Artemisium, was considered one of the Seven Wonders of the ancient world. We are given an important picture of the passionate devotion that Artemis inspired in Acts 19. Worship of the goddess was widely spread throughout the Mediterranean world. Indeed, one writer maintained that in private devotions Artemis of Ephesus was the most widely worshiped deity in the Mediterranean world. Though possessed of a bizarre stiff form, covered with many breasts, her adherents maintained that the configuration had a peculiar sanctity.[6]

The cult of the Greek Artemis in particular had associations with ritual murder. The goddess herself visited death upon mortals with her terrible arrows. The most famous case of human sacrifice is the mythical one in which Artemis demanded the sacrifice of Agamemnon's daughter, Iphigenia, before the goddess would permit the Greek fleet to continue its expedition against Troy. The story is told by several ancient authors but is given its most complete treatment by Euripides in his tragedy, *Iphigenia at Aulis*. In the sequel to the story, Artemis substitutes a deer for the girl and transports her to the land of the Taurians. There she becomes a priestess of the goddess. In this capacity, it is her duty to consign to death any foreign men who may arrive on those remote shores. Iphigenia herself is accompanied by a group of exiled Greek maidens who serve under her as priestesses in the death cult. Euripides' *Iphigenia among the Taurians* tells the story of how her own brother is captured and is supposed to be sentenced to death by his priestess-sister. According to Euripides' story, they all manage to escape to Greece and there establish memorials of the ancient practice.

The cult of Artemis at Haloa required that a man be nicked in the throat with a knife in token of human sacrifice as it had been practiced by the Taurians.[7] In Sparta the tradition of the Taurian death sentence was commuted to a ritual beating that youths endured before the statue of Artemis Orthia. A priestess carried the statue and complained that the statue was unbearably heavy if the beating was not severe enough.[8] In the temple of Artemis at Brauron, goats were substituted for the human victims that had originally been required.[9] Shipwrecked sailors and strangers were said to be sacrificed to her by the Taurians on the shores of the Black Sea.[10] Pythocles, in the third book of his *On Concord*, said that the Phoceans offered a man as a burnt sacrifice to the Taurian Artemis.[11] Apollonius of Rhodes told of how Medea, a priestess of Artemis, lured her brother to the temple of Artemis on an island sacred to the goddess. She arranged for her lover to slay him there. In the vestibule of the temple Jason slew him as an ox is slain for the sacrifice while Medea, the priestess, stood by.[12]

Human sacrifice, especially to Artemis, was still being practiced at the beginning of the Common Era. The famous temple of Diana (Roman name for Artemis) at Aricia was presided over by a priest-king who was in fact a runaway slave who had gained his position by killing his predecessor.[13] In the second century A.D. Scymnus Chius mentioned human sacrifice as still being used to propitiate the goddess.[14] Tatian (A.D. 110–72) announced that after he had been initiated into the mysteries and studied the various rites, he discovered that near Rome Artemis was worshiped with the slaughter of men.[15] The Albanians offered a temple slave each year to the moon goddess, Selene, a deity sometimes identified with Artemis.[16]

The shrine of the Ephesian Artemis was said to have been founded by the Amazons who brought to Ephesus a statue of the Tauropolian Artemis. One of the epithets applied to the Amazons was "man-slaying." In keeping with this tradition, Amazons were not allowed to marry until they had slain a man of the enemy.[17] During the classical age, four enormous statues of Amazons stood in the temple of Artemis of Ephesus; and for centuries after Christ, the Amazons were commemorated yearly in a marvelous dance at Ephesus. In Ephesus women also assumed the role of the man-slaying Amazons who had founded the cult of Artemis of Ephesus. The dance may have contained a simulated attack on males, especially as the dances were performed with spears.[18] Evidence of actual human sacrifice has been discovered at the lowest level of the great Artemisium, and the tradition of a man who served as scapegoat for the religious community of Ephesus was long perpetuated.[19]

An ancient record of martyrs preserves a curious tradition about the cult of Artemis of Ephesus. It is contained in the work of a famous Byzantine scholar who flourished in the last half of the tenth century (i.e., 950–99). This scholar, Symeon Metaphrastes, gained his nickname because, although he sometimes retained earlier histories of saints and martyrs verbatim, he frequently paraphrased the older material to produce a more uniform effect. His account of St.

Timothy describes a festival of Artemis of Ephesus that was known as the *katagogion* or bringing home of the goddess. It seems to refer to a yearly procession in which the cult statue was carried through the streets and back to her temple.[20]

Metaphrastes described the procession in which people walked through the streets with idols in their hands and masks on their faces. They were also said to carry *rhopala,* understood by later martyrologists to mean clubs or cudgels—the instruments with which Timothy was to meet his fate. The word also means "phalluses," however, and the representations of the male member were frequently carried in such processions.

The next part of the description grows more curious. These citizens were said to walk around the more prominent parts of the city as they chanted hymns, apparently in honor of the goddess. This, too, accords well with what we know of such celebrations, but here the tale takes a strange turn: "In the manner of brigands they fell upon both men and women and worked great slaughter among them. The wretches believed that in this way they honored their goddess, so that they might appear men of the sort whose greatest religious service was the death of worshippers."[21] There may well be a grain of truth in the concept that Artemis was most honored by an action that secured death to her worshipers.

Ancient writers struggled with a tradition that presented Artemis both as demanding human sacrifice and also as abhorring human blood. In some cases this paradox was resolved by pretended murder in connection with the temple cult, as seems to be indicated by Achilles Tatius.[22]

But human sacrifice could be made to male gods as well as female. A number of ancient authors attest to grizzly sacrifices of young children offered in times of crisis.[23] The Phoenicians and those colonies settled by them offered young children to their deities. Hundreds of infant burials have been recovered from sacrificial burying grounds, especially at Carthage. The remains of one, two, or even three children were found inside urns interred close together in the precinct of Baal Hinnom and of his consort, Tanit. One archaeologist, Lawrence Stager, estimates that the infant sacrifices averaged one hundred a year. Diodorus of Sicily (20.14, 6) described a time of emergency when hundreds of infants from the city's first families were selected for sacrifice. The hapless babes were placed in the arms of a bronze statue of

Kronos, known as Baal Hinnom among the Punic speaking Carthaginians. The children rolled off the idol's arms and into a pit of fire. Tertullian, the church father, remonstrated against the practice:

> But, indeed, the world has held it lawful for Diana of the Scythians, or Mercury of the Gauls, or Saturn of the Africans [a later name for Kronos], to be appeased by human sacrifices; and in Latium to this day Jupiter has human blood given him to taste in the midst of the city (*Scorpiace*, III, trans. S. Thelwall).

Infant rites, he says, were abolished under the proconsulship of Tiberius and thereafter were conducted only in secret. There is evidence that, increasingly, animals were substituted for children.[24]

▼ The Violent Behavior of Religious Devotees

Stories from the realm of myth made a powerful impression on the ancient (and modern) mind. Other incidents of murder or mutilation on the part of religious devotees are reported as historical fact. Camma, a Galatian priestess of Artemis, managed to slay Sinorix, the murderer of her husband, during a rite dedicated to the goddess. She administered a cup containing a potion, which W. M. Ramsay considered "part of an old Anatolian ritual."[25] The cup, however, was poisoned. Tatian's comment that "Artemis is a poisoner"[26] may give some insight into the ramifications of the tradition.

Melitta, an aged priestess of Demeter, dwelt on the Isthmus of Corinth. She was initiated into the mysteries of the goddess but refused to share her knowledge with the local women. They first begged and later demanded that the secrets be shared with them and finally, in a rage, pulled her to pieces.[27] Both Pentheus and Orpheus were said to have been pulled to pieces by crazed female followers of Dionysus. The slaughter of King Pentheus by the women of Thebes was memorialized by two statues in the marketplace of Corinth. They were said to be hewn out of the very tree from which the king was pulled to his death by the murderous maenads.[28]

The world traveler Pausanias (second century A.D.) told of Aristomenes, who, during a ravaging expedition near Sparta, came to a sanctuary of Demeter at Aegila in Laconia. Inside, women were holding a festival and were inspired by the goddess to attack the intruders with sacrificial knives and roasting spits. Aristomenes himself was beaten with flaming torches but managed to escape alive, though some of his companions were not so fortunate.[29]

King Battos I of Cyrene wished to satisfy his curiosity as to the nature of the Thesmophoria. These were special ceremonies celebrated by women in honor of the goddess Demeter, the giver of the laws of marriage. At first the priestesses tried to explain that the rites were open only to feminine worshipers and dealt with him gently. When he persisted, they performed those rites that might be viewed by all but refused the sight of that which was forbidden to men. Finally, the female officiants, their faces and hands covered with blood and brandishing swords, suddenly bore down upon Battos and emasculated him so that he was no longer a male.[30] This same attitude finds expression at the entrance of a man into the Athenian Thesmophoria in Aristophanes' play, the *Thesmophoriazusae*.

The Greek historian Herodotus (c.484–20 B.C.) knew of an underpriestess of Demeter who effected the discomfiture of a general, Miltiades, as he was laying siege to her city, Paros. On her advice, he climbed over the wall that enclosed Demeter's sanctuary. Her strategem apparently was to lure him into an impiety that would justify his execution by the temple staff. Suddenly panic overwhelmed him as he found himself in a situation to which no male should be admitted. He jumped down from the wall, injured his thigh, and sailed home to Athens, where his wound became gangrenous and caused his death. The Delphic oracle forbade the Parians to punish the priestess.[31]

Dionysus could inspire male adherents to violence as well as women. A most egregious instance is the attack upon a Roman governor by a group of Dionysiac worshipers dressed as women in the second century A.D. So great was their fury that they dismembered the unfortunate official and consumed him as well. Cannibalism is not ordinarily associated with Dionysus, and yet Euripides' *Bacchae* carries the same message. Both mythic and actual reports point to a violent savagery lying deep within the unrestrained human consciousness.

▼ Disenchantment with the Gods

If the behavior of human devotees was appalling, frequently the behavior of the traditional gods was worse. Women in particular suffered outrageously at the hands of gods and goddesses. Jose-

phus, at the very beginning of the second century, declared that
Jews traditionally refrained from the criticism of other religions.
In this case, however, when Judaism was under attack, he would
say no more than what many Greek philosophers and thinkers had
said before him. The most famous of their poets were culpable
because of the way in which they have misrepresented the gods,
and the reproach heaped upon these myth-makers is just. The
philosophers find their tales preposterous:

> The Father himself [Zeus], the foremost and most noble [of the gods],
> allows the women who have been seduced by him and made preg-
> nant to be imprisoned or thrown into the sea, and he is unable to save
> those whom he himself has begotten, since he is held in the grasp of
> Destiny, unable to endure their deaths without tears (Josephus, *Against
> Apion*, II.245).

A number of ancient writers were wrestling with behavior in the
gods that they thought was not acceptable in human beings. Even
the pagan ancients expressed revulsion at the immorality of the
mythic material.

Euripides

Perhaps Euripides expressed this problem most perfectly in the
Ion. The hero himself struggles with the notion of the god whom he
serves (in this case Apollo) as being a rapist and betrayer of both the
woman and her child.

> I must remonstrate with Apollo; what can have come over him? He
> ravishes girls by force, then abandons them? He begets children by
> stealth, then leaves them to die? Apollo, no! Since you possess power,
> pursue goodness! Why, if a man is bad, it is the gods who punish him.
> How can it be right for you to make laws for men, and appear as law-
> breakers yourselves? Why, if—suppose something impossible, for the
> sake of argument—if you, Apollo, and Poseidon, and Zeus King of
> Heaven, are to pay to mortals the lawful indemnity for every rape
> you commit, you will empty your temples in paying for your mis-
> deeds. You put pleasure first and wisdom after—and it is sin!

How can a god live in defiance of a law that he himself has
established? It is unfair to condemn mortals who follow this
example.[32]

Euripides' Amphitrion vows that in vain has Zeus availed himself of another's marriage bed, and in vain should he also be named as father of one for whom Amphitrion himself claims paternity.

> I, a mortal, am superior in virtue to you who are a great god. For I did not betray the children of Herakles. You understand quite well how to come secretly to a couch, taking as your own marriage beds which no one has given you, but you do not understand how to save those who are dear to you. You are some sort of ignorant god, or else you are not by nature righteous (Euripides, *Heracles Furens,* 342–47).

Of all Zeus' manifold rape victims, the worst-treated was Antiope, whose sufferings became proverbial in the ancient world. The myth of her ordeal is not well known in contemporary circles, but the ancients understood its implications as a moral condemnation of not only Zeus but other predatory gods as well. The story line is similar to the format of many other tales called by Walter Burkert, "The Maidens' Tragedies." The lovely Antiope, daughter of Nycteus, king of Thebes, was raped by Zeus in the form of a satyr. Like many another victim of rape, she experienced intense persecution and rejection from her own family. Her enraged father threatened her life when he discovered that his daughter was pregnant, and Antiope fled to Sicyon, where she was received by King Epopeus. Nycteus died shortly thereafter of grief and rage but on his deathbed extracted from his brother, Lycos, a promise that he would adequately punish both Antiope and Epopeus.

Lycos marched on Sicyon, slew Epopeus, and led back Antiope as a captive. On the way, she came to Mount Cithaeron, a site intimately associated with the god Dionysus. There she gave birth to the twins and was forced to abandon them. Antiope was taken to a dungeon in Thebes, where every type of deprivation and punishment was heaped upon her by her uncle Lycos and especially by his wife Dirce. The newborn twins were discovered by a kindly herdsman and raised to young manhood. Amphion was highly musical and received from Hermes the gift of a lyre with which he sang inspired verse. Zethos, on the other hand, was of a more practical bent and saw little use in his brother's artistic and philosophical leanings. One day as they were arguing the merits of the active versus the contemplative and philosophic lifestyle, a woman, dirty, disheveled, and travel-worn burst upon the scene.

It was Antiope, who had escaped from her imprisonment and the excessive abuse that she had received at the hands of Dirce. Only with difficulty did she persuade her sons that she was indeed their mother and not, as they had at first supposed, a runaway slave. The twins found more implausible yet her story of corruption by Zeus in the guise of a satyr. Amphion protested that it was unthinkable that the noble king of the gods would approach her by stealth in the base form of a creature so notorious for lechery and trouble making. This was not the only time that Euripides' human characters were to possess a morality higher than that of the gods, and that the playwright must find means to justify divine actions.

But a Dionysiac festival was in full swing, and Dirce herself arrived with a train of maenads to celebrate the rites of the god. Here Dirce discovered the newly escaped Antiope and commanded the young men to bind her to a raging bull. When the lads understood that this was actually their mother's chief persecutor, they seized Dirce instead and bound her to the bull, which dragged her to her death. They must now defend themselves from Lycos, who would surely seek to avenge his wife's death.

Their stratagems lured Lycos into the herdsman's cave, where they were about to slay him; but suddenly Hermes appeared as a *deus ex machina*, an emissary from Mount Olympus. The twins were declared to be the sons of Zeus and their mother Antiope his beloved. The life of Lycos was to be spared, but he was to yield his kingdom to the joint rule of Amphion and Zethos, who would build the walls with the help of Amphion's wonderful lyre. Lycos must sprinkle the ashes of the slain Dirce into a fountain in Thebes that would forever after bear her name. The repentant king obeyed the command and explained that he had not understood the truth of Antiope's story, that it was she who was truly blessed.

Fortunately the last hundred lines of the play were discovered in a papyrus, and there remain as well quotations and allusions to the play in other ancient literary and artistic works. A summary in Hyginus is explicitly said to be a summarization of the play by Euripides, so that the general outline can be reconstructed with a reasonable degree of certainty. Antiope's story became an increasingly popular motif for writers and artists, but it developed as well a religious and mystic significance beyond the mere myth.

In Euripides' treatment of the story, Antiope's son, Amphion, voices an objection to the despicable way in which Zeus treats Antiope. At one point he shouts to his indifferent sire:

> You who inhabit heaven's shining plain,
> do not copulate thus for your pleasure
> and then abandon those who are dear to you,
> when you should fight alongside them as ally.[33]

Zeus has not only raped and impregnated an unfortunate mortal, but he has abandoned her to some twenty years of persistent persecution by her family. The sons, rather than the father, save Antiope from a frightful death, and Hermes appears only to affirm the paternity of the twins and to grant them the rule of Thebes. Ovid refers to the action as a "celestial crime." Perhaps the Roman Propertius states the problem most poignantly.

> For the vicious Dirce will be witness with her actual accusation
> That Antiope daughter of Nycteus had slept with Lycos.
> Ah, how many times the queen tore her beautiful hair,
> Her pitiless hand drove into her soft face.
> Ah, how many times she burdens the slave with an unfair workload
> and orders her to place her head upon the hard ground.
> Frequently she allows her to live in filth and darkness,
> frequently denies even brackish water to the fasting woman.
> Jupiter, will you never help Antiope who suffers so many ills?
> The cruel chain mars her hand.
> Are you a god to treat your girl so shabbily?
> On whom should Antiope call in her chains
> if not upon Jove?
> The obligation, though too late, is fulfilled at last (3.15).

As we noted, Antiope fares far worse than other victims of divine rape. Like Melanippe and Hypsipyle, she is separated from her children. Like Danaë she experiences the wrath of her father, like Io she wanders in madness, like Alcmena, she narrowly escapes death.

Most victims undergo a year or two of troubles and then find a variety of rewards. Some are placed among the stars, and almost all are given human husbands, other children, and a happy home life.

Antiope is given none of these rewards. Her life was ruined as she languished for years in jail as the slave of the vicious Dirce, abused and separated from her children. Things take a turn for the better only when she has been brought to the very brink of death, and then her sons, rather than Antiope, receive the compensations for all that their mother has suffered.

The Censure of Later Authors

Many of the later authors refer to the story in ways that are critical of Zeus.[34] How can one reconcile such crassly indifferent and irresponsible behavior with the justice of Zeus? The story of Antiope became a prime example of the fundamental immorality not only of Zeus but of Greek religion in general. The story could not be accepted at face value by enlightened pagans, Jews, or Christians. In late antiquity Antiope became a focal point in arguments over the justification of Zeus. Her tale provided a fertile field for Jewish and Christian apologists, those writers of the second century A.D. and later who defended their faith against paganism. The story also posed immense problems for thoughtful pagans. It must be denied, denounced, or spiritualized.

There were several elements of the tale that were totally untenable to religious thinkers in late antiquity. These were the violence of the rape, the deceit perpetrated by Zeus through the bestiality of the satyr form, and the total lack of concern on the part of the king of the gods for the consequences of his own misdeed.

The Violence of Rape

The first element for censure was the violence of rape and the extent of the injury that it inflicted upon a helpless woman. Amphion sees Zeus as a malefactor in his role as rapist. Sexual violence is an oft-repeated theme in the stories of heroines, and the impregnation of Antiope is by no means unique in this respect. By late antiquity, however, writers were concerned for the harm done to the victims and spoke feelingly of their suffering. Increasingly divine rape was considered a "celestial crime" rather than a light-hearted escapade. There was an examination of the consequences of the amours of the gods.

By the second century A.D., there is evidence that there was a ritual calling of Zeus to account for his rape of the mother goddess,

Demeter. At Eleusis there was said to be: "a goat-legged mime enacted about the testicles; for Zeus, making expiation for the violence done to Demeter, cut off the testicles of a goat and placed them in her lap as though they were his own."[35]

Apparently the wrath of Demeter formed an integral part of the mystery. Indeed, Clement of Alexandria derived the term "orgy" from the wrath of Demeter against Zeus. Within the Phrygian mysteries of Deo, the king of gods was also said to have thrown the genitals of a ram in her lap in pretended repentance over the deed and thereby to have appeased her.[36]

By late antiquity even Zeus could not behave so reprehensibly without some show of conscience or compunction. Texts reveal a growing awareness that rape is a crime that could not be condoned even in the king of gods. He was no longer admired for his sly manipulation of the trusting young girl but condemned for his despicable tricks. Sometimes rape was spiritualized into celestial union with the god, but increasingly the ancients viewed such behavior as totally unacceptable in the deity who was said to dispense ultimate justice.

The Deceit Perpetrated by Zeus

A second element that drew the censure of later writers was the crass deceit with which the king of gods took advantage of his victim in the seduction.

The disguise of Zeus drew far more condemnation than one might expect from a literary and artistic device. His treacherous transformations served Christian and Jewish authors well in their arguments against the morality of Greek religion, and especially of the pagan gods.

Zeus, who swallowed Metis, possessed the power of infinite transformation.[37] His was the power of wily cunning, of taking his unsuspecting prey by surprise. He was the master of trickery and deceit, outwitting men, gods, and especially women. Disguise was a fundamental element of his wiles, and no disguise can be more appropriate to his *metis* than that of a conniving satyr, grandmaster of the erotic arts.

Antiope, like many another heroine, was simply no match for so experienced a trickster. But how could this side of Zeus' nature be reconciled with the fundamental integrity and justice that he was otherwise said to possess?

It is hard to find another story in which Zeus appears in so base a form. Satyrs were not in general looked upon with admiration. For the most part their image denoted degradation, drunkenness, and lechery. The satyr was often viewed with disgust.[38] Antiope is the more demeaned that she was violated by so outrageous a figure of ribaldry and degradation.

The Example Set by Zeus

These divine activities described by the poets left a burden upon the more philosophically minded. Although the gods and goddesses had captured the poetic and artistic imagination—and still continue to do so—their attitudes and actions were scarcely worthy of emulation by ordinary mortals. Frequently their exploits were characterized by caprice and cruelty. Well before the beginning of the Common Era, Greek philosophers, dramatists, and poets were torn between their own sense of integrity and the images of the gods that classical mythology had projected. Xenophanes, raised in Asia Minor under Persian rule, complained that the gods were depicted in the tales of Homer and Hesiod as thieves, adulterers, and deceivers. These tales were not worthy of deity.[39] The Athenian orator, Isocrates, declared that Orpheus told more scurrilous tales about the gods than any other poet.[40]

Only shortly after the time of Euripides, Plato's Socrates maintained that the felonies and conflicts of the gods should not be divulged except to a chosen few. Mothers and nurses should tell children stories that condemn quarreling, and poets should represent divinities in a favorable light.[41]

While the poets might be castigated for their representations of the gods, they dealt for the most part with myths that were already shaped by tradition. The playwright Euripides, as we have seen, was painfully aware of the injustice inherent in the story that he told. He was wrestling with behavior in the gods that simply was not acceptable in human beings. His dramas express revulsion at the immorality of the mythic material that he as a poet was constrained to use. His Heracles vehemently repudiates the tales of divine adulteries as being the lies of poets:

> I do not believe the gods commit adultery, or bind each other in chains.
> I never did believe it; I never shall; nor that one god is tyrant of the

rest. If god is truly god, he is perfect, lacking nothing. These are poets' wretched lies (*Heracles,* 1341–46).

Beginning with Euripides a new theme developed: that of condemnation of Zeus for his crass treatment of the unfortunate heroine. By the first century B.C., the wrong that was done Antiope became cause for concern. The stories of Antiope, the worst abused of Zeus' rape victims, and of the young boy Ganymede, whom Zeus abducted, came to be representative of the accounts of all the mortals defiled by the king of the gods. The reproofs were at first restrained and were originally voiced by pagans.

The Roman poet Ovid's mention of Antiope is encompassed in a series of stories of rapes by Zeus and other deities. Indeed, Leo C. Curran points to no less than fifty divine rapes that are chronicled in the *Metamorphoses*.[42] The Antiope vignette occurs within the story of the contest between Athena, goddess of household crafts, and Arachne, the fabulous weaver. Arachne boasted that her spinning was finer than that of Athena. Angered by Arachne's boasts, Athena, disguising herself as an old woman, visited Arachne's home and challenged her to a weaving contest in order to humble the arrogant mortal.

Athena crafted a tapestry depicting the contest in which she bested Poseidon over the naming of Athens. The twelve gods sat in judgment at the event. The two consultants, as well as their gifts, a spring of salt water, and an olive tree were worked into the fabric along with a figure of Victory. The work of Athena left no doubt as to her intentions for the outcome of the present contest. At each of the four corners was woven a scene showing the dire fate of mortals who had displayed *hubris* in comparing themselves favorably with the deities. The whole constituted a warning not to be lightly ignored.

Then she demanded that Arachne produce a piece of equal merit. With trembling hands, the girl executed a piece demonstrating the sins and injustices of the gods toward mortals. While the piece of Athena glorified the supremacy of the gods, the work of Arachne depicted their perfidy and victimization of women. Each scene showed a rape accomplished through treachery. First she crafted the story of Europa tricked into trusting the seemingly mild bull who was Zeus in disguise. Leda is raped by Zeus in the form of a swan, and Asterie is his victim when he assumes the guise of an eagle.

Antiope is the fourth victim: "She added how Jupiter disguised as a satyr filled the womb of the beautiful daughter of Nycteus with twins."[43]

In all, Arachne's handiwork comprised a total of no less than twenty-one rapes. Ovid calls them "celestial crimes." The tapestry contains a monumental charge against the very deities who preside with such majesty in Athena's weaving. The goddess is enraged not only by the faultless skill of the mortal but more yet by her audacious allegation of immorality on the part of the gods. She rends the precious web and transforms Arachne so that she must forever after do her spinning as a humble spider.

The criticisms of the pagans paved the way for more severe censure from monotheists. Both Jewish and Christian writers attacked the morality of Zeus in his rape and neglect of Antiope. They argued that such a tale proved the degeneracy of paganism. The myth was often selected as indicative of the misbehavior of the gods.

A late work, *Barlaam and Josaphat,* preserves within it one of the earliest Christian apologies, *The Apology of Aristides,* which dates to the middle of the second century A.D.[44] It was said to have been presented before the Emperor Hadrian on behalf of Christians by an Athenian philosopher known as Aristides.[45] He writes that the Greeks are more degenerate in their biases than the Chaldeans, and a prime example is the conduct of Zeus:

> Next Zeus is brought in, whom they say rules over these gods and is metamorphosed into creatures so that he may commit adultery with mortal women. For they show him metamorphosed into a bull for Europa and into gold for Danaë and into a swan for Leda and into a satyr for Antiope and into a thunderbolt for Semele.[46]

While the report is highly critical of Zeus' adultery, the repeated emphasis upon his metamorphoses reveals that this in itself was a dominant motif of Greek religion in late antiquity. The degeneracy of the gods and its deleterious influence on their worshipers is the fundamental theme of the argument. Aristides harks back to the Antiope story and deplores the utilization by pagans of the old stories of the gods to justify their own outrageous conduct.[47] The philosopher views the problem as compounded because thieves and adulterers address their prayers to deities who have set them their example.

Another second-century apologist, Justin Martyr, addressed his *First Apology* to Antoninus Pius and his sons about A.D. 150. Antiope's story provides a prime example of depravity on the part of the pagan gods. In contrast, as Christians: "We have dedicated ourselves to a God who is unborn and not subject to passion, whom we are convinced has come neither upon an Antiope and other such women, nor upon a Ganymede through lechery" (*Apology*, 1.25). Christians are superior because they do not worship a god who could abuse someone like Antiope so shamefully.[48]

▼ Conclusion

God's goodness and spiritual nature were the reasons Judaism and Christianity were superior to the pagan religions. Unlike the pagan deities, God's nature and form are always the same. Violence, deceit, and injustice by the deities established for humans attitudes and actions not worth emulating. Sexual freedom did not bring human happiness. Because pagans, Jews, and Christians became agreed on this point, the God described in the Bible came to claim the hearts and minds of the ancient world. The positive traits expounded today, as we shall see in the next chapter, were not prominent in the ancient deities. Few are the authors today who tell us in published form the actual myths of the past and their consistent ramifications for today.[49]

4

GOD IS UNIQUE

*L*iberty Hyde Bailey wrote a beautiful introduction to the 1947 *Woman's Home Companion Garden Book*. This Garden Book is simply a reference book explaining climatic regions, garden making, and plant material. When I need to find out if and when I should trim my rosebush, I check the section called "Roses." But in the foreword Bailey gives the book a surprising theological twist. She sets gardening into the context of the garden or paradise of Eden. She decides that the earth is for people's pleasure, and that people may live in a paradise. Plants

> have been man's to choose and to adapt, and to modify to his liking . . .
>
> It would be indefensible if man did not gather these benefits to himself. He does not need to exercise restraint. He has the opportunity to partake. Only indifference or blindness can prevent . . .
>
> To grow a plant to perfect maturity is a triumph. The plant has met the man's wishes. It is with him every waking hour and it waits for him at the dawn. He sees the young shoot, the priceless flower, the full seed. He covers it for the deep sleep of winter in confidence; it will come back to him in the spring . . .
>
> The paradise or the garden provides diversion and occupation.[1]

Rereading this foreword in the 1990s, after our introduction to God/dess worship, I see it with new eyes. Would an ecofeminist be repelled by Bailey's view that the garden is here for us to choose, adapt, modify, benefit from, partake, enjoy, and work? Or is it, rather, we humans who need to give to and be adapted and modified by the earth? Bailey's view seems too human-centered, now. Moreover, what was then the generic "man" has now come to represent for some patriarchy, a force of subjugation, violence, and destruction.

But to conclude so glibly would leave us misreading Bailey's words. We would miss the enchantment, care, and love toward the garden: the gardener observing and enabling the plant's growth from seed, shoot, to flower, and the gardener taking care of the plant in winter. If the garden is seen as diversion and occupation, the garden is then nurtured and appreciated. Yes, she says, we humans need not "exercise restraint." But, the next sentence explains what this means: "partake." To have dominion means you take care of plants so that you can appreciate their beauty and eat their fruits.

God/dess worship is, at times, reacting to excesses of the past.

- where dominion meant destruction, rather than nurture;
- where the deity was portrayed as so transcendent, wholly different, solely masculine, war-like, and judge-like, that humans, especially women, feel unloved, and female power does not appear legitimate or beneficent;
- where the church's authority has been so overtaken by men that women have felt excluded;
- where women's bodies and their life cycle were seen as carnal, fleshly, and earthly, and therefore were not affirmed;
- where women were taught to devalue their wills and to believe that they could not achieve their will through their own power;
- where women's relations to other women (such as mother-daughter) were ignored or distorted.[2]

God/dess worship also has its own history: as a continuation of the 1960s God-is-dead movement,[3] Carl Jung's anti-Judaeo-Christian monotheism,[4] and as a newer evolution of the new age movement.[5]

We humans can all so easily misread and misunderstand one another. Our views are often much more subtle and complex than we care to acknowledge. Hopefully, we as writers have accurately explained what we have read about the God/dess. We also think that Christianity itself has been misrepresented in many of the texts we have read. At times some feminists have repudiated Jung's and Freud's view of women while appropriating their negative view of Christianity, yet feel perfectly free to write that the same discernment should never be applied to their stereotypes of Christianity. For example, Naomi Goldenberg concludes: "Jesus Christ cannot symbolize the liberation of women. A culture that maintains a masculine image for its highest divinity cannot allow its women to experience themselves as the equals of its men. In order to develop a theology of women's liberation, feminists have to leave Christ and Bible behind them." However, even though Goldenberg gives proof for both Sigmund Freud's and Carl Jung's sexist and racist views, she still wants to benefit from their theories: "We do not have to accept all of Freud's terms to see the significance of his theory," and "Although Jung deserves sharp criticism for those areas of his work that fall short of his ideals of respect and dignity for individual psychic values, he ought not to be dismissed on account of his worst work."[6] We hope none of our readers will bring this closemindedness to their study of the Bible.

Our goal for chapters 4–8 is to understand God's nature as revealed in the Bible. Those who reject Christianity may have some true complaints to make of Christians. We need to be open to those complaints. But we believe that not only can we as Christians respond to these complaints, but also that the God of the Bible offers the greatest joy, love, and freedom to humans.

▼ Connotations of Goddess Spirituality

Most of the literature on goddess spirituality agrees that certain ideas are good while others are bad. For instance, Asoka Bandarage, in the introduction to the Fall 1991 issue of *Woman of Power*[7] makes these evaluations:

Positive Concepts	*Negative Concepts*
a new world of peace, harmony, and beauty	the global military-industrial complex
visionary	confusion
diverse	individual freedoms
egalitarian	abstract academic theorizing

ecologically sustainable	games of New Age spirituality
global consciousness	gender, race, and class domination
harmonious planetary community	dominant political, economic, and cultural forces
cooperative, democratic	hierarchical
we decade	me decade
exquisite	rampant biases
a beacon of light	
social change activists	sexual politics
inner empowerment	greed
wisdom	hatred
nonviolent	violence, destruction
courage	poverty
resilience	repression
wondrous process of growth and expansion	mechanistic
a dance of life	military superpower
a celebration of spirit	decaying world order
truth, compassion, generosity	ignorance, delusion
free, spontaneity	control
inspired	technocapitalist
decisive	
exciting, vitality	
organic	separation
oneness of all life, holistic	dominant
inherent connection	above nature
interbeing, reciprocity	impersonal
interdependence	dualism of self and other
cycle of nature	
complex	
everchanging ebb and flow of nature	permanence

Gaia—one living, breathing
   organism, indivisible, synergic

▼ Biblical Concepts Are Similar to Goddess Concepts

Ironically, so many of the positive concepts are biblical ones.

"Blessed are the *peacemakers*, for they will be called children of
   God" (Matt. 5:9).[8]

"The kings of the Gentiles lord it over them; and those in authority over them are called benefactors. But not so with you; rather
   the greatest among you must become like the youngest, and
   the leader like one who *serves*" (Luke 22:25–26).

"The Lord God took the man and put him in the garden of Eden
   to till it and keep it" (Gen. 2:15).

"You must not destroy [a town's] trees by wielding an ax against
   them. Although you may take food from them, you must not
   cut them down. Are trees in the field human beings that they
   should come under siege from you?" (Deut. 20:19).

"Above all, clothe yourselves with *love*, which binds everything
   together in perfect *harmony*" (Col. 3:14).

"Happy are those who find wisdom, . . . She is more precious
   than jewels, and nothing you desire can compare with her.
   Long life is in her right hand; in her left hand are riches and
   honor. Her ways are ways of pleasantness, and all her paths
   are peace. She is a tree of life to those who lay hold of her,
   those who hold her fast are called happy" (Prov. 3:13, 15–18).

The Word is "the *light* of all people. The light shines in the darkness, and the darkness did not overcome it" (John 1:4–5).

"I will pour out my spirit on all flesh; your sons and your daughters shall prophesy, your old men shall dream dreams, and your
   young men shall see *visions*. Even on the male and female
   slaves, in those days, I will pour out my spirit" (Joel 2:28–29).

"There is no longer Jew or Greek, there is no longer slave or free,
   there is no longer male and female; for all of you are *one* in
   Christ Jesus" (Gal. 3:28).

"The Spirit of the Lord is upon me, because he has anointed me
   to bring good news to the poor. He has sent me to proclaim
   release to the captives and recovery of sight to the blind, to let

the *oppressed* go free, to proclaim the year of the Lord's favor" (Luke 4:18–19).

"You will receive *power* when the Holy Spirit has come upon you" (Acts 1:8).

"One of them struck the slave of the high priest and cut off his right ear. But Jesus said, "No more of this!" And he touched his ear and *healed* him" (Luke 22:50–1).

"Be strong and of good *courage*. Do not be afraid or dismayed before the king of Assyria and all the horde that is with him; for there is one greater with us than with him. With him is an arm of flesh; but with us is the Lord our God" (2 Chron. 32:7–8).

"For we are the aroma of Christ to God among those who are *being* saved and among those who are perishing" (2 Cor. 2:15).

Praise God "with tambourine and *dance*" (Ps. 150:4).

"So do not worry about tomorrow, for tomorrow will bring worries of its own" (Matt. 6:34).

"Grace and *truth* came through Jesus Christ" (John 1:17).

"The Lord, the Lord, a God merciful and *gracious,* slow to anger, and abounding in steadfast love and faithfulness, keeping steadfast love for the thousandth generation, forgiving iniquity and transgression and sin" (Exod. 34:6–7).

"Do not lord it over those in your charge, but be examples to the flock" (1 Pet. 5:3).

"So if the Son makes you free, you will be *free* indeed" (John 8:36).

"For just as the body is one and has many members, and all the members of the body, though many, are *one body,* so it is with Christ (1 Cor. 12:12).

"We know that the whole creation has been groaning in labor pains until now; and not only the creation, but we ourselves, who have the first fruits of the Spirit, groan inwardly while we wait for adoption, the redemption of our bodies" (Rom. 8:22–23).

In the biblical text we find strong exhortations for peace, service, care of nature, equality, harmony, wisdom, light, visions, diversity in oneness, concern for the oppressed, power, healing, courage, a right process, dance, immediacy, truth, compassion, freedom, an interdependence between humanity and creation. Why then is the Judaeo-Christian faith placed along the side of the violent, hierarchical, destructive, repressive, mechanistic, decaying world order? The core of the criticism and the core of the defense lies with the nature of God. Again and again the God of the Bible is described in the goddess literature as (Yahweh) the male warrior God.[9] What is God like as described in the Bible? How does God's description compare to these positive concepts as listed earlier? In this chapter we will study the biblical claim that God is unique and God is one. In the next two chapters we will study God as spirit without sexuality.

▼ God Is a God of Gods

"The God of gods (and goddesses)" occurs about ten times in the Bible. For the biblical writers "the God of gods" was a key reminder of the biblical God's uniqueness. Ironically, for others, the title "God of gods" was a vestige, not of God's uniqueness, but of a polytheistic belief remnant in the Bible text. For example, Tikva Frymer-Kensky writes: "Early Israelite poetry shows that in the early stages of biblical religion, Israel believed in other divine beings, none of whom could compare to YHWH."[10]

However, the best way to understand any term is to study the context of that term. What does "the God of gods" mean in its biblical contexts?

The first reference occurs in the Book of Deuteronomy, where Moses summarizes God's message to him. Moses was raised in an intercultural, interreligious setting. His natural mother and sister, devout Hebrews, kept up contact with Moses in his early years, but he was adopted by Egypt's Pharaoh's daughter (Exod. 2:7–10). Moses must have had some training both in the God of the Bible and the gods of Egypt (Acts 7:22, 25). He was able to see certain powerful acts done by the Egyptian sorcerers, for instance, seeing them turn sticks into snakes. But, we are told, "Aaron's staff swallowed up theirs" (Exod. 7:12).

Power and Compassion Are Combined in the God of the Bible

So, Moses, as the Hebrews, had seen the deities of his age demonstrate a certain power, but the God who created the world was greater. Therefore, Moses teaches the people that "the Lord your

God, he is God of the gods and Lord of the lords" (Deut. 10:17). The
title "God of gods," rather than acknowledging polytheism, repri-
mands a potentially polytheistic audience, the Hebrews. Not only is
"the Lord" greater than any sorcerer, the Lord is greater than any
presence or entity in the world. "The God, the great, the mighty"
can not be bribed to ignore the righteous pleas of the powerless,
symbolized by orphans, widows, and strangers. The Lord is greater
than the power of money or status to corrupt and to oppress those
who are most defenseless. The main point here is to show that the
Lord who has the greatest power of all uses it in a compassionate,
socially active manner. This understanding of God then becomes a
model to all of us, to use what power we have to serve others with
less power (Deut. 10:19).

In contrast, the first emphasis in God/dess is on *inner* empowerment. For example, Jean Shinoda Bolen, author of *Goddesses in Everywoman,* as well as other books, writes that the women's spirituality
movement: "is an interior, empowering movement that was being
ignored until the concept of the Goddess became more wide-
spread."[11] Starhawk, even though she herself was involved in a
blockade of the Livermore Weapons Lab, states that the model of
earth-based spirituality is "one of personal power. We each strive to
increase our power-from-within." Magic is "the art of evoking
power-from-within."[12] One issue of *Woman of Power* even includes
an essay by a believer in American Indian deities who claims she
has been oppressed by white spiritual feminists as they demand that
she teach them her religion. Andy Smith writes: "New Agers see
Indians as romanticized gurus who exist only to meet their con-
sumerist needs." White "feminists" "do not want to be part of our
struggles for survival against genocide, and they do not want to fight
for treaty rights or an end to substance abuse or sterilization abuse."
She concludes: "White feminists should know that as long as they
take part in Indian spiritual abuse, either by being consumers of it
or by refusing to take a stand on it, Indian women will consider
white 'feminists' to be nothing more than agents in the genocide of
our people."[13] Even though some authors write both of inner
empowerment and social activism, Smith objects that, in her experience, concern for oneself rarely leads to concern for others.

At least in some of the goddess literature, one reason for women
to be empowered inwardly is so they can thereby be empowered

outwardly. Certainly any Christian should agree that God's power must work within us as we act outwardly. However, the God we worship makes a key difference in who we are, how important we are, and what we do. What is never made explicit in the goddess literature is that if the Goddess is indeed the cosmos "in whose being we all partake, who encompasses us and is immanent within us" and, as well, we humans are also the Goddess, in reality, only the whole cosmos or the whole pattern has most importance. We humans are only one part of that pattern and therefore important only inasmuch as we are part of a whole. Each human has no importance in her/himself: "What is valued is the whole pattern." That is why the ethics Starhawk promotes are of "interconnection." "The ethics of immanence are based on the recognition that all is interconnected." "Earth-based spiritual traditions are rooted in community" *not* "individual salvation." That sounds good and we can see a certain truth in it. What is not said, however, is that a single human in herself/himself has no value. That is why individually we are not worth "saving," only insofar are we worth saving as we are a part of the pattern. That is why ritual is so prominent in goddess worship. "Ritual is patterned action." Adherents need to enter patterned action in order to become part of the larger cosmic pattern of action.[14]

Only the God of the Bible Has Power to Create

The biblical title "God of gods" is addressed to a polytheistic audience. This God models an inner power that results in individual care. In addition, wherever the Lord is contrasted with gods, soon thereafter the author will explain that these other gods do not exist. In 1 Chronicles the Lord is great and greatly praised and "is to be revered above all gods" (16:25). Again, the author repeats Moses' point that the world has no greater presence, power, or entity than the Lord.[15] Immediately thereafter, as an explanatory note, the author comments: "for all the gods of the peoples are idols" (1 Chron. 16:26). "Idols" or *ĕlîlîm* literally are "nothings." *Ĕlîl* in the singular signifies "null, vain, nothingness, feebleness."[16] Why is the Lord to be feared over all gods? That is because the gods are "nothing." Only the Lord can create the world (1 Chron. 16:26). Without God we have nothing (Gen. 1:2).

In almost every passage where the Lord is compared to the gods, somewhere in the context the contrast is made that only the Lord made the world:

> "For all the gods of the peoples are idols, *but the Lord made the heavens*" (1 Chron. 16:26).
> "For the Lord is a great God, and a great King above all gods." In God's "hand are the depths of the earth; the heights of the mountains are his also" (Ps. 95:3–4).
> The Lord "is to be revered above all gods. For all the gods of the peoples are idols, *but the Lord made the heavens*" (Ps. 96:4–5).
> "The heavens proclaim [the Lord's] righteousness . . . all gods bow down. . . . For you, O Lord, are most high over all the earth; you are exalted far above all gods" (Ps. 97:6, 7, 9).
> "For I know that the Lord is great; our Lord is above all gods. Whatever the Lord pleases he does, in heaven and on earth, in the seas and all deeps" (Ps. 135:5–6).
> "O give thanks to the God of gods, for his steadfast love endures forever. O give thanks to the Lord of lords, . . . who alone does great wonders, . . . who by understanding made the heavens" (Ps. 136:2–5).

The Lord is great because only the Lord can create and maintain the world. Since idols are "nothing," they do not have the power to create and maintain the world. The authors also use personification, using human action or feeling to describe something inanimate, to describe the great contrast between the Lord and the idols: "all gods bow down" before God (Ps. 97:7).

A few believers have been trying to work out a compromise between Goddess spirituality and Christianity. For instance, the authors of *Wisdom's Feast* have taken a quality of God—wisdom— and made it into an intermediary figure not quite God, definitely not human (similar to an angel). Assuming the Hebrew God is male (which is debated in the next two chapters), they designate creation to Wisdom or Sophia. Yet we have seen that a key biblical thought is that only one God, one unique God, can create. In addition, at the practical level Sophia replaces God in worship and preaching as the one, not God directly, to whom one prays.

Moreover, what have women gained? God appears as some sort of immaterial male, whom men reflect. Women simply reflect a demiurge, an inferior to God. When the apostle John fell down to worship at the feet of a glorious angel, the angel (if Sophia were angel and not simply personification) declares: "You must not do that! I am a servant together with you and your brothers and sisters the prophets, and the people observing the words of this book. Worship God" (Rev. 22:9).[17]

God creating the heavens and the earth is a central truth about the world we live in. The first words of God's self-revelation in Genesis declare this truth. Only one presence in the world is able to accomplish this goal, as the Reubenites, Gadites, and half-tribe of Manasseh emphatically shout: "God God the Lord, God God the Lord" (Josh. 22:22). Not to give credit to the author of this world is blasphemy. To confuse subject and predicate is blasphemy. The Bible text declares: *"God* created the heavens and the earth" (Gen. 1:1), *not* "the heavens and the earth created God" and *"God* created humankind" (Gen. 1:27), *not* "humankind created God." Such a slight difference in language is a crucial difference in meaning. We have often heard about giving credit where credit is due, but now that maxim takes on macrocosmic consequences.

▼ God Is One

Moses was charged to teach the Hebrews what came to be called the "Hear" (in Hebrew the *šĕmaᶜ*). Both the adults and the children were to learn this message. The *šĕmaᶜ*, or Deuteronomy 6:4–9; 11:13–21, and Numbers 15:37–41, had to be recited two times every day in the first century of our era by free adult Jewish males if they wanted to remain in good religious standing.[18] But the Bible does not exempt women, children, and slaves. It also does not require people to repeat daily this crucial message, except to say they are to keep it in their will or inmost being ("heart"), to recite it to or inculcate it in their children, to talk about it at home and when traveling, and to make symbolic reminders of it to keep on their person and on their houses and gates (Deut. 6:6–9). Learn this message they must if they want to appreciate and not forget the God who does good actions on their behalf (Deut. 6:12). The "Hear" or *šĕmaᶜ* begins, literally: "Hear Israel, Lord is God, Lord is one" (Deut. 6:4). Then,

Moses continues: "Love Lord your God with all your heart and with all your life and with all your trembling" (Deut. 6:5).

"Hear" in the Bible signifies not only "hear" with your sense of hearing, but also "hear" with your will (Deut. 6:6). To hear with one's will means to obey or observe or follow and do. For instance, earlier Moses says: "Hear Israel and guard" (Deut. 6:3). The term "guard" repeats and amplifies the meaning of "hear."

The Lord Is Holy

What is Israel supposed to hear, watch, and obey? "Lord God, Lord one." The word we translate "Lord" is the Tetragrammaton, four consonants (YHWH) to which the appropriate vowel pointings have never been written in the authoritative Masoretic text. When God gives Moses a name in Exodus 6:2–3 it is a name that is unpronounceable (at least by us). In order to acknowledge God's greatness and holiness the Hebrews would recite "Lord" whenever they saw the Tetragrammaton. The ancient editors of the Hebrew text, the Masorites, also wrote down the vowels for the Hebrew *Adonai* or "Lord." Even in the first century A.D. the correct vowel endings were pronounced only by the high priest during services at the temple in Jerusalem.[19] When the people and the priests heard the correct vowel and consonantal name of God expressed by the High Priest at the Temple Court in Jerusalem during the once a year Day of Atonement service, they would kneel and bow and fall down on their faces and say: "Blessed be the name of the glory of his kingdom for ever and ever!"

Any attempt to reconstruct the vowels today is purely hypothetical (e.g., "Yahweh"). Devout Jews today continue to translate YHWH as "Lord" and I think we Gentiles should follow their practice. First of all, we do not know how accurately to pronounce YHWH. Second, the early church followed in the same practice. Ancient New Testament Greek manuscripts dating from the first century through the middle ages abbreviate the name of God, Jesus, and Spirit. Instead of *theos* ("God"), *Iēsous* ("Jesus") and *Pneuma* ("Spirit"), for example, the scribes wrote: *Ths, Is, Pna.*[20] Their intention was the same as the writers of the Tetragrammaton, to express God's holiness, very unlike today's practice of removing "Christ" from "Xmas." Today in the United States abbreviations for names are less formal and less respectful. "X" symbolizes a secularizing process today, but not in ancient times. Third, since the term "Yahweh" has no significance today, people often end employing "Yahweh" as a name for a lesser deity, whether consciously or subconsciously.[21]

YHWH may be related to the Hebrew "to be" (*hayah*). When Moses wants to know how to call "God" when speaking to the Israelites, God answers "I will be who I will be" (Exod. 3:14), in the qal imperfect tense, a tense of incompleted action. I have always thought this reply was affectionately humorous on God's part, indicating that no name is complete enough to explain fully God's nature. In addition, by using the imperfect tense God is implying that God is a God of the future, God can not be restrained from acting, and God is consistent in nature. No wonder Paul Tillich described God as "being itself or as the ground of being."[22] However, the "ground of being" or the translation "I am who I am" do not communicate well that action orientation of the imperfect tense.

The Lord Is God

What Moses has written[23] as the essential message to be taught from generation to generation, then, is that this God with this unique name has two key characteristics that must be maintained together: the Lord is *God*, the Lord is *one*. The Hebrew for "God" is *ʾĕlôhîm*. *ʾĕlôhîm* is surprisingly a plural noun. And, it can refer to more than one god or goddess, as we saw earlier in Deuteronomy 10:17: "God (*ʾĕlôhîm*) of *the gods*" (*ʾĕlôhîm*) or as in Genesis 35:2, "the foreign *gods*." In Deuteronomy 10:17 "the gods" takes the article showing that Moses speaks of a whole class ("the gods") as compared to the individually unique "God."[24] Only context can clarify which God or gods or goddesses the author writes about.[25] The singular form (*ʾelôha*) is very unusual, more often used in poetry.[26] When *ʾĕlôhîm* refers to one God, it is an abstract plural noun. The plural ending indicates not number, but an intensification of the characteristics inherent in the stem. *ʾĕlôhîm* may be translated "Godhead." In other words, whatever makes God be God is very present in this God. In the same way, "womanhood" or "manhood" are two abstract forms of the simpler nouns "woman" and "man," intensifying gender. The grammarian W. Gesenius explains that *ʾĕlôhîm* is not "a remnant of earlier polytheistic views" because Hebrew has many similar abstract plural nouns. For example, "the Most Holy" (*qĕdōsîm*) is an abstract plural noun that refers clearly to the one Lord (Hos. 11:12 [12:1]).

"Lord" ('ădônîm) in the plural can also clearly refer to one person (Gen. 42:30). In addition, the plural abstract 'ĕlôhîm, when it refers to majesty, not number, takes a singular verb or a singular adjective. For example, in Genesis 1:1 "God" or 'ĕlôhîm (plural) "created" (third person singular verb). In Psalm 7:9 'ĕlôhîm is modified by the singular adjective "righteous" (ṣadîq, Heb. 7:10).[27] Moreover, in Deuteronomy 6:4 'ĕlôhîm is immediately explained as referring to "one" ('eḥād). It can not, therefore, refer to more than one god.

The Lord Is One

"One" is a number. It can very literally refer to one being, as Jacob ("We are all one man's son's" [Gen. 42:11]), one unit of time, one day (Gen. 1:5; 27:45), or one locale (Gen. 1:9). It can also refer to unity of purpose. The people at Shinar were "one" because they spoke the same "one" language and wanted to make a name for themselves apart from God (Gen. 11:1, 6). "One" can also be symbolic. The attachment of a husband to his wife will be so great as to make them "one" flesh (Gen. 2:24). Thus, Moses is telling his listeners that, unlike the polytheistic culture around them, they are to get it into their heads that the God they are to obey is one God not many gods. However, the terms 'ĕlôhîm and *one* leave open the additional truth that this one God is multidimensional, as the church has come to explain, three Persons but one God.

Humans Mirror God's Oneness

The oneness of the deity (a one in diversity) is mirrored in the oneness of humanity (also, a one in diversity). Even though the plural 'ĕlôhîm takes a singular verb (God "said"), when God speaks in Genesis 1:26 God uses the first person plural verb: "let us make." In order to help us understand the way in which humans reflect God, God here for the first time in the series of creations described in Genesis 1 uses a plural verb and plural suffixes ("*our* image," "*our* resemblance"): "And God said, '*Let us make* Adam in *our* image according to *our* resemblance and they will rule over . . .'" (Gen. 1:26). The God who is powerful and great enough to create everything in the world (Gen. 1:1) also has some aspect of diversity or multiplicity or multidimensionality. No wonder God's creation is all good (that is its unity) yet diverse. The light is divided from darkness (Gen. 1:4–5). The firmament divides waters from waters (Gen. 1:6–7). The waters are gathered into seas leaving dry land (Gen. 1:10). Some lights are used for daytime, others for night (Gen. 1:14–18). But all of it is "good," none of it is evil.

Humans are the first and the only creation explicitly made in God's diverse trinity image. God's nature affects our nature. First of all, we, all of us, are "Adam," or the Human. Before we should ever be gender-specific, we must be "human" first. Our humanity precedes our maleness or femaleness. The same point is repeated in Genesis 1:27: "And God created the Adam in his image, in the image of God he created him, a male and a female he created them." The same message is repeated after the fall: "God was creating Adam in the resemblance of God he made him, a male and a female he created them, and he praised them and he named their name Adam in the day of their being created" (Gen. 5:1–2).

Believing in polytheistic deities today appears generally to augment gender-specific ideas, actions, and groups. Nelle Morton typifies Goddess gatherings where women gather to gain a sense of community or oneness: "The words used in the service were exclusively female words" given in a circle, an egalitarian womb symbol, in contrast to being delivered from a podium, "the phallic symbol up front." Genevieve Vaughan contrasts male "phallic aggressiveness," violence, competition with "women's ways," which are others-oriented, gentle, merciful, kind, loving, trusting, peaceful, and life nurturing.[28] These are the traditional stereotypes for men and women. Yet, very few men are as aggressive while driving as a mother driving her child to school! Many fathers have devoted themselves to their children. These are all stereotypes that rarely are true for all women and men.

Joan B. Townsend agrees that the Goddess movement "perpetuates the male/female dichotomy and merely replaces one sexist hierarchical model (the dominance of males and a male God) with another (the dominance of females and a female Goddess), and so perpetuates the insidious stratified dualism. The objective, I believe, should be equal responsibilities and rewards which are based on ability, not on gender."[29]

Humans Mirror God's Multidimensionality

God's intention is for males and females to set a priority on their humanity over their gender because humans were created to reflect or mirror *one* God. Further, in Genesis 1:26–27 who is the "Adam"? Adam or Human is a "they," "a male and a female," a "them" (Gen. 1:26–27). "They" have one name: "Human" (Gen. 5:2). There is the diversity: male and female. The analogy should be clear. In the same way as Human is one entity, but two genders, so too God is one God, but three Persons.[30] The Jewish thinker Frymer-Kensky concludes similarly that our humanity has more priority than our sexuality by comparing Genesis 1 to the Epic of Gilgamesh. When the gods of Mesopotamia want to create an equal for Gilgamesh, the mother-goddess creates another male, Enkidu. Similarly, when the goddess Ishtar needs a companion, Enki creates a female, Saltu. In contrast, she writes, in Genesis 1: "The differences between male and female are only a question of genitalia rather than of character. This view of the essential sameness of men and women is most appropriate to monotheism." Marcia Falk, also a feminist-Jewish theologian, agrees: "Monotheism means that, *with all our differences,* I am more like you than I am unlike you. It means that we share the same source, and that one principle of justice must govern us equally. Thus, monotheism would seem to imply that if we are all created in the image of divinity, the images with which we point toward divinity must reflect us all."[31]

The New Testament similarly explains that God is one, but God is three Persons. Jesus commanded his disciples to baptize the new students: "in the name of the Father and of the Son and of the Holy Spirit" (Matt. 28:19). First of all, God has only one name. "The name" (*to onoma*) is singular. "The name" is a frequent biblical synecdoche, a part, a name, representing the whole Person.[32] God does not have three names, but only one name because God is one. But that one name has three entities or Persons: Father, Son, and Holy Spirit. These three entities, although one, are also distinct from each other. Jesus says, and Matthew records,[33] that each noun is connected by the same conjunction "and" (*kai*). *Kai,* according to grammarian A. T. Robertson, presents the words it connects as on a par with each other. They are equal. They are closely related. Moreover, when the article "the" is repeated and the nouns all have the same number, gender, and case the speaker is emphasizing that each noun is distinguished or distinct from each other.[34] In Matthew 28:19 "of the Father," "of the Son," and "of the Holy Spirit" are each in the singular, masculine, genitive case. Thus, grammatically we are told

Father, Son, and Holy Spirit are distinct from each other, equal, but one. Thus, what is nascent/implicit in Genesis 1:26 is more explicit in Matthew 28:19.[35]

The danger of god/dess worship is its conservatism. In god/dess we are returning back to societies even more gender-specific than we have today. For instance, in Frymer-Kensky's insightful study *In the Wake of the Goddesses,* she notes that every aspect of ancient Sumerian thinking, culture, nature, and society was perceived along gender lines: "The male/female division of the animal (and human) world was projected on to the cosmic sphere and permeated philosophical reflection. As a result, gender was an immediate and inescapable aspect of Sumerian thought." She explains: "The natural elements that the goddesses controlled were as gender-specific as the social relationships that they exemplified. Control over the natural world was not gender-neutral, and there was no free variation between gods and goddesses. All reality and all power are gender-structured." She writes similarly of the Greek deities: "The male-female distinction was one of the great polarities of the Greek dualistic system."[36]

▼ Conclusion

People are looking for good concepts, but in the wrong places: themselves. Inner empowerment and social change can most wholistically, powerfully, and healthily be found in the God of the Bible. Only by holding corollaries can we become fully mature humans. The Lord of the Bible is clearly presented as one God creating one united Human. This unity is the appropriate oneness of all life. We humans are all one because we have the same ancestry. We all mirror the same God. Yet God is not human, nor are all gods or goddesses the same. Only one Power in the universe can create the world and humans. According to the Bible that power is not an impersonal effect of plants and animals. Nor is that power a personified Mother Earth whose metaphorical basis has been forgotten. Nor is that power we humans. God is distinct from all other entities and is unique. We humans, too, are distinct from God. In contrast, Melissa Potter explains, the goddess she knew had no one name because she was part of her creative self and she represents the cycles and transformations of life and nature. As in magic there is no separation between humans and the universe.[37]

However, only a very superficial reader of the Bible can therefore conclude that God is impersonal, abstract, uninteresting, and detached. If we are interested in process and vitality, we can find it in the "name" God gave Moses: "I will be who I will be." Although God is unique, God is also dynamic, surprising us humans and making us marvel.[38] "Interbeing" and "interdependence" can be reinterpreted in light of the Trinity: one God in three Persons. Again this interdependence is mirrored in Human who was created male and female. The idea of inner empowerment and social change is modeled by this God who has great power, but uses that power for others who need empowerment and change. That is compassion, taking one's power and using it for others. We see no hierarchy in the Trinity, nor hierarchy in the humans God created.[39]

But is it true the God of the Bible is a masculine or male deity? Let us explore that question in the next two chapters.

GOD IS INVISIBLE

*R*eading the literature on god/dess largely entails reading the exclamations of many people in revolt against the God of the Bible. Carol Christ speaks for many when she says she rejects the patriarchal God of the Bible—his sex, his warlike nature, his religious intolerance, his destruction of peoples of other religions.[1] Mary Daly explains: "If God in 'his' heaven is a father ruling 'his' people, then it is in the 'nature' of things and according to divine plan and the order of the universe that society be male-dominated." The fictional character Shug Avery in *The Color Purple* is frequently quoted when she explains to Celie: "When I found out I thought God was white, and a man, I lost interest. You mad cause he don't seem to listen to your prayers. Humph! Do the mayor listen to anything colored say?"[2]

If we are to respond that "father" is metaphorical language for God who is spirit, we would then hear the opposite complaint by professor of Psychiatry Jean Shinoda Bolen that such a god is disembodied, a powerful, white, male, sky god. Therefore, women must worship a female goddess of color in her body.[3] No wonder Emily Erwin Culpepper can say "Yahweh the warrior god/father is revolted and repulsed toward female bodies."[4]

In this chapter, we will respond to these complaints by studying God as spirit and human, and in the next chapter, God as known by actions, adjectives, and metaphors. We will conclude by looking at the function of language as a way to speak about God.

▼ God Is Spirit

One complaint about God is true. God, by nature, is "disembodied," in the sense of being without a body. God, though, never had a body. ("Disembody," according to *Webster's Dictionary* is "*to divest* of the body.") Jesus teaches quite explicitly: "God is Spirit," with the application that the place of worship is of no consequence ("neither on this mountain nor in Jerusalem" John 4:21, 24). Therefore, we must worship God in Spirit and in truth. Jesus speaks about "true" worshipers in verse 23. Possibly he might be referring to the Jews who knew whom they worshiped (v. 22). They had the truth. However, they, like the Samaritan woman, now needed to worship the Father or Parent in *spirit* as well as truth (v. 23). Jesus refers back to verses 10 and 14 where he offers eternal, living water, and forward to verse 24 "God is Spirit." True worshipers now need to be filled by God's Spirit, their own spirit reaching out to God. Where we worship is irrelevant, but who and how we worship is crucial. Since God is spirit and the place of worship is of no importance, what is Jesus saying? "But [the] hour comes, and now is, when the genuine worshipers will worship the Father in Spirit and truth; for also the Father seeks such worshiping him" (John 4:23). If the hour "now is," Jesus must have been referring to himself. By worshiping Jesus, the woman of Samaria would be worshiping the Father.

God Can Be Worshiped in Any Place

In Psalm 139 David explains he can never escape God's presence because God is Spirit (v. 7). God is everywhere. The apostle Paul, similar to David, can therefore agree with the ancient Greeks that God is not far from any of us since in God "we are living and we are moving and we are existing" (Acts 17:28).[5] No matter where we live, we can approach God even without the use of deities made of matter or deities from our imagination (Acts 17:29).

In the Old Testament, the tent or temple, especially the holy of holies, was primarily a place of God's special presence (Exod. 25:8; Lev. 16). Whereas, when Jesus died, the curtain separating the holy of holies from the holy place was torn in two from top to bottom (Matt. 27:51), signifying that God's Spirit no longer dwells in a place (Heb. 9:11–14) but in a people. Christians have become a moveable tent. Paul explains to the Corinthian believers: "Do you (pl.) not know that you (pl.) are a sanctuary (*naos*) of God and the Spirit of God dwells among you?" (1 Cor. 3:16), or "we are a sanctuary of the living God" (2 Cor. 6:16). Therefore, we Christians "create sacred space" by gathering together in Jesus' name: "For where two or three are being gathered in my name, there I am in their midst" (Matt. 18:20).[6]

In contrast, for many Goddess worshipers, "creating a sacred space" is a very important series of actions. For instance, Carol Leonard burns sage and fans the smoke east, west, north, and south with a large feather. Starhawk explains that "ritual takes place in space and time marked off from the everyday." Witches must "cast a circle," draw a circle with a wand or ritual knife to contain the energy raised and to protect themselves from unwanted energies or entities. Luisah Teish teaches Yoruba-Lucumi initiates that: "The first step in communicating with your ancestors is building a shrine."[7]

God Has No Form or Evil

Another ramification of God being "Spirit" is that everything able to be perceived by the five senses will be inadequate to represent God. Moses is very explicit to the Israelites: "Since you saw no form when the Lord spoke to you at Horeb out of the fire, take care and watch yourselves closely, so that you do not act corruptly by making an idol for yourselves, in the form of any figure—the likeness of male or female, the likeness of any animal that is on the earth, the likeness of any winged bird that flies in the air, the likeness of anything that creeps on the ground, the likeness of any fish that is in the water under the earth. And when you look up to the heavens and see the sun, the moon, and the stars, all the host of heaven, do not be led astray and bow down to them and serve them, things that the Lord your God has allotted to all the peoples everywhere under heaven" (Deut. 4:15–20. See also Isa. 44:9–20). Deuteronomy 4 is a key passage. God does not have the form of anyone or anything on earth. God is neither male *nor* female. God also does not have the form of any animal, bird, fish, or of constellations, the sun, moon, or stars. God has no "form" at all. Moses reminds the Israelites that they heard a voice, but never saw a form. They could see the mountain blazing and hear God's voice, but they saw no form that was God's (Deut. 4:10–12). To conceive God as having any earthly form is not only to displease God (Exod. 20:4–5) but also to misrepresent God.[8]

The metaphor of "wind" is an appropriate one by which to understand God. The wind can not be seen by the human eye, but its effects can be perceived by all the senses. God can be heard. God's *actions* can be seen: "You have seen what I did to the Egyptians" (Exod. 19:4). Hearing is the one sense that humans may use to perceive God. When Jesus spoke to Paul, Paul's companions, too, heard a voice but saw no one (Acts 9:7). One crowd thought God's words were "thunder" (John 12:29). But not every human is holy enough (humble enough) and courageous enough even to hear God. The Israelites who heard God once were too terrified to do so again. They demanded that the humble and courageous Moses listen in their behalf (Deut. 5:23–37). Therefore, God uses visions, sometimes, as a less terrifying manner of communication (Num. 12:3–8).

Since God is not human, in addition to being without a human body, God is not evil in any sense. In contrast to humans, God is compassionate (Hos. 11:9). Unlike humans', God's words can always be trusted and God's intentions will always be accomplished (Num. 23:19; 1 Sam. 15:29; Isa. 46:9–10). Since God is not human, God is all-powerful to create and personally know everything (Isa. 40:25–26).

Many Christian feminists have noted that to talk of God as male or masculine is idolatry. A number of writers have repeated almost the same sentence word-for-word: "Christian theology has always recognized, theoretically, that all language for God is analogical or metaphorical, not literal." Rosemary Radford Ruether goes on to conclude: "To take one image drawn from one gender and in one sociological context (that of the ruling class) as normative for God is to legitimate this gender and social group as the normative possessors of the image of God and representatives on earth. This is idolatry."[9] Elisabeth Schüssler Fiorenza agrees that the Old Testament prophets considered idolatry whenever any definite form was fixed to God, whether of god or goddess, divine couple, or masculinity or femininity as ultimate absolute principles.[10]

▼ God Became Human

One thing the god/dess movement makes clear is that some people need a deity in a body, a God like themselves, a God in human flesh, a God like us. That is the marvel of Christianity. This God who is Spirit, who has no form, chose to become incarnate in human form. Jesus is "the image of the *invisible* (unseen) God" (*aoratos* Col. 1:15; 1 Tim. 1:17; Heb. 11:27). Jesus is Emmanuel, "God with us" (Matt. 1:23). Jesus, who is truly and fully God *(morphē),* who always existed *(huparchō)* equal to God, chose not to retain looking on the outside what he was on the inside *(morphē),* emptied himself of the Shekinah glory and became fully human. For God to be human is analogous to any one of us becoming a slave; therefore, the Apostle Paul writes: "Christ Jesus, who being in form *(morphē)* of God did not consider the being equal to God a treasure to retain, but emptied himself, taking on a form *(morphē)* of a slave, having been born in human likeness and having been found in appearance as a human, he humbled himself, having become obedient to the extent of death, even of a cross-death" (Phil. 2:5–8).

God Became "With-Us"

Philippians 2:6–8 is one long sentence in Greek. Christ Jesus is described by three extended adjectival clauses. Christ Jesus who

a. being *(huparchō)* in form *(morphē)* of God, he considered not a treasure the being equal to God,
b. but emptied himself taking a form *(morphē)* of a slave, having been born in likeness *(homoiōma)* of humans,
c. and having been found in appearance *(schēma)* as a human, he humbled himself having become obedient to the extent of death, even of a cross-death.

This passage has several synonyms, each with a slightly different emphasis. *Morphē* refers to the external appearance or form that can be seen of a person or thing. This external form reflects the essential and permanent nature or being of someone or something.[11] For example, the Jewish philosopher Philo described the neurotic attempts of the Roman Emperor Gaius/Caligula to dress up each day as a different Greek deity. Philo describes Apollo as with a crown with sun rays because noble and beautiful things need noonday brightness to show them forth. Apollo's bows and arrows are to render justice. Apollo's medicine was for promoting health. Gaius, on the other hand, was lawless, greedy, and unjust, bringing "disease to the healthy, crippling to the sound of limb and in general death to the living." Therefore, Philo concludes, let Gaius cease once for all to mimic Apollo "for a form *(morphē)* of god cannot be counterfeited as a coin can be" *(Embassy to Gaius,* XIV). In other words, Gaius' external form did not reflect his own internal nature. In contrast, Jesus is truly God. Having the Shekinah glory that can not be seen by humans was having the external "form" of God. Once during his life on earth Jesus took on *(metamorphoō)* some of that glory when he became intensely white, as white as light (Matt. 17:2). The divine glory was an outward sign of Jesus' equality with God (Ps. 104:2). Jesus emptied himself of this glory when he took on the form *(morphē)* of a slave (Phil. 2:6–7).

Being a slave is a metaphor, but a metaphor that reflects truth. Jesus looked outwardly (he had the likeness of a human) what he was inwardly, he was humble and obedient. He genuinely was "a slave" in action. For God to become incarnate was analogous to a free human becoming a slave. Paul used *homoiōma* and *schēma* to describe Jesus' humanity. *Homoiōma* is a word of comparison ("like") indicating the similarity between a copy and an original, as when God creates Eve, a helper like Adam (Gen. 2:20; LXX *homoios*). *Schēma* highlights the outward form perceptible to the senses.[12] With both *schēma* and *homoiōma,* the outward form may or may not reflect the inner true nature. For instance, Paul writes about the false apostles. They change *(metaschēmatizō)* or disguise themselves as apostles of Christ. Satan, too, changes himself *(metaschēmatizō)* into an angel of light (2 Cor. 11:13–14). Outwardly, to the senses, false apostles look like Christ's apostles, as Satan, outwardly, to the senses, looks like an angel of light. In the case of these false apostles and Satan, their outward appearance does not reflect their inner true nature.

Jesus was at the beginning already existing *(huparchō)* as God. He also became, to all sense perception, fully human. However, he was inwardly not "human" because he was fully humble and obedient, unlike all other humans. Paul uses similar language in Romans 8:3: "God sent his own Son in likeness *(homoiōma)* of sinful flesh and concerning sin he condemned the sin in the flesh." Jesus was human, but he was not sinful.

Thus, God's answer to human desire for a God-like-us was to become God-with-us. But in the process, God had to leave behind God's overwhelming majesty of outward appearance and action. The marvel portrayed throughout the gospels and the New Testament letters is that even so, when God became flesh and "pitched his tent" among humans, God's glory was still perceivable in all of Jesus' actions. Jesus was overflowing with God's grace and truth (John 1:14).

Jesus Became Human

But why did God become a man? Why not a woman? Does the fact that Jesus became a man, therefore prove that God is a man or God is masculine? We have already looked at the biblical passages explaining that God must not be represented by male or female forms because God has no form. Therefore, God becoming incarnate as a male can not reflect back on a male deity. Similarly, even though angels become incarnate often as men (Acts 1:10; 10:30), they too as spiritual beings have no sex (Mark 12:25).

The New Testament is very clear to accentuate Jesus' humanity over his maleness by using the Greek generic term *anthrōpos* ("human") overwhelmingly, not the more sex-specific term *anēr* ("male"). *Anthrōpos* may be used to speak of humans as opposed to God, Jews and Gentiles as opposed to a Jewish male only, and of a person representing a group.[13] For example, Peter refers to himself as a Jewish male *(anēr)* in contrast to anyone Gentile or Jewish *(anthrōpos)* in the same sentence: "You believe as forbidden for a Jewish man *(anēr)* to associate with or approach a non-Jew; but to me God has shown no human *(anthrōpos)* should be called common or unclean" (Acts 10:28). Paul, in contrast, says: "Indeed I, a human *(anthrōpos),* I am a Jew" because he may be highlighting his human-ity as opposed to being Egyptian (Acts 21:38–39). Consequently, the Bible's emphasis is God becoming "flesh" (*sarx,* John 1:14) or "human" (*anthrōpos,* Phil. 2:7). That is why the one mediator between God and humans must be both God and human *(anthrōpos).* Paul describes Jesus as "human Christ Jesus" (1 Tim. 2:5).

Jesus never once uses *anēr* ("male") for self-description. The "Son of Man" should really be the "Heir of Humanity." Even in parables Jesus uses "human" for self-description. I have found only six pas-sages from among the very many references to Jesus where Jesus is described as a "man" or "male." In three of these "male" is used to develop a metaphor. In the gospels, John the Baptist describes Jesus: "After me comes a man (*anēr*) who comes before me, because he was before me" (John 1:30). However, in the context John has been continuing the imagery of Jesus as "the Lamb of God, the one taking away the sin of the world" (John 1:29). John appears to refer to the Passover lamb, a year old male lamb, which gave protection to the first-born children of Israel (Exod. 12:5, 12–13). Sin offerings also included female goats (Lev. 5:6). Purification offerings used red female heifers (Num. 19:1–10). But John the Baptist alludes here to the Passover offering so therefore he uses male language for Jesus. One reason, therefore, Jesus may have been born male was to remind people of the Passover lamb, a prominent symbol of his life's mission.

In the letters, Paul describes Christ as the "one man" to whom the church is betrothed (2 Cor. 11:2). The only Greek word, as far as I know, for "husband" is *anēr* with a clarifying modifier, here, "one." ("*Anēr*" is also used of God as a "bridegroom" in Rev. 21:2.) If the church is described in feminine imagery in 2 Corinthians 11:2, in contrast it is described in masculine imagery in Ephesians 4:13. The church is "a mature man" because it is the body of Christ.

When Jesus is described as a prophet by Cleopas and companion (Luke 24:19) and Peter, Jesus' humanity is augmented by *anēr.* Peter describes Jesus as "a man" in his speech at Pentecost: "Jesus, the Nazarene, a man *(anēr)* rewarded by God among you by deeds of power and wonders and signs which God did through him in your midst, as you yourselves know" (Acts 2:22). Peter seems to use "man" here as a way to highlight Jesus' humanity. He was a mere male, as it were, just like many in his audience, through whom God worked powerfully. He speaks of Jesus' maleness as representing the simplest, least symbolic level of his existence, as the point where the listeners can most identify (even though women were probably also present, Acts 1:14; 2:17). But Peter goes on persuasively to build up to the idea that this mere mortal was also God when he cites David describing: "The Lord said to my Lord" (Acts 2:34).

Paul also uses *anēr,* when speaking to the Athenians, to highlight Jesus' humanity and function as judge: God will judge the world "in righteousness in a man *(anēr)* whom he appointed" (Acts 17:31). In Greco-Roman times women could not be judges or legal witnesses (in contrast, Deborah, Judges 4:4). Earlier in the same sentence, Paul uses "human," *anthrōpos,* to refer to all who need to repent. Other than these very few references, *anthrōpos* or "human" is the term used in the New Testament to describe Jesus. For instance, the woman of Samaria is certainly careful to preach: "Come, see *a person* who told me everything I have ever done!" (John 4:29).

The difficulty with perceiving the carefulness of the New Testament writers has come from past English translations when "man" was considered generic, for example, Christ Jesus became "a man" in Philippians 2:8 (KJV, NIV,[14] TEV) or "one mediator between God and men, the man Christ Jesus" (1 Tim. 2:5, KJV, NIV, NEB, TEV, NTME). No wonder people came to be confused. In English we have both the Anglo Saxon and Germanic heritage ("der Mann," "man" as human being or an adult male) or French and Latin and Greek heritage ("peuple," "plebs," the common people, "humanus," human, civilized, or *polys*, many) to choose from.[15] Unfortunately, the Germanic heritage instead of the French heritage became prominent in English.

The Bible linguistically and theologically highlights the importance of understanding Jesus first and primarily as human. That he was male is also true, but that fact should never be said to reflect God's sexuality. We can only guess why Jesus became a male rather than a female. Possibly, he symbolized the male Passover lamb, as I suggested. Possibly, he became a (free Jewish) male in order to make a strong contrast between the usual prerogatives for free Jewish men and the service he taught (Mark 10:42–45).[16] Possibly, he wanted to be more mobile in a traditional ancient society. (No woman could have taught in the male-only synagogue classes).[17] Nevertheless, Jesus' maleness was a limitation imposed on the incarnate God, not a reflection of God's essence. Jesus' maleness was not *morphē* (Phil. 2:6). His outward maleness or humanity did not reflect what he was inwardly. Only Jesus' deity and service (Phil. 2:6–7) were outward manifestations of inward realities.

6

GOD IS NOT MALE

od is Spirit and we must be careful as we try to perceive God. We saw in chapter 4 that God is one, yet diverse. Thus, as well, we will need to understand God through diverse images. But ultimately we need to accept the fact that we bodily humans can not in this life directly, fully, and literally perceive God who is "invisible." The Bible that claims to record reliable accounts of God's self-revelation attests that God, in addition to the incarnation, can be known only through a multiplicity of ways: actions, descriptive adjectives, and metaphorical language. (Even in the incarnation, Jesus continually pointed to his actions and used adjectives and metaphors for self-description [e.g., John 10:37–38]).

▼ God Is Known by Actions

The very first line of the Bible is an action statement about God. God is the One who created the heavens and the earth (Gen. 1:1). In the same way, we may speak about one another. Even though we (or most of us) can see, hear, touch, smell, and (in case of dogs) taste one another, we really learn what we are each like by our actions.

I teach at a graduate school. I remember one night years ago when I was fighting a sore throat. I was lecturing in a large auditorium. I was starting to lose my voice, coughing, and pausing, when I looked up and saw coming to my podium a student limping along carrying

103

a cup of water. I will never forget that act of kindness which was of great effort physically to that student. By an act of empathy, I learned how compassionate a person could be. So too with God. We can learn about God through God's actions. That is why assigning an evil act to God is blasphemy, for we have called God "evil." The most fundamental way to understand God (and each other too) is through action.

The first action by which we know God is as the creative, powerful, personal being who makes from nothing good things and, moreover, allows those created things to have a freedom and capacity to create of their own. God commands the earth "to put forth vegetation: plants yielding seed, and fruit trees of every kind on earth that bear fruit with the seed in it" (Gen. 1:11). Even the lights, the sun and moon, have their own rulership, one to rule the day, one to rule the night (Gen. 1:16–17). Humans too were commanded jointly to take care of both animals and the land (Gen. 1:26; 2:15). Ironically, we humans could never choose to worship any beings other than God, if God had not created us free to choose and to act.

The God of the Bible is not described by Goddess worshipers as creative, personal, and good, a God who allows freedom in creation. Rather, they say the God of the Bible is patriarchal, a male, warlike, intolerant, a dominating male repulsed by female bodies. Starhawk in *Truth or Dare* describes such a God as one "who stands outside the world, outside nature, who must be appeased, placated, feared, and above all, obeyed." That God represents "power-over" consciousness, not "power-from-within," the mysteries that awaken humanity's deepest abilities and potential, or "power-with," the influence people wield among equals.[1] But, what in reality do we learn about God if we were to list and study all the descriptive adjectives used by or about God as self-revelation?

▼ God Is Known by Adjectives

The very first name ever given to God is given by a woman. When Hagar runs away from Sarai because Sarai has poorly treated her, an angel of God seeks her out and promises her many descendants. She gives God the name "a God of Seeing" (Gen. 16:13). The name is acceptable to God because it is true, calling God by one attribute that is especially meaningful at that time. God seems to repeat this practice many times. In communicating to humans, God chooses an attribute to highlight in the communication process. When God wants Abram to trust the promise that at ninety-nine he could be the ancestor of a multitude of nations, God uses the description: "God Almighty" (Gen. 17:1; Exod. 6:3). God is saying, trust me and my promise because I am powerful.

Certainly God is portrayed in the Bible as powerful, but is not this what the women's spirituality movement is all about? Power? Women of Power? The paradox is that a God who indeed has "power-over" can use that power for power-for-within and power-with. Because God has power-over, therefore Hagar and Abraham have power-from-within to have many descendants. Starhawk portrays the God of the Bible in a deistic manner. In contrast, when she writes about the Goddess, she writes about paradox: "For what we call Goddess moves always through paradox, and so takes us into the heart of the mysteries, the great powers that can never be limited or defined."[2] Yet, why, then, can not the God of the Bible also be portrayed in paradox? God is outside the world and outside nature and God seeks obedience; however, God is also immanent. God also cares for everything created, all which is created with its inherent worth and its freedom. Rather than estranged from God, we are related to God and to one another. We humans are of value for who we are, but we only become fully ourselves if we are related to God, our outside standard.

God Is Intimate

"Power-over" does not communicate God's intimacy and care and personal concern. Why does God use the term "I am the God of Abraham your father" (Gen. 26:24)? God uses this self-description because God speaks to Abraham's son, Isaac, and God wants to remind Isaac of his father's relationship with God and of the promise God made to Abraham for many descendants. Then, when God speaks to Isaac's son, Jacob, God becomes "I am the Lord, the God of Abraham your father and the God of Isaac" (Gen. 28:13). Moses too is reminded of God's relationship with Moses' ancestors: "I am the God of your father, the God of Abraham, the God of Isaac, and the God of Jacob" (Exod. 3:6). The fact that God used these names does not limit God only to these people. Rather, the principle is that God makes covenants with specific individuals. No one need be excluded if they are willing to enter into covenant with God. We, too, today might appropriately call God by the name of significant family believers, adding our name, as trust in God is taught generation by generation.

God uses not only family members, but also places and actions as points of contact for communication. "I am the God of Bethel, where you anointed a pillar and made a vow to me" is meaningful only to Jacob because Jacob responded from his heart ("within") to acknowledge God ("without") and God noticed and appreciated it (Gen. 31:13). This is not a God who simply must be appeased, but this is a God who responds in love.

God Does Not Affirm Evil

Probably, the most extensive listing of God's attributes may be found in Exodus 34: "The Lord, the Lord, a God merciful and gracious, slow to anger, and abounding in steadfast love and faithfulness, keeping steadfast love for the thousandth generation, forgiving iniquity and transgression and sin, yet by no means clearing the guilty, but visiting the iniquity of the parents upon the children and the children's children, to the third and fourth generation" (vv. 6–7). Most Goddess worshipers affirm compassion, and generosity, but they do not affirm the concept of sin, guilt, or punishment. God may be a healer (Exod. 15:26), a deliverer (Exod. 20:2; Isa. 43:3), a comforter (Isa. 51:12–16), but God should not be a jealous, holy, and just God.[3]

Some writers clearly state that no concepts of sin, good, and evil exist in modern witchcraft. Naomi Goldenberg summarizes twelve key differences between the Craft and the Judaeo-Christian religion. Among these she includes: "Witchcraft has no concept of a primal sin committed by our ancestors nor does it have a concept of a covenant against which one can sin." She also writes that witches have "no division of good and evil."[4] That is because, in contrast to the God of the Bible, the Great Mother "is both Dark and Light, both matter and spirit, heaven and earth."[5] "Sin" then becomes simply fear of freedom.[6] "Sin" becomes any kind of restriction. Sherry Ruth Anderson and Patricia Hopkins explain that for women to develop spiritually: "Clinging to ideals about how one ought to be blocks the gateway to mystery, while honoring what is personally true in each moment brings one into relationship with the sacred."[7] Starhawk repeats: "When we are free, we can speak the unspeakable and think the unthinkable. To liberate ourselves, we must challenge the internal Censor and find the voice that will let us express the power that comes from within."[8]

Certainly, if they do not like the internal Censor, they will not like the external Censor: God, a holy, just, and jealous God. All of us want mercy for ourselves, but, if we are honest, deep down we want justice for our oppressors, whoever they may be. The game of "Truth or Dare" from which Starhawk draws a title of one book is a game of collective demand to speak the unspeakable, to reveal what people have always been warned not to reveal.[9] It sounds exciting, if one imagines oneself as the powerful person demanding that others answer intimate, embarrassing questions. But, it is not so enjoyable if one is "it." One problem of the conflict dynamics movement was the assumption that truth (meaning honesty) is greater than love (meaning maturity). I participated in one group where an elderly African-American gentleman used to turn his tape recorder on whenever the teacher spoke and off when the students spoke. This practice was insulting to the students, but it also was meaningless. We always imagined what the tape sounded like: "You feel angry," "And what do you think?," "How does that make you feel?," "What do you think?" One day a young white woman, before the whole group, tore into him, criticizing him soundly for his taping. The elderly man's sweet exterior dissolved while he unleashed stories of years of white thoughtlessness, prejudice, and discrimination on that young woman. Neither of them were ever able to participate in the group again. Yes, the truth needed to come out, but this manner was not the most maturing way for it to happen.

"Let everything private be made public" is a cruel game of excitement.[10] It sounds similar to Jesus' words: "Nothing is covered up that will not be uncovered, and nothing secret that will not become known." But Jesus' words are warnings of impending judgment (Luke 12:2–5), therefore we must not live hypocritical lives. Our evil deeds will be exposed, therefore, do no evil (John 3:19–20).

Freedom without morality is cruel and evil. For Starhawk and others, the pleasure-giving force of sexuality is sacred.[11] When one believes in many gods, that too affects actions. One then will accept many intimate relationships. In contrast, in Christianity, belief in one God results in belief in one committed marriage.[12] If multirelationships are so good, why do so many problems arise? As Starhawk notes from experience: "In any small group in which people are involved sexually, sooner or later there will be problems." She adds that "subsequent conflicts between lovers will be less threatening."[13] But I doubt people will feel "very safe" when they know their actions of intimacy are not done on the basis of any kind of commitment. Moreover, if sexuality was not intended to be monogamous, why then are "heterogamous" relationships so unhealthy? In the United States, over twenty sexually transmitted diseases run rampant. In a study by G. D. Searle, we are told that "two out of six Americans sexually active have been infected" with the virus Papovavirus. Viral-induced diseases can be the most difficult to treat. Papovavirus may cause warts in the thousands. Genital Herpes Simplex (HSV) affects more Americans than syphilis and gonorrhea combined. It is the source of organic and psychological complications. No drug cures herpes.[14]

Not to believe in a holy God means that we too need not be holy. Not to believe in a just God means that one need not be just. Not to believe in a jealous God means that one need not be monogamous. Have all participants in this kind of polytheistic spirituality weighed the consequences for themselves, their friends, and their society? Compassion is meaningful only in the light of justice. Compassion without justice is mere sentimentality. When justice has been recognized, then forgiveness is significant. Forgiveness is probably the most cleansing of all actions because it recognizes sin and justice. Yet forgiveness is rarely mentioned in the Goddess movement because sin is not recognized.

In any movement, one can find truth too. The internal Censor may be merely one's self-hatred, the Accuser's voice, which is always criticizing and limiting: "You aren't good enough to deserve——." Or, it may be merely a barometer of our feelings: "I'm terrified to try something new." But, it could be God affirming one in what is good. I remember once a teenager told me how on one day he resisted stealing from a store and he felt so good as his parents affirmed him. The next day, as he and a friend were "borrowing" a neighbor's bike, the neighbors came out and beat them up and brought them to the police. All of a sudden he felt a tremendous feeling surge within him, that he knew was from God, indicating how awful was today's experience, as opposed to yesterday's experience. In his case, the internal Censor, from God, was a wonderful exhilarating experience of true freedom. That is the mystery. True freedom comes in true holiness, a holiness from outside us, not limited by self-centered others.

God Is Just

One aspect of God's holiness and justice that has repelled many is God allowing or commanding nations to be punished for rank immorality and idolatry. God is denounced as the "war-like" God. God is not "war-like" simply to be domineering or oppressive. Rather, God wants people to be just and if after repeated warnings they are not, God may allow them to be destroyed. Most people do not complain about God bringing the Jews into exile because they oppressed foreigners, orphans, and widows, killed innocent people, broke the Sabbath rest, enslaved their own people, and worshiped other gods. For example, Jeremiah records God saying: "How can I pardon you? Your children have forsaken me, and have sworn by those who are no gods. When I fed them to the full, they committed adultery and trooped to the houses of prostitutes. They were well-fed lusty stallions, each neighing for his neighbor's wife. Shall I not punish them for these things? says the Lord; and shall I not bring retribution on a nation such as this?" (Jer. 5:7–9).[15] God warned the people through prophets for many years before allowing any punishment: "Yet the Lord warned Israel and Judah by every prophet and every seer" (2 Kings 17:13).

God was no less charitable to the original inhabitants of Canaan. God told Abram that his descendants would not live in Canaan for four generations because the Canaanites had not yet done enough evil (Gen. 15:16). But when the Canaanites continued to kill their own children and worship other gods, then their time was up: "When the Lord your God thrusts them out before you, do not say to yourself, 'It is because of my righteousness that the Lord has brought me in to occupy this land'; it is rather because of the wickedness of these nations that the Lord is dispossessing them before you" (Deut. 9:4).[16]

Great evil demands justice or punishment. But because God is loving as well as just, God warns people continuously. God's goal is repentance or change of behavior. God wants to forgive, because God takes no pleasure in the death of humans or animals or nature. (See God's concern for animals as well as humans in Jonah 4:11.)

We humans never have God's patience. For instance, the whole Book of Jonah is a historical piece recording Jonah's frustration that the Assyrians who were renowned for their cruelty might be forgiven by God.[17] Jonah had not wanted to go to Nineveh to preach because he knew God was gracious and merciful, slow to anger, and abounding in steadfast love, and ready to relent from punishing (Jon. 4:2). And just as he suspected, the Ninevites did repent and God forgave them. Thus, when we disparage justice or limitations on ourselves, we must also, to be consistent, allow injustice against ourselves and others. Even Starhawk agrees that the importance of justice must be reclaimed: "If we participate in a Native American sweat lodge, we are obligated to aid their struggles for land and treaty rights and their battles against forced relocation. . . . The immanent value of the individual cannot be separated from a concern for social justice."[18] The ethics of immanence demand concern because everything and everyone is connected. As Christians, we would agree that everything is connected, but, as well, we have a Creator who connects these things and people and then models how to treat each one with justice and love.

▼ God Is Known by Metaphors

Outside of knowing God through actions and adjectives, God is known by metaphorical language: Father, Lord, Rock, Seeing One, Peace, Glory, Most High, Shepherd, Teacher, Offspring, to name a few. A metaphor is a comparison between two things of unlike nature that yet have something in common so that one or more properties of the first are attributed to the second. A metaphor is an *implied* comparison because no word of comparison is used, whereas a simile is an *explicit* comparison because a word such as "like" or "as" is used.[19] "God is a shepherd" is a metaphor. "God is like a shepherd" is a simile. The key principle to remember is that metaphorical language is used with two things of *unlike* nature that yet have something in common. A figurative term or image, such as "shepherd," is used to illumine a literal term or concept, such as God. God has no body, unlike a shepherd. God keeps no literal sheep, unlike a shepherd. But God does protect and care for living things, as does a shepherd. In other words, a metaphor needs to be carefully analyzed, to discern the analogies being made and the degree of corre-

spondence between the image and the concept.[20] Originally James
Lovelock used Gaia as a metaphor to describe the Biocybernetic Universal System Tendency/Homeostasis.[21] Yet, in time, his metaphor
came to be taken literally. Are metaphors true? Of course, they are
true, but only insofar as the analogy holds.[22] They are true, but not
literal.

Something could be literal, but not true. For instance, I could say,
literally, I have a million dollars. That is a literal statement, but it
certainly is not true. Unfortunately, people have come to confuse
literalness with truth ("that's literally true!") and metaphor with lies
("that's fiction!"), possibly as a result of our pseudoscientific culture.
A friend of ours, a minister, was at a book signing where a patron,
giving a long eye at the pile of novels an author was signing, said,
"I only read nonfiction. Is this book fiction?" "No," the author
snapped, glaring, "This is truth!"

Thus, to conclude that Father, Lord, Son, Creator, Redeemer,
Judge, and Savior are literal terms as opposed to Good Shepherd,
True Vine, Rock, Fortress, and motherhood, which are metaphorical and symbolic, is nonsensical.[23] All metaphors and images are figurative analogies. Possibly, some metaphors may be more common
than others (such as Lord), but they can not be *less* metaphorical.
Some metaphors may be more developed or have more degrees of
correspondence, but they still are metaphors.

Both interpreters at the far right and the far left seem to agree
that the God of the Bible is essentially masculine. Those to the right
then tend to use that conclusion to prefer male leadership. For example, Donald G. Bloesch, in contrast to many feminists, sees God as
primarily masculine and transcendent. His view of God seems to
affect indirectly his view of women. He supports having women in
ministry and supports partnership in marriage, but still he maintains
that the husband in team ministries should "have a certain precedence in authority."[24] Some Goddess worshipers because they have
essentially agreed with his analysis about God therefore have rejected
Christianity.

The Bible Uses Feminine Images for God

As we have seen earlier, God is one God, yet diverse. Male and
female reflect this diversity of God. If indeed males and females
reflect God's image, then conversely God will use the characteristics

and roles of both females and males to help people understand God's nature. Most biblical metaphors are not clearly sex-specific. However, we can find in the Bible many metaphors for God that must be female because only women can become pregnant, bear, and nurse children. To communicate God's great love, power, righteousness, and uniqueness, God uses the extended metaphor of a mother carrying a child from before birth to death. No false deity can have the power of such a mother-God (Isa. 45:24–46:6). Handmade deities in contrast must be carried around on human shoulders and animal backs. Although ancient Amazonian women warriors have been found,[25] for many cultures most soldiers were men. The power of God and the need to punish injustice are communicated by a dual image: a warrior shouting aloud against his enemies and a pregnant woman shouting aloud as her child moves through the birth canal (Isa. 42:13–17). The nine months of pregnancy are like the times of God's patience, but the time of labor, which comes suddenly, is like the sudden, unpredictable time of God's judgment. The hope for the future is compared to a mother nursing. God will never forget God's people, even as most mothers will not, even can not, forget they have a child to nurse (Isa. 49:14–15).

Phyllis Trible, by paying attention to the meanings of words and stylistic analysis, has given us numerous examples where "motherly-compassion" is embedded in what superficially looks to be abstract concepts. For example, Jacob blesses Joseph by "the Almighty." Parallel to "Almighty" are "breasts" and "womb" (Gen. 49:25). The plural for "womb" is "compassion." The concrete physical organ of the female body, the womb, is a synecdoche for the abstract psychic mode of being, compassion. Trible explains: "To the responsive imagination, this metaphor suggests the meaning of love as selfless participation in life. The womb protects and nourishes but does not possess and control. It yields its treasure in order that wholeness and well-being may happen. Truly, it is the way of compassion."[26] God's great power to help is like that of maternal nourishment.

"Father" tended to be used by the ancients metaphorically for the idea of conception, whereas "mother" for the idea of labor and actual birth. For instance, God as "maker" *(yāṣar)*, potter, is compared to both a father and a mother. The "father" "begets" *(yālad)*, the mother "is in labor" *(ḥûl)* (Isa. 45:9–10). These same two verbs were used by Moses in his song: "You were unmindful of the Rock that bore you *(yālad)*; you forgot the God who gave you birth *(ḥûl)* (Deut. 32:18). *Yālad* may refer to a father or mother (as in Prov. 23:22, 25; Gen. 4:18, Enoch; Gen. 22:20, Milcah). However, *ḥûl* refers only to a woman in labor. Trible concludes that Deuteronomy 32:18 presents either "complementary or identical parental metaphors. In the first instance, the Rock is the father who begot, and God is the mother who writhed at birth."[27]

God is like mothers and all females in that God has the capacity to bear burdens, to produce life, to save, to perform the inexplicable, to be decisive, to be thorough and careful, to be constant, to be compassionate, to calm, to comfort, to care, to protect, to help, to love, to bring joy, to command fear and immediate response, to intimidate, to destroy, to guide, to educate, to feed, to preserve, to develop, to rule, and to be merciful. Not only does the Bible use images of motherhood (human, eagle, lioness, bear), household management, and sovereign or queen, but also these female images are both powerful and caring.[28] Since these female images may be found throughout the Bible, possibly as early as Genesis 1:2 with the Spirit "hovering over" the waters and Exodus 19:4 with the eagle carrying her young on her back, and "hovering over" her young (Deut 32:11), why then do they not get more publicity? How could God be "male"? One reason some people propose is that in the New Testament God is called "Father."

Bible Readers Misunderstand "Father"

First of all, the term "father" is no less a metaphor than "light" or "bread" or "shepherd." God is not a literal father nor a literal mother. God has no body. God does not conceive children through intercourse. As we saw in chapter 3, many ancients did think that Zeus, who was also called "father," did have a body and could literally conceive children. Zeus himself had Titan parents: Cronus and Ops. Pallas Athene sprang from Zeus' head completely armed. Zeus was quite a busy father, siring Hephaestus and Ares (with Hera), Phoebus Apollo (with Latona), Aphrodite (with Dione), Hermes (with Maia), Dionysus (with Semele), and the Muses Calliope, Clio, Euterpe, Melpomene, Terpsichore, Erato, Polyhymnia, Urania, and Thalia (with Mnemosyne).[29] So when Zeus or Jupiter was called "Father," the Greeks really meant *father*. He also was not much of an example of monogamy. When the Bible uses the term "father" for God, it is *not* intended in the same literal sense because the Bible emphatically teaches that God has no form or body. Even when God became incarnate, Jesus did not marry but remained celibate.

Second, the Greeks did not have any noun that served in the generic *singular* as "parent." The very few rare occurrences of *goneus* before or during New Testament times all serve as synonyms for "father" (Diodorus of Sicily, IV.30; XVII.2; XXXVI.16). All three references refer to human fathers. In IV.30 Iolaüs is honored as "progenitor" (*goneus*) of a people. At his death he became a god addressed as "Father Iolaüs" *(patēr)*. Only in the plural does *goneus* (as well as *patēr*) include mother and father.[30]

Nevertheless, the verb *gennaō*, to bear, is used of God. Even though Liddell and Scott say *gennaō* refers "mostly to the father," in the New Testament this verb is used mainly of the mother "bearing" a child, as from Mary *came* Jesus (Matt. 1:16), Elizabeth *will bear* a son (Luke 1:13), wombs that do (not) *bear* children (Luke 23:29; Matt. 19:12; John 16:21). In John 3:4 *gennaō* for God is clearly based on the mother image. Nicodemus uses *gennaō* to refer to birth from the womb of a mother. Jesus responds that birth from a watery uterus is not enough, but that birth is also needed from out of [the womb of] the Holy Spirit (John 3:5–6).[31]

Third, how frequent is the metaphor "father" for God in the Bible as compared to other metaphorical terms? I am in the process of writing a Concordance of New Testament Images. At this point I have completed one-half (50 percent) of the New Testament. "Father" is the most frequent term for God in the New Testament portions I have studied thus far only because of the frequent use of it in the Gospel of John. But outside the Gospel of John, "Lord" is the most frequent metaphor for both God and Jesus.

Since "Lord" is, across the New Testament, the most frequent metaphor for both God and Jesus, that indicates that a relationship of obedience and submission is key to understanding people's relation to the God of the Bible. The God of the Bible is *not* a god who equals oneself. "Namaste," Jean Shinoda Bolen explains, means "the Goddess in me beholds and honors the Goddess in you." Barbara Sciacca describes the Goddess as the Spirit of Life: "I understand that life is a circle and I am one with it—I AM it!" Janet L. Jacobs describes a neo-pagan chant: "Woman am I, Spirit am I, I am the Infinite within

Jesus	Luke, Acts	John	1, 2, 3 John	2 Cor., Eph., Phil, Philem., James, Jude	1, 2 Tim., Titus	Total
lord (kurios)	24, 43	14		45	8	134
son (of God) (huios)	12, 2	28	24	2		68
name	8, 30	12	3	2		55
son (of humanity)	26	13				39
light	1	23		1 (Eph.)	1 (1 Tim.)	26
savior/ ransom	4, 2	1	1	2	5	15
food/bread	1	12				13
life		5	6			11
face	5, 1			2		8
bridegroom /husband	2	3		1		6
shepherd		6				6
word		4	1			5
child	4[33]					4
king/reign	1	1			2 (1 Tim.)	4
stone	2, 2					4
head	1			2 (Eph.)		3
master	2			1		3
righteous	3 (Acts)					3
water			3			3
Images that occur twice	Christian, doctor, Elijah, holy, son (of David), strong	after, ahead, full, gate, glory, lamb, vine	blood	offering, rich	glory	34

God[32]	Luke, Acts	John	1, 2, 3 John	2 Cor., Eph., Phil., Philem., James, Jude	1, 2 Tim., Titus	Total
father	29, 3	117	15	18	3	185
lord (kurios)	38, 42	2		47	13 (2 Tim.)	142
name	3, 3	8	1	2 (James)	2	19
sender	2	16				18
(most) high	7, 2					9
above		4		4		8
savior	1			1 (Jude)	6	8
heaven	2, 1	2				5
judge		1		3 (James)	1 (2 Tim.)	5
grace					3	3
light			2	1 (James)		3
master (despotes)	1, 1				1 (2 Tim.)	3
rich(es)				3		3
planter	2	1				3
beginning			2			2
face	2 (Acts)					2
hand(s)	1, 2	1				4
knower, hearts	2 (Acts)					2
one			1	1 (James)		2

my soul; I have no beginning and I have no end, all this I am."[34] One thing at least that the metaphor "Lord" shows is that God should be obeyed. God is outside of oneself and superior to any female or male.

Since both God and Jesus are referred to with the same term, that also reinforces their unity. John composed his gospel in an interesting way. Most of the references to Jesus as "Lord" occur at the end of the gospel, after the resurrection, as if John writes from the disciples' growing awareness, Jesus was not only the Messiah, but also God.[35] Yet, the distinctiveness of the Trinity is also shown by the metaphors "Father" and "Son." So far in my study, these terms are unique to each person of the Trinity (except possibly 1 John 2:1). "Savior" is common to both. If one were to interpret the metaphors of the Bible merely quantitatively, then all of us would need to use the synecdoche "name" more frequently. Metaphors such as "light" and "life" are also hardly used in the United States, but they are quite frequent in the New Testament. Jesus as "head" certainly is used more frequently in the Western world than the total references warrant. Of course, all such thinking is ludicrous. God is not literally any one of these metaphors. God is both like and unlike all of them. On the other hand, we should not say that to use any biblical metaphor is wrong. What is wrong is to use the metaphor literally. In other words, to treat God as a literal father, lord, name, savior, high one, and judge, or to treat Jesus as a literal lord, son, name, light, food, savior, life, face, above one, word, husband, king, water, or head, that is idolatry. How is this idolatry? God, unlike a father, has no sexual organs.[36] God, unlike a lord, allows freedom of choice. God, unlike a name, is alive. God, unlike a savior, has no sword or gun. God, unlike a high one, is not limited to one space. God, unlike a judge, needs no chair, stool, and no jury. To treat God literally as any one of these metaphors limits God to the earthly equivalent, making a false image of God, an idol.

Fourth, if "father" is indeed a metaphor, in what way is it like and unlike the reality "God"? Literally, "father" refers to a man who can conceive children, as Herod was the father of Archelaus, Zebedee the father of James and John, and Zechariah the father of John. "Father" also is a synecdoche, one person, who came to represent someone who begins something, such as a nation, or someone who had been a father of one of one's ancestors, such as Abraham, the "father" of Israel, or David, Jacob, or Isaac, past covenant partners with God.[37]

In ancient times, the roles of a father had some similarities to today's father in industrialized societies, but, as well, some differences. God, like any average good father of then or today, teaches (John 6:45; 8:28), has an occupation ("works" in John 5:17 and "farms" in Matt. 15:13 and John 15:1), gets glory when the children do good (Matt. 5:16), loves when obeyed (John 10:17), disciplines (Heb. 12:7–11, but God disciplines only for the child's good), forgives (Ps. 103:13), provides and protects (Ps. 68:5–6), appreciates thanks (Col. 1:12; 3:17), and is unique (Matt. 23:9). Everyone has only one natural father.

But God is more than your average father. This "father" creates the world, gives only good gifts to children, and knows what people need before they ask.[38] When Jesus exhorts his listeners to be perfect, as their heavenly Father is perfect (Matt. 5:48), the term "perfect" is no understatement to describe the image of this "Father." Unlike Josephus' reference to Zeus called "nominally Father, but in reality a tyrant and a despot" (*Against Apion*, II. 33[241]), the biblical metaphor "father" draws out a paradoxical picture of a very powerful "father" who is also very tender. The ancient "father" to which Jesus alludes is more than your usual small village Dad.

Unlike most dads today, "Father" God is a ruler of a vast reign, a judge, with heirs. For instance, the rulers described in the history of 1 Maccabees all could have armies, appoint ministers of state or "Friends," give rewards of robes, crowns, and money, expect obedience, have heirs. Their ambassadors or "Friends," with whom they had intimate conversations, could represent the ruler.[39] Similarly, the "father" of the Bible has a kingdom, with an army (of angels). This ruler, like ancient rulers, was also a judge.[40] The heir or "son" is Jesus Christ, who represents the king, and who intimately communicates with the king.[41] This ruler has a will that should be obeyed, gives rewards, and grants peace.[42] But, God as ruler is not limited to national interests. This "father" has an impartial love, loving and caring for friends and enemies alike. This judge is partial to oppressed people so as to balance the scales. This judge is merciful, not wanting even one person to be lost.[43]

Thus, when the Bible uses the metaphor "Father" for God, many good qualities are implied: creation, education, working, appreciation, love, forgiveness, generosity, perception, power, justice, communication, and mercy. But not every father is like God. Many fathers (like mothers) do not always help their children mature, they are not always loving and impartial. They certainly can not create the world. Not all rulers are like God either. A king *needs* allies, but God chooses to use humans. An ancient king's allies were equals, but God's "ministers of state" are unequal. Rulers expected loyalty from their allies. God expects total love (John 15:12–13). A ruler must be concerned with the nation and the large mass of people (or, the powerful citizens). God is concerned for everyone, and especially the powerless, because God created everyone: "Have we not all one father? Has not one God created us?" (Mal. 2:10).

Since women were rarely inheritors among Jews, the metaphor "mother" would not include the double image of father-ruler. For instance, the rabbinical teachings in the Mishnah reproved any father who wanted his daughter to inherit when he had a son. Such an inheritance would be illegal because it was contrary to what was written in the rabbinical laws (m., *B. Bat.,* 8:5). Job, in contrast, after all his suffering, divided his inheritance among his sons *and* his daughters (42:13–15).

The metaphor of a father and a son goes back to the prototype David. God tells David: "I will be to him as a father, and he shall be to me as a son." What does that mean? That means that David's inheritance is guaranteed. David might still be punished when he sins, but the monarchy, the covenant line, will not be removed.[44] Even in New Testament times, among the Romans, the father-son metaphor was used to indicate the formal adoption and the loving care of an heir. For instance, the Roman Emperor Gaius promises his cousin that he will be "more than a guardian, a tutor and a teacher" of Tiberius Gemellus: "I will appoint myself to be his father and him to be my son" (Philo, *Embassy to Gaius,* IV). Gaius was lying. However, his metaphorical language communicated to his listeners that Gaius intended to instruct Tiberius, prepare him for leadership, and give him full power.

The father-son metaphors communicated to ancient listeners the intimacy, love, and care of a parent and the power of a ruler. Since few Western nations are monarchies with inheriting heirs, we may find difficulty in thinking of a dynamic equivalent for our cultures. "Ruler-heir" would be a nonsexist way to say "father-son." But, how many ruler-heirs do we all know? Possibly, the Queen of England and the prince/princess might be an apt equivalent, but does the Queen have the power of an ancient ruler? Can she call on the army to fight? I believe the prime minister has ultimate power over the army. The United States president has ultimate power over the army, but the president has no heir. Moreover, God has no congress with whom to muster support. What we need is a word with the intimacy of a father or mother, with the power of a ruler in a monarchy. No word today is adequate.

What I am trying to communicate is that if God is Spirit, neither male nor female, then the metaphor "father" can not be intended for its sexuality. Rather, as we have seen, by looking at the immediate contexts of its uses in the Bible, the metaphor communicates some aspects of God's character. "Father" by itself is insufficient. That is why the Bible has a great variety of metaphors to describe God. The Old Testament also has many, many metaphors. The Book of Isaiah, for example, has a great variety of figurative language for God, contrasting images standing side-by-side with each other, from the rejected parent, rejected lover, frustrated farmer, the vineyard owner with no yield to the master farmer and builder, powerful feller of trees, and strong mother. God is described by many occupations: potter, seamstress, business person, judge, sweeper, ironsmith, washer, doctor, winepresser, warrior.[45] God is also described by nature: storms, thunder, earthquakes, great noises, tidal waves, whirlwinds, tempests, wild fires, rocky mountains, heat, shade, streams, dawn, darkness, and bright light.[46] God can also be symbolized by animals, a lioness, a bird, and parts of the human body.[47] All of this figurative language teaches us that God is indeed majestic, just, righteous, and powerful, but also compassionate, patient, perceptive, and protective. These metaphors certainly do *not* teach us that God is a father, mother, tempest, bird, or body part. To what or whom, then, will we compare God? God is like, and unlike, many, many images on earth.

▼ God Is Not Limited by Pronouns

What about language? Why is "she" never used of God in the Bible? Why is "he" for God so frequent? The Old and New Testaments were written originally in Hebrew and Greek, respectively. Simply having a translation can limit our perception. The third person singular Hebrew or Greek verb does not need a pronoun, unlike English. For example, Romans 1:1–2 in English reads: "the gospel of God which *he* promised," whereas the Greek literally says: "gospel of God which promised." "He," "she," or "it" are implied subjects of the verb "promised." Sentence after sentence these "he's" added in translation may gather up creating a subconscious feeling for some people that God must be male. But, if we simply take Romans 1 and compare the original Greek text with several translations, this is what we will observe:

Masculine Referents for God and People in Romans 1

	Greek[48]	NRSV[49]	KJV	NIV	NTME	REB	Living Bible	TEV
Personal Pronoun	6	9 (10)	8	12	7	19 (16)	16	21 (19)
"man" or *anēr* for generic	0	0 (2)	1	3	2	1 (4)	4	0 (8)
"brothers" (*adelphos*) v. 13 only	1	0 (1)	1	1	1	0 (1)	1	0 (1)

The different translators of the Greek vary in the amount of "he," "his," "him," and "himself" they used for God. *The New Testament in Modern English,* which was published in 1924 (and still is in print), but was translated by a woman, Helen Barrett Montgomery, is closest to the Greek text. The *King James Version* and *New Revised Standard Version* have only two and three more uses, respectively, than the Greek. The popular *New International Version* of 1985 has twice the number of masculine pronouns. *Today's English Version* of 1992 has more than three times the masculine pronouns for God. The 1966 TEV had eight times the number of "man" and "men" than the Greek does.

The Significance of Gender in Language

But even more foundational than the number of "he's" is the question, what does "he" mean in each language? In English (as well as Persian and Chinese) grammar, gender plays a relatively minor part. When "he, she, it" are used in English, they refer almost every time to natural gender,[50] as in "the man, he fell," "the woman, she fell," and "the book, it fell." Therefore, when English readers see gender, they tend to project their own understanding of gender to language: "If 'he, she, it' refers to sexuality, in English, then all gender in all languages must refer to sexuality!"

However, projecting one's own views on other worldviews can create great misunderstanding. The renowned linguist John Lyons writes: "The recognition of gender as a grammatical category is logically independent of any particular semantic association that might be established between the gender of a noun and the physical or other properties of the persons or objects denoted by that noun."[51] The authoritative Hebrew grammarian W. Gesenius says the same thing about Hebrew: "The language, however, is not obliged to use the feminine ending either for the purpose of distinguishing the *sex* of animate objects, or as an indication of the (*figurative*) gender of inanimate things which are regarded as feminine."[52] Even though the Greek grammarian A. T. Robertson guesses that grammatical gender probably arose from the natural differences of sex and the poetic imagination of early peoples, he observes that Sanskrit, Latin and Greek "developed rules that are difficult to apply, with many inconsistencies and absurdities." He points out, for example, that "sun" in Greek *(hēlios)* is masculine, but "sun" in German is feminine *(die Sonne)*. "Wife" in German is masculine *(das Weib)*![53]

In other words, what the grammarians are trying to explain is that what we call "gender," which comes from the Latin *genus,* simply refers to "class" or "kind." Most languages divide words into categories. These categories have some basis for classification, but it is not necessarily sex.[54] The categories preceded the term "gender" or *genus,* kind. The Greeks had been happily grouping words as they desired before Protagoras, a Sophist, in the fifth century B.C. noticed three categories. Aristotle in the 300's B.C. called these three: masculine, feminine, and neither (*Poetics,* XXI). From "neither" or "intermediate" comes our word "neuter." It took the Greek grammarians six centuries to analyze their own language![55]

Gender in Biblical Languages Signifies "Class"

Different dialects were providing different forms of even the same word. Some grammarians have found as many as ten or more noun categories. Even though Greek *Koine* grammarians today may popularly talk about three kinds of nouns: masculine, feminine, and neuter, we would more accurately call them $\bar{a}$ stems, the o stems, and the consonant and close vowel (i, u) stems. Rather than sex, these categories may be based on shape, texture, color, edibility, and being animate or inanimate.[56]

Hebrew has two categories: masculine and feminine. Hebrew and Arabic grammarians have been expending much effort on trying to figure out the basis for these categories. They have noticed that the feminine is frequently used for names of countries or towns, including personification of nations and towns, a circumscribed space, instruments, parts of the body, natural forces, abstract ideas, titles of offices, collectives, a single example of a class, death, and the artificial. The masculine tends to be used for names of peoples, instruments for binding, names of heavenly bodies, and the natural. The grammarians also may themselves be sexist in their observations, declaring that the masculine gender is for the strong, courageous, dangerous, savage, respected, great, and powerful, whereas the feminine gender is for the weak, timid, motherly, productive, sustaining, nourishing, and gentle.[57]

Would a dog (masculine in Hebrew) be strong and courageous, but a bee (feminine in Hebrew) be weak and timid? A hare, dove, and stork are feminine in Hebrew. Rather than "weak and timid," I might classify hares, doves, and storks as *"gentle* and timid." A bee is small, but neither weak, timid, nor gentle. An ox is masculine, but so is a cow when pregnant. A bear is masculine, but so is a bearmother bereaved of whelps. "Masculine" in Hebrew seems to refer to a big aggressive animal, whereas "feminine" seems to refer to a smaller animal that is not likely to attack if one leaves it alone. Therefore, in this case, knowing the category may save one's life. Yes, if you want to take a short-cut through an empty field with rabbits, doves, storks, bees, and ants, you will be safe as long as you stay away from the bees and ants. (That is the feminine category.) But, if you want to take a short-cut through an empty field with oxen, pregnant cows, bears, bears whose whelps have been taken, wolves, and dogs, you may not be so safe, so you had better walk around them. (That is the masculine category.)

But no classification works completely. Oxen are masculine in Exodus 21:37 and feminine in Genesis 33:13. A "camel" is masculine in Genesis 24:63, but feminine in Genesis 32:16. "Sun" may be feminine or masculine. A mother eagle is described by a masculine pronoun (Deut. 32:10–14). A sword is feminine, but a girdle in Hebrew is masculine. A shoulder is feminine, but a nose is masculine. For every general rule are a host of exceptions. Sex, though, is a minor consideration, especially in Hebrew, when the feminine form is used for abstract ideas even if they refer to men.

The masculine plural in Hebrew and Greek "not infrequently" refers to feminine nouns, as *anēr* ("male") in the plural may include women, and "father" (*patēr*) in the plural may refer to parents.[58] In Hebrew and Greek the generic form, or prior gender, will often later become the masculine form when a second category, the feminine, is developed.[59] In other words, the masculine can not exist until the feminine has been created. Hebrew, as an ancient Semitic language, has more "masculine" generic words than does Greek. *ʾĀdām* and *ʾîs* are frequently used for both men and women. Greek, on the other hand, generally uses *anthrōpos,* "human," as opposed to *anēr,* "male," for the generic.

An example of a word in the process of change is *diakonos,* "minister." It is a "masculine" noun because of the *os* ending. However, in the New Testament, it is used of men and women, such as Paul, Timothy, and Phoebe (Rom. 16:1; 1 Tim. 4:6; Eph. 3:7). However, in the next two to three centuries so many women became "ministers" that first *diakonos* was given a feminine article and then a feminine ending, *diakonissa,* or "deaconess."[60]

ʾĔlôhîm can refer to male or female deities. *Theos* can also refer to male or female deities, although when *theos* refers only to the female deity Artemis, the Ephesian town clerk keeps *theos* but gives it a feminine article (Acts 19:37 vs. 19:11). In contrast, Demetrius, the silversmith calls Artemis by the Ionic dialect, *thea* (Acts 19:21).[61] In English, we too are struggling over this question. "God" is not a masculine term in English, yet since some people have come to see "God" as masculine, they are highlighting the feminine "Goddess" or creating new forms, "God/ess."[62]

We have seen already that *patēr* could refer to literal fathers. The plural usually refers to "parents." The Greeks had no singular generic term "parent." *Goneus* in the singular also refers to begetter or father. It emphasized the physical act of producing offspring.[63] Yet, in English we can use the term "parent" in the singular as a generic term to refer to a father or a mother.

Language is like a glove. As long as it fits and keeps you warm, it is great. But, if it shrinks or gets too big, it can be changed. God is authoritative, not language in itself.

Therefore, when we analyze language, we need to evaluate it in light of its function. If we are to take the grammarians and linguists seriously, God is not called "he" because God is a male. Rather, God is "he" because God is powerful and personal. In Hebrew, "Spirit" *(rûaḥ)* is grammatically feminine because the word is a metaphor for "wind," a natural force. We can not be sure why *pneuma* in Greek is neuter in form. A. T. Robertson suggests that -*ma* nouns are result words. In that case the neuter noun *pneuma*, "breath," or "wind" would be the noun resulting from the action of the verb "blow," *pneō*.[64] Grammatically, God is described by masculine *(theos)*, plural *('Ělôhîm)*, singular, feminine *(rûaḥ)*, and neuter *(pneuma)* nouns. These nouns do not tell us about God's sexuality. They are simply classes or categories of grammatical substantives. God simply must communicate to us humans within the confines of our own languages. We should learn about God by looking at God's own self-revelation, and in those self-revelations God clearly tells us that the God of the Bible has *no form*.

▼ Conclusion

Sometimes I wonder how God can be patient with us. We often ignore God's explicit self-revelations and draw our theologies only from our subjective intuitions. The church may be to blame for some of the grave misunderstandings that are wandering around our world. Why is metaphor so frequently misunderstood? Aristotle thinks that using metaphors well "cannot be learnt; it is the token of genius. For the right use of metaphor means an eye for resemblances" (*Poetics*, XXII). God, though, does not require that we use metaphors well. We need only recognize them. We have seen that God has no sexuality because God is spirit, a God who can be worshiped anywhere, who in these days chooses as sanctuary two or three Christians. God is unseeable, and unlike us humans, fully good, compassionate, trustworthy, purposeful, able to create and know. The great message of the Jewish men and women eyewitnesses of the first century is that this great God chose to become human. But seeing Jesus, by itself, was not self-evident proof of God's existence.

Both before, during, and after the incarnation, God is known by actions, adjectives, and metaphors. God allows humans to create names and titles for God, and, as well, God chooses attributes for self-description with particular listeners in mind. Of course, God is powerful, but what we need to highlight is how that power is used: to help those in need, *not* to domineer over the weak. Of course, God is holy, just, and jealous, and, when we model our own lives on these qualities, we humans become healthy and happy, not oppressed and deprived.

Language and human "bodyness" do provide some limitations to God's self-revelation. However, metaphor and language are accurate only in so far as they are not stretched beyond their intentions. God uses a great variety of metaphors, only one of which is "father." Every metaphor must be studied for its analogies and disanalogies. "Lord" teaches us that because God is so good, God should be always obeyed. "Father" is part of a constellation of connotations, the everyday parent, the all-powerful idealized Parent, and the intimate but powerful ruler. Ultimately, when referring to God, "he" in Hebrew or Greek is not *masculine*, but rather genderless, since "masculine" gender is simply an androgenous pronoun or noun. As well, the "masculine," "feminine," and "neuter" genera all symbolize different qualities about God. God is powerful, personal, forceful, causing results—one, and diverse.

Language Should Be Individualized

How then shall we communicate today about God in each of our own languages, each with their enabling aspects and disabling aspects? First of all, we need to keep in balance who God is when communicating to specific humans with their own specific needs. In the *Priscilla Papers*, Greg Boyd has written a poignant account of his upbringing by his abusive stepmother. He explains that he subconsciously blamed God for taking away his real (and idealized) mother when he was two years old. However, when he finally opened up himself at twenty years of age to receive from God what he had always longed for, that "motherly love," which he defines as unconditional love, he "could finally be cradled, hugged, kissed, and loved in a way that no earthly mother ever could." He also explains how a friend who had been abused by her father could approach God first only as mother. Eventually she was able to see that God as father was not like her own earthly father. He concludes: "The complementary usage of diverse metaphors saves all the metaphors from becoming literalized, and hence destructive idols." Complementing the traditional metaphor of God as father with the metaphor of God as mother "affects a deepening of a believer's wholeness on many levels." It opens up doors for God to be our "all in all." "Reclaiming all biblical imagery assists women in experiencing themselves as being as much in the image of God as males," and "it enables both sexes to attain a wholeness which breaks through the barriers of stereotypical cultural expectations imposed on them."[65] Joe LaMadeleine agrees. As a teenager, he used to pray to Mary instead of God when he was really desperate: "I felt that as a woman she would be more compassionate than God the Father. Now that my image of God has both male and female attributes, I find God more approachable."[66]

Similarly, Deborah Detering, after parenting about seventy-five foster children "few of whom had fathers who satisfied even minimal standards of fatherhood," was very apologetic about using "Our Father." She did not use the term "father" for a daughter who was raped by her human father. God instead, was "savior" only to her. Detering concluded that "God is not like a father, but a father is supposed to be like God."[67] A variety of images about God, metaphors chosen to communicate to our specific listeners, can help them (and us!) understand God much more, as well as feel good about themselves. Thus, if readers choose to continue to use "he" for God, as the Bible does, they still need to be careful not to use the masculine pronoun so much that their listeners misinterpret God to be male.

"He" for God Should Be Avoided

Most readers by now probably are aware that I try not to use "He" for God because in today's world, in English, that "He" is no longer by many understood as the original writers intended, as a generic, nonsexual term. Paul's principle is here applicable: "To all I became all so that by all means some I might save" (1 Cor. 9:22). Supposedly, in English the pronouns "he," "his," and "him" refer to common gender when the antecedent has no apparent sex, sex is not important, or males and females are included. In 1850 the British Parliament had to pass a law declaring that "Words importing the Masculine Gender shall be deemed and taken to include Females, . . . unless the contrary as to Gender . . . is expressly provided." Even then John Stuart argued one year later that the law should be repealed because the women would be entitled to a vote. Similarly, when "he" is used of God, many speakers today do not clearly understand the antecedent "God" to be without sex. They argue, as does the *Oxford English Dictionary* about "man": "he" primarily and inclusively denotes the male sex, indirectly the female sex. Dennis Baron documents "the deep antifeminist tradition that underlies our ideas about language," even though, he thinks: "There is nothing inherently sexist about the English language." Unfortunately, the masculine has been treated by many as the more worthy and superior gender: "The concept of worthiness is no longer a rule of thumb to resolve the syntactic puzzle of what to do when an adjective refers to nouns of differing genders, but a reflection of a natural order that places man at the head of creation, with woman in a subordinate, subservient, and frequently invisible second place."[68]

That is why other evangelical writers have chosen to use "She" for God. Marchiene Vroom Rienstra explains in her introduction to the devotional *Swallow's Nest: A Feminine Reading of the Psalms:* "My goal is not to replace masculine God-language with feminine God-language in the Christian tradition, but to encourage the use of feminine language" because "God finally is neither male nor female, but far more than both, and that God's nature includes qualities attributed to both male and female in varying ways in all cultures."[69] I believe this practice in itself does not contradict the intentions of the biblical language. Pastor Paul R. Smith prefers using both "him" and "her" and both "Father" and "Mother" for God (such as baptizing "In the name of the Father, Son and Holy Spirit, the One God who is Mother to us all") to nonsexist language ("Godself," "Parent, Child, Spirit") because the metaphor "father" is a foundational biblical metaphor, a God who is neither male nor female would be less personal, and a nonsexist God would remain a male-only image of God because of our culture's intensive and life-long cultural inclination toward God as being masculine. He believes: "Perhaps one of the chief values in calling God 'she' is that it is so shocking. Idols are sometimes more effectively shattered with lightning bolts than with endless debates." He concludes that using both inclusive language for God and people and including both women and men fully in the church's worship will be a result of the Spirit's revival and renewal of the church.[70]

Language about God Should Be Monotheistic

The only danger may arise when both "She" and "He" are used for God, each in a different way, so that we end up having two gods, a great female one, and a great male one. This sense comes across in some of Andrew M. Greeley's novels. The priest Blackie Ryan calls God "She" to accentuate God as immanent, intensely personal, capricious, physically loving, "a God who is pathetically eager to forgive at the slightest hint of any emotion that can be called compunction." When Greeley calls God the "Lady God" who dances and the "Lord God" who lurks, even though Greeley may intend one God, the reader sometimes feels like he writes about two deities.[71] In contrast, both Tikva Frymer-Kensky and Susanne Heine explain that the biblical revelation accentuates that one God can meet *all* our human needs: "Why do you need a mother goddess? Yahweh, the father, judge and warrior hero, can also give birth, breast-feed, care for and have mercy."[72] That is the danger to calling God the Father "he" but God the Spirit "she." Again, we will begin to worship, even if subconsciously, two or three deities. God is one, and that fact must be represented in all our actions and terms.

Some writers have suggested that the Shaker's Holy Mother Wisdom (Holy Spirit) and God the Father might be a model for us today. Linda A. Mercadante's study of their theology concludes that the Shakers subordinated the feminine or female element (the Holy Spirit) to the masculine Father element: "To seek a solution to male dominance by rooting gender stereotypes in God only causes a further hardening of them." Rather, the Trinity holds most promise for contemporary theology: "God as a coequal, interconnected community of divine persons, operating in a completely harmonious and mutually loving manner. Freely and out of this abundance, the divine love spills over to create, and then to intimately love, that creation. Such a trinitarian community avoids the gender dualism endemic to the two-elements approach. The process it suggests can also be productively used in describing and providing a model for human relationships."[73]

But, we do have to watch out, who we are addressing. If we take a term for someone or something who is not the God of the Bible and we use it, we may very well end up worshiping another deity. To use a variety of attributes as names for the one God is totally different from using a variety of gods/goddesses as different names all for one God.

GOD IS A PARADOX

*W*ho is God? God is unique. God is a spirit and has no sexuality. But is God a God who is near by or is God a God who is far off? With our limited minds, this is the question we pose. As I mentioned in the introduction, people tend to respond in reductionist answers. On the one hand, Judith Ochshorn, noting that the God of monotheism is pictured as both immanent and transcendent, decides that God as transcendent should be abandoned: "In this time of global ecological crisis, it is important that human beings abandon a paradigm of the divine as above nature, existing eternally whether the natural universe lives or dies; rather let us return to the earlier reverence for all nature as sacred."[1] Starhawk proposes the Goddess as "a living religion of immanence." Even the artist Meinrad Craighead who remains in institutional Catholicism agrees that because Mothergod "was a force living within me, she was more real, more powerful than the remote Fathergod I was educated to have faith in."[2] On the other hand, Donald G. Bloesch has developed in an abstract manner what many people actually feel, that even though God is both transcendent and immanent, God "is primarily and originally transcendent and secondarily and derivatively immanent." Karl Barth has had quite an effect on both Bloesch and the Christian world in his emphasis of God as "the Wholly Other."[3]

In effect, one excess leads to another excess, one heresy leads to another. Some people overemphasize God's transcendence through the metaphor of father, degenerating into picturing an absent, tyrannical sovereign father. In reaction, other people overemphasize God's immanence through the metaphor of mother, arriving at a present, caring, but also capricious, mother. Some people, brought up in a more liberal setting, have become tired of a deistic impersonal deity. Others, brought up in a more conservative setting, have revolted against an oppressive setting for women. Some may find themselves emphasizing God's otherness because they are driven by fear to protect God in today's pseudoscientific culture. For them, God is so *Other* that no amount of human perception can ever even approach God, no less question God. Rather, we need to embrace both transcendence *and* immanence in our conception of God because God is *not* us, yet God is *in* us.

What does immanence and transcendence mean in our English language and in the Bible? After defining these terms we will look at several key biblical passages in order to discover how God is "all in all," close, powerful, and not dark and light.

▼ Transcendence and Immanence Are Defined

According to *Webster's Unabridged Dictionary* both "transcendence" and "immanence" are derived from Latin terms. "Transcendent," according to *Webster's,* is "surpassing, excelling, extraordinary," "beyond human knowledge," "that exists apart from the material universe," and "divine spirit."[4] The Latin *transcendere* means "to climb or step over, surmount,"[5] "surpass," "go beyond." According to Elizabeth Achtemeier, "transcendence" refers to God's holiness. God is "other from all things, creatures, persons, and processes."[6]

"Immanent" is "living, remaining, or operating within; inherent" and "present throughout the universe." The Latin *immanere* means "to remain in or near," which comes from *in* plus *manere,* "to remain."[7] The verb *manere,* in Latin, can mean "to wait for, await, stay, remain; to stop off, pass the night; to last, endure, continue, persist."[8]

The Greek has a verb very similar to the Latin, *emmenō,* to "*abide in* a place," "*stand by,*" "remain fixed, stand fast."[9] *Emmenō* is *menō,* to "stand fast," "stay at home," "stay," "remain," "abide," "sojourn," "endure," "wait for," intensified by "in," "to stay *in.*"[10] *Menō* is a common New Testament word as in "Mary *remained* with [Elizabeth] about three months" (Luke 1:56). *Emmenō* occurs in the Greek Old Testament, but is used only metaphorically, as in God "*will fulfill*"

God's promise (Num. 23:19) or one witness is not enough *to abide* against someone (Deut. 19:15). *Emmenō* refers to the ability to act on one's intentions.[11] Neither the Greek or Latin verbs are used exactly as we use the concept of "immanence" today. However, the Greek verb *emmenō* highlights the idea that when we say God is immanent we mean that God "abides" with us, or is present with us, no matter where we are.

Theologians define immanence as the nearness or presence or indwelling of God in the creation, God sustaining and preserving creation generally, and more particularly, energizing the wills of believers. Van A. Harvey contrasts immanence with deism, where God created the world but does not intervene in it, and with pantheism, where "all things and beings are modes, attributes, or appearances of one single reality or being." Bluntly put, the neo-pagan Goddess movement is largely pantheistic. For example, Gloria Anzaldúa explains: "We've been taught that the spirit is outside our bodies or above our heads somewhere up in the sky with God. We're supposed to forget that every cell in our bodies, every bone and bird and worm has spirit in it." Or, the character Shug Avery believes: "God is inside you and inside everybody else. You come into the world with God. But only them that search for it inside find it. . . . I believe God is everything, says Shug. Everything that is or ever was or ever will be."[12] Alice Walker's novel *The Color Purple* has extensively publicized the belief of pantheism because she is a genius as a stylist. (Some adherents may be panentheistic: the world is included in God's being, but the world does not exhaust God's being.)[13] Philip Edgcumbe Hughes, in contrast to Van Harvey, sees pantheism as "a familiar form of the theology of immanence." Moreover, he understands "immanentism" as maintaining that God's activity takes place solely within the normal course of nature (which appears to be deism)![14] In the textbook *Introducing Christian Doctrine* Millard J. Erickson defines immanence as God being "present and active within his creation, and within the human race, even those members of it that do not believe in or obey him. . . . He is at work in and through natural processes."[15]

All these Christian theologians agree that the Bible teaches God as being immanent *and* transcendent. Georgia Harkness explains that God "is *in* the world but also *other than* the world." "God is not far off looking down from above or from without upon millions of separate human folk. God is immanent in his universe, and that means that he is already within each one of us. 'Closer is he than breathing.' In prayer we strive to become conscious of a Presence that is already part of our very nature!"[16] Millard Erickson helpfully mentions both the excesses and the implications of both doctrines: "If we emphasize immanence too much, we may identify everything that happens as God's will and working." If we emphasize transcendence too much, "we may expect God to work miracles at all times," "we may tend to mistreat the creation, forgetting that he himself is present and active there," and "we may depreciate the value of what non-Christians do."[17]

The ultimate sense of God being with us has been fulfilled in the incarnation, God becoming human. The Greek "immanuel" *(emmanouēl)* is a transliteration of two Hebrew words, *ʾēl,* "God," and *ʾimānû,* "with us."[18] God was near to humans, literally near, and near in the sense of being fully human. John expresses Jesus' presence beautifully as Jesus "pitched a tent among us" (John 1:14). Jesus was immanent "near," but not immanent "present throughout the universe." Jesus, though, promised the disciples that after the resurrection, he would be both "near" and "present throughout the universe" by means of the Spirit (John 14:16–19, 23, 28; 16:12–16; 2 Cor. 3:17).

Several Bible passages are key ones for understanding God's immanence: Ephesians 1, 4; Acts 17:24–28; Psalm 139; Isaiah 57:15; 66:1; Colossians 1; Jeremiah 23:23–24; and 1 Kings 8:27. Ironically, almost every one of them also teaches us something about God's transcendence.

▼ God Is All in All

In Ephesians, a letter written to encourage unity, Paul explains that God seated Jesus "far above *(huperanō)* every ruler and authority and power and lordship and every name being named, not only in this age but also in the one coming; and he subjected all under *(hupo)* his feet, and he made him head over *(huper)* all the church" (Eph. 1:21–22). Here is transcendence accentuated! The words "far above," "under," and "over" are spatial words that highlight Christ's surpassing power over any human. But, then, Paul adds that the church "is his body *(sōma),* the fullness of the one filling for oneself all in all" (Eph. 1:23). The incarnation was one occasion of God's immanence. The church is a continuing presence of Christ, along with the Spirit. The church, two or three Christians, continue to be Christ's moveable "tent." Wherever the church goes, Christ goes, too. When Paul is stopped by a great light on the road to Damascus, Jesus tells him: "Saul, Saul, why do you persecute me?" (Acts 9:4). Saul never directly persecuted the human Jesus. But when he persecuted the church, he was persecuting the immanent presence of Christ. The church, Christ's body, is the fullness *(plērōma)* of Christ. "Fullness" is another spatial word. It, too, fits in the concept of immanence. *Plērōma* refers to that which is filled full as a ship is filled with sailors, rowers, and soldiers, or a stomach is filled with food.[19] The church is "filled with" not many people, but with one person, Jesus (Eph. 1:23).

And who is this Jesus? "The one filling for himself all things in all ones." "Filling" is a participle that indicates that what Jesus does ("fill") occurs not just once but continually. It is a process. "Filling" is in the middle voice, which indicates Jesus himself does the filling, acting for his own concern. T. K. Abbott explains: "If Christ is to fill all things through the medium of the Church, He must first fill the Church. And with this the figure of *sōma* agrees, since in a man the head fills the body with its thoughts and purposes, so that each member is determined by it and filled by it, and that the more, the maturer the man is."[20] If this passage is interpreted in the light of Ephesians 4:8, 11 the neuter "all things" would include spiritual gifts given to "all ones," the people of Christ.

But Paul may not simply be writing of "gifts" for service. Whenever we act out of love, Christ then "dwells" all the more in our "hearts," our inmost selves (Eph. 3:17–19). When we act in unity with other believers and are mature in our beliefs and our actions, we have experienced "the fullness of Christ" (Eph. 4:13). As Jesus explained, the church may be known by the world as his disciples if we "have love for one another" (John 13:35). We are also filled with the Spirit when we are mature, not drunk, obeying the Lord's will, communicating with one another joyfully, singing from a united heart, thankful, and submissive to one another out of respect to Christ (Eph. 5:17–21). Jesus' filling is paradoxical. It definitely comes from Jesus, but it is also developed by humans. I understand it to be analogous to being given muscles from creation, but these muscles must be continually in action for them to stay in shape.

God is not the only transcendent being. The Devil is also transcendent in some way: "the ruler of the authority of the air, the spirit now working among those who are disobedient" (Eph. 2:2). We believers will also ourselves be transcendent: we will be raised up and seated among the heavenly places in Christ Jesus (Eph. 2:6). Transcendence is an image of affirmation for believers.

I remember the first time I attended a college fellowship meeting. I had recently begun studying at Douglass College, an all-women's school. I had been invited to go to a Christian InterVarsity Fellowship meeting one Friday night at Rutgers College, then an all-men's college. I was terrified, but I went anyway led by a magnificent undergirding cloud of comfort that later I came to understand as God's Spirit. Alone, I climbed onto the intercampus bus. Alone, I trudged up three flights of an abandoned old classroom building to find the meeting room. And, of all topics, the guest lecturer spoke against Christianity, how none of the Messianic promises of the Old Testament were fulfilled in Jesus. As a conducive setting for acknowledging Jesus as Lord and Savior, this night was a flop! But what struck me was the love of the Christians for one another and for me. I was treated as a regal princess, someone of worth. They were interested in my thoughts and they invited me to join them for refreshments. Their love for each other helped me to recognize God's love for me.

▼ God Is Immanent

Paul writes to the Ephesians about the importance of the unity of Jew and Gentile (Eph. 2:11–21). This unity is again accentuated in Ephesians 4:4–6 by the many things or beings who are one. As Jesus is one, so too Jesus' body, the church, is one. Only one Spirit, one hope, one Lord, one faith, one baptism, one God exist. The metaphor of father here closely refers to creation: "one God and father of all." God created Jew and Gentile. Paul may be hearkening back to 3:14–15 where he states that every race in heaven and on earth takes its name from God the Father. If Jesus had been described as "the one filling for himself all things in all people" (Eph. 1:23), now Paul describes God as: "the one over (*epi*) all and through (*dia*) all and in (*en*) all" (Eph. 4:6). God is "the one," the unique one with three different spheres. These three phrases are parallel, exactly identical except for the different prepositions used: *over* all and *through* all and *in* all. By repeating "and" Paul accentuates the all-inclusiveness of God. These three prepositions suggest increasingly closer distances, a multidimensional presence of God.

God Is Close

The grammarian A. T. Robertson suggests that the way to interpret a preposition is to hold on to its root-idea and work out from that in each special context. The root-idea of *epi* is "a real resting upon" and, with the genitive case, it may refer to kind or genus and sometimes vicinity, before, in the presence of. *Epi* contrasts with *huper* which signifies "over."[21] So Paul is suggesting that God is not simply "over and beyond" people, but resting upon them. This distinction reminds me of those scales one finds at the doctor's office. When we stand on the scale, straight, the nurse or doctor drops on our head a metal ruler that exactly measures our height. God is that close to us, so close to us that God rests on our head. Paul uses the plural "all." This fact is not just true for me or for you, but for everyone. God's closeness is certainly true for believers. Paul is writing to a church. However, we have seen from Ephesians 3:15 that every family of people takes its identity from God. God is close to all people. However, not all people have God's "fullness" or overabounding presence, as does the mature church (Eph. 1:23; 4:13).

Paul is writing metaphorically here. God is not a hat we wear on our head. Even in the introductory textbook *Introducing Christian Doctrine* Millard Erickson explains: "'Up' and 'down' do not really apply to a spirit, who is not located at some specific place within the universe."[22] Paul is trying to explain God's omnipresence. God is so close to us as to rest upon us.

If that were not close enough, God also is the one "through all." The root-idea of *dia* is *duo* or two. A. T. Robertson reiterates how very persistent is the etymological force of this root. *Dia* refers to "by twos" or "be-tween" (by-twain). It can refer to an interval of time, as in Acts 1:3, Jesus appeared at intervals within the forty days. It can refer to location, as passing between or through two objects or parts of objects. It can more abstractly refer to intermediate agent, the one who comes between the attainment and nonattainment of the object.[23] Thus, in this case, God is between two people, God is next to us as we stand next to our neighbor. If we want to communicate to our neighbor, God moves between us. This verse falls in the context of a continuing exhortation by Paul: "I am exhorting you, I, the prisoner in Christ, worthily to walk the calling to which you were called, with all humility and gentleness, with patience, bearing with one another in love, making every effort to guard the unity of the Spirit in the bond of peace" (Eph. 4:1–3). That bond or "chain" is one body, one Spirit, one hope, one Lord, one faith, one baptism, one God. That chain binding all believers finally ends in this three-dimensional bond: over, between, and within. Remember, Paul is in prison, and, everyday, a new praetorian guard comes to him and is himself lightly chained to one of his wrists.[24] Handcuffs are very ancient. As Paul looks at his guard, and the guard looks at Paul, the handcuffs become for Paul a synecdoche of God's presence. (A synecdoche is a small item representing a larger concept.) As the handcuff both unites and separates Paul and his guard, so too God is there between the two of them. And Paul need only whisper to God, who is as close as that handcuff, so that Paul might be empowered, as he walks around that day in his apartment, to bear with that guard in love. God apparently did empower Paul because the whole praetorian guard came to learn that Paul was not imprisoned for criminal behavior, but he was imprisoned for the sake of Christ (Phil. 1:13).

God is very close, close over us and close between us, and, even, close within or among us. The basic idea of *en* is locative, the location of something is within the bounds marked by the word with which it occurs. *En* is *not* "near," rather, it is "inside."[25] "All," here, again, is plural. God is the One "among us," or, literally, "within all of us." God is not limited to a presence between *two* people, but God is present in all groups. Air certainly is an apt metaphor. It rests over us, next to us, and even inside us. We can not live without air. Even though Paul in Ephesians addresses believers, when he spoke at Athens he communicated a similar thought to skeptics. In God, "we are living and we are moving and we are existing" (Acts 17:28). In Ephesians 4, Paul has now reached the most intimate of all spheres. Every step the Ephesians take is in God's very presence. They (and us) need only stretch forward those legs and swing those arms and breathe in the air to be able powerfully and confidently to walk, humbly and patiently, bearing with each other and guarding unity. The Christians at Ephesus are guards who are tied up (*"to guard* the unity of the Spirit in the *chain* of peace" Eph. 4:3). Looking at a guard manacled to a prisoner, who is to tell who is guard and who is prisoner?

Thus, Ephesians 4:6 does not so much teach God's transcendence and immanence. Rather, all three prepositions hearken to God's closeness, closeness to all people to help them live loving lives. What a misunderstanding that Craighead can claim she was taught in the church to believe in a "remote" God! The biblical God is certainly concerned with all creation. But in none of these prepositions does Paul ever say God *is* us or God is all people or God is all things. God rests upon us, stands between us, stands among us, but God still is God, and humans are human.

In Psalm 139 David also describes God's omnipresence using locative imagery: "Behind and before you press me in and you place upon me your palm" (Ps. 139:5). God is here compared to either companions in walking or to a girdle for walking. On a cold, windy day a larger person might want to block the wind from blowing away someone slight. God walks both behind and before David. God presses him in. But God also walks next to David with a soothing intimate palm on his shoulder. The ancients used to wrap a "girdle"—a cloth or leather belt from two to eight inches wide around their middle to help them walk long distances,[26] to give them support, even as some walkers do today, or as weight lifters who wear a comfortable belt for support. God, like that girdle, presses David both in the back and the front binding in David's thoughts and words (Ps. 139:3–5). No matter where David goes, God is with him: "If I ascend to heaven, you are there; if I make my bed in Sheol, you are there. If I take the wings of the morning and settle at the farthest limits of the sea; even there your hand shall lead me, and your right hand shall hold me fast" (Ps. 139:8–10). David communicates God's closeness with the metaphor of a hand, comforting, leading, and holding.

Only a Transcendent God Can Be Immanent

In Ephesians, the focus has been unity, one God, one human race (4:1–6). Paul goes on to describe diversity and transcendence: "Having ascended into a height, [Christ] captured captivity, he gave gifts to the people" (Eph. 4:8) and "the one having descended is also the one having ascended far above all the heavens, in order that he might fill all" (4:10). Here clearly immanence is dependent on transcendence. The image is of a military victor. Both in Israel and in Greece hills were used for fortress cities. Jesus, the conqueror of all conquerors and conqueror even of conquering situations (4:8) shares the treasures that were gathered from the vanquished with his army. But these treasures are not gold or silver. They are diverse gifts, people who can serve (apostles, prophets, evangelists, pastors, teachers), all with one purpose, to equip believers for ministry, to help mature, to build up "the fullness" of Christ's presence (4:8, 11–13). Only when someone is "transcendent," here signifying someone victorious and powerful, can that person then be concerned for everyone, "immanent."

In very different words, Paul here has reiterated the idea expressed by Moses in Deuteronomy: "For the Lord your God is God of gods and Lord of lords, the great God, mighty and awesome, who is not partial and takes no bribe, who executes justice for the orphan and the widow, and who loves the strangers, providing them food and clothing" (10:17–18). Only a transcendent God can be powerfully, immanently present. The same idea is expressed in Isaiah. The "high and lofty one who inhabits eternity, whose name is Holy: I dwell in the high and holy place," this surpassing God, Wholly Other God, who dwells in "high and holy places" also dwells "with those who are contrite and humble in spirit" (Isa. 57:15. See also 66:1). In contrast, Starhawk explains, *we* need to help the Goddess! "The Goddess, who is the soul of earth, of sky, of the living being in whose body we are cells," "unlike other deities," "does not come to save us. It is up to us to save her—if we choose. If we so will."[27]

▼ God Is Powerful

Transcendence is not the only way to express God's power. Immanence too describes God's power. In Paul's letter to the Colossians, written at about the same time as Ephesians, during Paul's same house arrest in Rome, creation and Christ are intimately related. All things were created in (*en*) Christ (Col. 1:16). Christ marks the bounds of creation. Nothing or no one was created outside of Christ's sphere of influence, as God declares in Genesis: "God saw everything that he had made, and indeed, it was very good" (Gen. 1:31). "All things," "the seen and the unseen," were not only created "in" (*en*) Christ, but also "through" (*dia*) Christ and "for" (*eis*) Christ (Col. 1:16). Christ was the intermediate agent, the one who came between the attainment and nonattainment of creation (*dia*). Nothing or no one could have been created without Christ's presence. Also, all things were created for Christ's purpose (*eis*). *Eis* is simply *en* plus the accusative case (direct object). It expresses motion towards. Metaphorically, it indicates aim or purpose.[28] Not only were all things created within Christ's sphere, through Christ as intermediate agent, but also they were created to please Christ. Christ is superior to all creation, firstborn, existing before (*pro*) all creation and superior to all creation (Col. 1:15, 17). Christ also holds together *(sunistēmi)* everything within (*en*) himself (Col. 1:17). Christ "places together," as wooden blocks in a building, everything. Christ's immanence is a statement of power in Colossians. Nothing or no one is beyond Christ's presence and pleasure and power. Creation does not have a life of its own. It must be held together by Christ and it moves toward Christ.

We began this chapter by alluding to Jeremiah 23:23: "Am I a God near by, says the Lord, and not a God far off?" It sounds like "near by" refers to God's immanence and "far off" refers to God's transcendence. However, the next verse explains God's meaning: "Who can hide in secret places so that I cannot see them? says the Lord. Do I not fill heaven and earth? says the Lord" (Jer. 23:24). God is immanent—or all present—because God is transcendent—surpassing humans. The categories immanence and transcendence are too limiting to help us here understand God. A God "near at hand" would be a god constructed by the people, a god who is limited, a god created by the deceit of the heart (Jer. 23:25–27). Because God is "far off" and fills "heaven and earth," therefore no person, no thought can ever escape God. How then can the prophets claim to prophesy in God's name and not expect God to notice!

Our study so far has shown us that we humans have created artificial divisions. We can not simply say that immanence is God's nearness, while transcendence is God's farness. Rather, we have seen that God's transcendence may refer to God's power, victory, and holiness, but so may God's immanence refer to God's power. God has the power to be very near to us only because God is very far from us. Rarely does anyone mention that only if God is very close to us can we humans be enabled to be loving and united. We have also been reminded of the fullness of Christ's presence in the world, in the church as the immanent presence of Christ, a presence more overflowing as the church is more mature. God as Spirit is present everywhere, but God also has a more full presence. In these days, that presence is in the church. In the past, God had God's fuller presence symbolized by the ark, the temple, the tablets, the manna, the bronze serpent, the sacrificial cult.[29] God can not be contained within space (1 Kings 8:27; 2 Chron. 2:6), but God can chose to be more present, in former days, in some places, in newer days, in some people. In the future, neither place nor people will be needed to contain God's special presence. John saw no sanctuary (*naos*) in the new heaven and the new earth. God is the sanctuary, pitched right among humans: "God, God's very self," will be among people (Rev. 21:3, 22).

▼ God Is Not Dark and Light

The neo-pagan movement is very hard to study because the adherents do not claim to be consistent nor even historically truthful. As Naomi Goldenberg explains, if the truth is not helpful, then a fiction may be devised: "A remembered fact and an invented fantasy have identical psychological value."[30] Many speak of God as within, others of God as also without. For some, goddess begins as an affirmation of the self, and eventually moves to an exhortation for the Goddess to come within. For example, Nelle Morton begins an essay: "When I speak of the Goddess as metaphoric image I am in no way referring to an entity 'out there.' . . . I am not even referring to a Goddess 'back there' as if I participate in resurrecting an ancient religion. In the sense that I am woman I see the Goddess in myself, but I need something tangible, a concrete image or a concrete event, to capture my full attention to the present and draw me into the metaphoric process." Nevertheless, she describes a handful of events where "as if intimate, infinite, and transcending power had enfolded me, as if great wings [Isis] had spread themselves around the seated women and gathered us into a oneness. . . . That is the first time I *experienced* a female deity." Starhawk explains that "Spirit [in immanent value] is not seen as separate from matter."[31] As in pantheism, neo-pagans believe in one single reality that appears in many different modes. What does appear inconsistent is that, if indeed the Goddess without (the Earth's cycles) and the Goddess within (the cycles of our own bodies) are all one,[32] who are those powers, energies or entities who can take over on the ungrounded, unsuspecting believer? Who are the universal energies that must be nourished? Who are the four powers invited to come? Why must the human in the ritual remain focused on what (s)he is doing from moment to moment so that "astral entities" do not "take over" and become "unfriendly" when "trapped in our realm"? Why are people in danger of being not "grounded," one foot "flailing in the heavens" and the other foot "floundering on earth"?[33] Mayumi Oda, a practicing Zen Buddhist, suggests that all of us have "a shadow side" that "has a lot of force" if "we can meet and embrace our evil." Unlike what Oda suggests, we Christians and Jews do feel free to talk about the evil we do, but we certainly do not think we should "embrace" our evil.[34] Is this Isis really, "a *gentle* potency"?[35]

The Spirits Appear in Different Guises

How can someone be overpowered if both the forces within and without come from one source? Is this source good into which people are tapping? Certainly the God of the Bible never claims to destroy someone, but rather to enhance one's own will.

As the apostle James explains, the "Parent of lights" has "no change of position or shadow cast by turning." Rather, every good gift and every perfect present comes down from above (James 1:17). God's *metaphorical* sun and moon ("lights" Gen. 1:16; Ps. 136:7) do not create a shadow, a dark side. God only causes life and growth. Therefore, when Jesus challenges his listeners to "hate their life in this world," giving them up as a grain of wheat falling into the earth and dying, their lives, their wills, are *enhanced,* not destroyed. They will keep their lives eternally and bear much fruit. They remain not a single seed, but a tall, healthy wheat plant sustaining many (John 12:23–26). The seed of their self-centered will has disappeared in the flower of God's will working through them. Jesus is our model as he chose to die for a covenant of forgiveness, but was resurrected from death and glorified and honored.

How can someone instead worship an unknown force(s) who is "both Dark and Light, both matter and spirit, heaven and earth"?[36]

These powers that can take over are the powers of the evil one, the Devil (Eph. 2:2), disguised not simply as an angel of light (2 Cor. 11:14), but as a Goddess, in Spanish, *la serpiente*. This Goddess may be invoked by the name of any of many goddesses: Gaia, Demeter, Isis, the Great Mother, Aphrodite, Juno, Hera, Astarte, Inanna, Persephone, Ariadne, Pallas Athena, Sophia, Artemis, Hecate, the child, shakti, Shinte, Amaterasu, Ishtar, Arachne, Lakshmi, Lucini, Oshun, Oya, Yemaya, Kali, Tara, Dakinis, and Asunge. Unfortunately, behind the guise of goddesses are evil spirits, as the apostle Paul explains, to whom pagans sacrifice, "to demons and not to God, I do not want you to become partners with the demons" (1 Cor. 10:20).[37] These mysterious energies and forces are really "the evil spiritual forces in the heavenly places" (Eph. 6:12).

We in the Western world need to learn from our Third World sisters and brothers. In a sociological study of the Ewe Christians in Ghana, Birgit Meyer concludes: "But 140 years after the coming of the first missionary church members still seem to hold ideas resembling those of the first converts." What are those ideas? Even when an African trained in the West might declare there are no idols, the church member is astounded and replies: "Surely there are idols, but the God of the Christians is more powerful than all of them."[38] When one calls on idols, one invites demons into one's life. Even in the last century a missionary to China, John L. Nevius, who originally did not believe in evil spirits, came to discover that the Goddess invoked by a farmer was an evil spirit. He has a firsthand account of a Mr. Kwo who was harassed by an evil spirit when he invoked Wang Mu-niang, the wife of Yu-hwang, the chief divinity of China at that time.[39]

Unfortunately, such intercourse with evil does not strengthen one's personal identity. It destroys it. In Sheila S. Walker's study of the African Harrist Church, she was told again and again that: "The major activity of the witch, or devil, is to eat the souls of their victims to make them sick or die."[40] What a tragic outcome that women who feel blocked out of God's good blessings should go to find fulfillment in a belief system that ultimately will destroy them even more! In C. S. Lewis' preface to his fictional *The Screwtape Letters* he suggests that devils have "a kind of hunger": "Even in human life we have seen the passion to dominate, almost to digest, one's fellow; to make his whole intellectual and emotional life merely an

extension of one's own—to hate one's hatreds and resent one's griev-
ances and indulge one's egoism through him as well as through
myself." In Hell, this desire is a ravenous hunger irrevocably to "suck
the weaker into itself and permanently gorge its own being on the
weaker's outraged individuality. It is (I feign) for this that devils
desire human souls and the souls of one another. It is for this that
Satan desires all his own followers and all the sons of Eve and all
the host of Heaven. His dream is of the day when all shall be inside
him and all that says 'I' can say it only through him. This, I surmise,
is the bloated-spider parody, the only imitation he can understand,
of that unfathomed bounty whereby God turns tools into servants
and servants into sons, so that they may be at last reunited to Him
in the perfect freedom of a love offered from the height of the utter
individualities which he has liberated them to be."[41]

Of course, very, very few believers in witchcraft or the Goddess
or goddesses or (neo) paganism would ever be attracted by Satan
worship. Repeatedly writers in goddess feminism repudiate
Satanism, the conscious decision to worship a malevolent power
and use one's power only for evil goals.[42] What I am suggesting is
that they are being deceived. The universe has only one true God,
all other deities, if they have power, come from the temporarily-
allowed-to exist Devil,[43] no matter how attractively presented. The
Bible claims that idols are demonic spirits, fallen angels, who are
obedient to Satan. As lexicographer Joseph Thayer explains: demons
"appropriate to their own use and honor the sacrifices offered to
idols."[44] Even the term "demon" can mean "power," similar to "powers," which is frequently used today. In the New Testament, the
appeal of magic is to an unhealthy curiosity, a kind of spiritual med-
dling. For instance, the young widows at Ephesus were not only
idle, they were gossips and magic-workers, speaking the things they
should not (1 Tim. 5:13, *periergos*). Several years earlier, at Ephesus,
where Artemis was worshiped, new believers burned 50,000 silver
coins worth of books on magic (*periergos* Acts 19:19). And after this
action, "The word of the Lord grew mightily and prevailed" (Acts
19:20). The Greek *pharmakeia* is the basis for today's "pharmacist."
Then as now "drugs" could be health-inducing or harmful depend-
ing on the goal of creator and user.[45] Fornication, idolatry, magic
(*pharmakeia*), fighting, jealousy, murder, and theft are examples of
works of the flesh (Gal. 5:19–20; Rev. 9:20–21).

In the Old Testament, the Canaanites who inhabited the land of Israel had been active in divination (Deut. 18:9–14). (These very same Canaanite deities are being resurrected today.) In a theocracy, such sorcery-working witches were killed (Exod. 22:18). However, when Jesus, God incarnate, lives out God's reign on earth, witches were not sought out and killed, instead demon-possessed people were delivered and set free.[46] God did not allow witchcraft because these powers were in conflict with worship of the one God. The interesting account of Saul's consultation with a witch shows her in a positive light (she wanted to abide by Saul's own law not to practice witchcraft). When she calls up the spirit of Samuel, she describes him as a "god." Saul worships him.[47] In the same way, today, witchcraft is related to idolatry or the worship of divine spirits, even, as in 1 Samuel 28, sometimes to ancestor worship.

Unfortunately women have been attracted to witchcraft, from the West's contemporary interest in the Goddess, to those in African traditional religions like the Ewe in Ghana,[48] to even ancient times when Hillel used to say: "The more women the more witchcrafts" (*m. Aboth*, 2:7). Some Ewe Christians think men are more spiritually strong than women. My husband Bill thinks many women are more spiritually sensitive than are men. The apostle Paul thinks women need to be spiritually educated so that they no longer will be susceptible to teachings other than the right ones (1 Tim. 2:11; 1:7).[49] How many women, like Lupe, who writes her story in the appendix, do not find a welcome in the church for their gifts and seek that welcome elsewhere? That certainly was true among the ancient Jews (who exempted women from the study of the Law), as it sadly is also true among some churches today in the United States, Ghana, and elsewhere.

Polarized Views Are Not Biblical

In addition, if the Bible does not appear to have these polarized views of transcendence and immanence, where do they come from? Rosemary Radford Ruether suggests that they come from the Greek Platonic religious heritage. These are the dualities inherited from the past:

mind	body
subject	object

individual	community
intellect	body
autonomy	subjugation
spirit	sensuality
transcendence	immanence
male	female
life-separating	life-affirming
meaning in a few sacred moments	meaning in everyday and ordinary moments[50]

These dichotomies are very old, inherited among Christians and Jews strongly influenced by Greek neo-Platonic thought. For example, the first century Hellenistic-Jewish philosopher Philo writes: "For among us a man *(anēr)* has reason *(logos)*, a woman sensation" (*On the Creation of the World,* LIX). That is why the serpent could deceive Eve, he thinks. In Philo's *Allegorical Interpretation of Genesis* he develops this dichotomy between male and female: "For just as the man shows himself in activity and the woman in passivity, so the province of the mind is activity, and that of the perceptive sense passivity, as in woman" (2.XI). Philo's basis is that woman was created from man. Even a man leaving his parents to cling to his wife (Gen. 2:24) supports his imported ideology: "For the sake of sense-perception the Mind, when it has become her slave, abandons both God the Father of the universe, and God's excellence and wisdom, the Mother of all things, and cleaves to and becomes one with sense-perception" (2.XIV). Throughout his *Allegory* he appeals to his Greek readers by continuing this same contrast: "For when that which is superior, namely Mind, becomes one with that which is inferior, namely Sense-perception" and "father and mother, his mind and material body" (*Alleg.,* 2.XIV).

Philo is attempting to appeal to Greek thinkers. For example, Plato describes reason as the superior godly trait: "Of Reason only the gods and but a small class" of humans partake (*Timaeus,* 51). In *Timaeus,* a description of the creation of the universe, reason is part of *psuchē,* the soul, the elder and ruler, as opposed to the *sōma,* the body, the younger and ruled (34). The male is the superior sex. Any men who "proved themselves cowardly and spent their lives in wrong-doing were transformed at their second incarnation, into women" (42, 90). Lower levels of incarnation were birds, wild-footed animals, and fish (91–92). The loss or "gain of reason and unreason" are the criteria for the stage of reincarnation one enters at death (92). The deity who is the Source he likens to the Father, while the deity who is the Recipient he likens to the Mother (50). No wonder his contemporary, fourth century B.C. Olympian Xenophon, explains in the character of Ischomachus: "For [God] made the man's body and mind more capable of enduring cold and heat, and journeys and campaigns; and therefore imposed on him the outdoor tasks. To the woman, since he has made her body less capable of such endurance, I take it that God has assigned the indoor tasks" (*The Oeconomicus: A Discussion of Estate Management,* VII). Therefore, he argues, the woman was given more affection for newborn babies and more fear than the man. The man was given more courage to be a defender.

The very conservative, actually reactionary, contemporary Goddess movement has not only accepted these artificial dualities, but has also embraced them, possibly because the conservative Carl Jung himself believed them. Anyone wise would simply say that these dualities, although interesting for abstract philosophical thought games, have nothing to do with reality. Neither women, nor men, nor God, nor thought, nor relationships can be carved up in this way. Or if they are carved up, they should be placed like cut animals of a two part covenant and burned up! Starhawk explains: "To restore immanent value, we can begin by affirming the body, not denying its needs or desires. Pleasure, humor, laughter, fun, art, sex, food, and beauty are our liberators. Spirit is not seen as separate from matter. When the sacred is embodied, spirituality, the means we use to connect with the sacred, takes us into the body, not away from it."[51]

I can not believe that women have been so deceived as to accept and embrace such sexist views! As we saw earlier, men and women are human first. Whatever of importance is true of one is true of the other.[52] Or, if anything, if one were to think literally, men should be the "earthy" ones since male was formed from the dirt, but women should be more "spiritual" since female was formed from another human. Since we have seen that the Bible does not create a dichotomy between transcendence and immanence, we can see that instead such a dichotomy comes from an ancient, very conservative Greek society. Unfortunately, such an unrealistic dichotomy falsely covers all we study. Better we take off that veil than thicken it.

▼ Conclusion

How ironic that in a search for love and unity and power people should abandon the very means for obtaining them! God can not be close, near, protective, victorious, powerful, loving, discerning, holy, good without being *both* transcendent and immanent. We as humans can not have the power to love, to be united, to be mature and pure without having a generous God who is other than us but close to us. Because God is transcendent, God can be immanent. Both immanence and transcendence are concepts of power and love, because we Christians do not worship two gods but one God. Who could imagine that God is very near *because* God is very far! And yet, God gives us humans authentic freedom. A transcendent God is not bad for ecology. We *humans* are bad for ecology! But, if we invoke into our lives polytheistic or mysterious powers, we will be worse off than ever before.

Nevertheless, a number of Christian feminists have discerned that we Christians can learn from the false battle between transcendence and immanence. The very same dichotomy that people develop between transcendence and immanence also may develop into an exaggerated dichotomy between humans and the earth, men and women. Human interconnection with nature and God is then lessened. Elizabeth A. Johnson explains that "hierarchical dualism" concentrates "on the one high God" to the "neglect of the indwelling, sustaining presence of God." She recommends instead a wholistic design, a kinship model of humanity and nature, and a theology of the life-giving Creator Spirit: "Moved by this Spirit, human beings are similarly configured to compassion, taught to be co-creators who enter the lists on behalf of those who suffer, to resist and creatively transform the powers that destroy."[53]

If God is immanent, as well as transcendent, then how can we learn about God from creation? We will explore that question in the next chapter.

GOD IS REFLECTED

*L*ast century when Thomas Bulfinch wrote *The Age of Fable or Beauties of Mythology* he began his book: "The so-called divinities of Olympus have not a single worshipper among living men."[1] Those days have certainly changed! Zeus, Apollo, Hera, Demeter, Artemis, Pallas Athene, Aphrodite, Hermes, and others are certainly being worshiped today, ironically as manifestations of self worship. In my readings I have discovered three main ways creation is treated:

A. creation mirrors the Creator
(metaphor is treated as analogy)
B. creation mirrors the self
(metaphor is treated as personification)
C. creation mirrors polytheistic deities or powers
(metaphor is treated as literal)

Creation is a mirror in every case, but human injustice or sin can be a barrier preventing creation in mirroring its proper author, the Creator. When sin becomes a barrier, people seek substitutes for the living God in their own creations and, paradoxically, become less like God in the process. In this chapter we will study in depth Paul's description of creation's relation to the Creator in Romans 1:18–21 and compare Paul's view to some uses of creation today.

▼ God Is Known through Creation

Paul's main purpose in writing a letter to the Roman Christians is to appeal to the Jewish and Gentile believers to live in harmony with one another because the good news "is God's power for salvation to everyone believing, to Jew first and also to Gentile, for in it God's righteousness is being revealed by means of faith to faith, just as it is written, 'But the righteous one out of faith will live'" (Rom. 1:16–17).[2] Paul appears to quote Habbakuk 2:4, where the righteous, faithful person can be content until God's promise is fulfilled, in contrast to the proud, wealthy, greedy, and arrogant person who never has enough (Hab. 2:5–6). Since Paul's goal is to bring harmony to the warring Jews and Gentiles, he begins by explaining that everyone, Gentile and Jew, needs salvation. The Gentiles need the good news that righteousness can come through faith because, although they can "perceive clearly" God in the created order, they do not glorify or thank God (1:18–32). But, as well, Jews are also without excuse for their (hypocritical) godlessness, breaking the Old Covenant Law (2:1–24). They knew what was right, but did not do it.

Romans 1 Teaches That Creation Mirrors the Creator

Paul embeds in Romans 1:18–21 a positive statement about nature reflecting God's power and deity in a negative introduction and conclusion:

> For God's anger is being revealed from heaven against all impiety and injustice of humans, the ones suppressing the truth with injustice, because what can be known of God is clear among them; for God made it clear to them. For his unseen attributes, namely his everlasting power and deity, are being perceived thoroughly since the world's creation, being contemplated by means of what is created, with the result that they may be without excuse; because having known God not as God they glorified or thanked, but they were given to worthless speculation in their thoughts and their dull hearts became darkened (Rom. 1:18–21).

Paul begins these two sentences with a shocking and depressing statement. Something is being revealed or disclosed from heaven, and what is being disclosed is not pleasant. It is anger or punishment.

That aspect of God's nature is making itself known. God does not want only or without discretion to punish. Rather, God punishes only human "impiety" (*asebeia*) and "injustice" (*adikia*). *Asebeia* is a noun. It is related to the verb "worship" or "revere" (*sebō*). *Asebeia*, literally, means "not to worship." Humans are not reverent toward God.[3] They also are "unjust." *Adikia* includes both lack of righteousness, evil, sin and injustice (as of a judge, Rom. 9:14). Who are the humans God is punishing? "The ones the truth—with injustice—suppressing." In other words, God is angry with those humans who suppress or "cripple" *(katechō)* the truth. *Katechō* means "possess," and technically refers to legal ownership of lands possessed. It can also mean "arrest," "lay hands on," "impress" for a public duty, and "hold back," "detain," "cripple," "bind," "restrain," as to detain in town.[4] In other words, these humans are the ones restraining or taking possession of the truth, and they do so by means of their own injustice or sin.

The outrageous statement, placing all responsibility on humans for God's punishment, is now explained by four clauses:

a. *because* what can be known of God is clear among them,
b. *for* God made it clear to them,
c. *for* his unseen attributes, namely his everlasting power and deity, are being perceived thoroughly since the world's creation, being contemplated by means of what is created, with the result that they may be without excuse,
d. *because* having known God not as God they glorified or thanked, but they were given to worthless speculation in their thoughts and their dull hearts became darkened.

Paul first explains that "what can be known" *(gnōstos)* of God, a common knowledge, is "manifest," or "visible" (*phaneros* Rom. 1:19) because God chose to make it manifest, clear, known (*phaneroō*).[5] "What can be known" may refer to "personal friends." For example, when Mary and Joseph could not find the twelve-year-old Jesus they looked for him among "the ones known," their friends (Luke 2:44). In contrast, family are *suggenēs* ("relatives"). The same neuter form, *gnōston*, occurs as a proclamation, as when Peter declared "let this be known to you," the believers were not drunk, but they were filled with God's Spirit, fulfilling past prophecies (Acts 2:14–17). God is making a revelation to us humans, common knowledge, as personal as one would reveal to friends.

Furthermore, God's self-proclamation is "clear" or "manifest." Both the adjective *(phaneros)* and the verb *(phaneroō)* come from the same root word. *Phaneros* refers to outward or visible things (e.g., circumcision) as opposed to inward or not so self-evident things (e.g., obedience to the law, Rom. 2:28–29). *Phaneros* is what is proclaimed or publicized as opposed to what is secret (Mark 4:22; 1 Cor. 14:25). The verb *phaneroō* can refer to bringing light on an object (Eph. 5:13), a visible proclamation, as part of a parade (2 Cor. 2:14), or as a present body (incarnation, 1 Tim. 3:16), or a verbal proclamation (Titus 1:3). The opposite is a mystery or lack of clarity (Col. 1:26; 4:4). In other words, God's self-proclamation *(to gnōston)* is proclaimed clearly *(phaneros)* because God made it clear and self-evident *(phaneroō)*. God's self-revelation is visible, self-evident, publicized, present, clear, not mysterious, not a secret.

This self-revelation has also some intimacy to it. Paul literally writes: "God, to them, made manifest" (1:19). By moving the prepositional phrase "to them" before the verb, unlike its more common place, after the verb, Paul accentuates this phrase. To whom God communicates is important. God communicates to every person individually ("to them") through what can be seen in the world.

Paul also implies a comparison between "the known" *(to gnōston)* of verse 19 and "the unseen" *(ta aorata)* of verse 20 by beginning both clauses similarly, with the direct object. What can be known of God is God's unseen or invisible nature or qualities. The author may be known by the creation.

My most appreciated drawing, from a very small collection, is of a rose. Many years ago in our garden in Newark I was captured by the beauty of a yellow rose with a red heart. I was inspired, in the sense that I had an exciting idea, as I drew it. When I showed the drawing to my husband, Bill, I explained that I identified with that rose. I saw the attractive but sedate yellow outside as my Dutch background, calm and serene. But the red heart was my Spanish background, because deep inside I felt my passions deeply. By looking at that drawing people might learn a lot about me.

But the drawing has a life of its own. Almost twenty years later, when I look at it, I am struck by the details. I showed Bill the picture today. He said it reminded him of beauty and eternal life. He pointed out that I did not choose to draw a picture of a bud, about to flower, or of a flower once it began to decay, but I chose to draw a picture of a rose in its full bloom.

In a drawing we are one step away from God's creation. The beauty, eternity, and wholesomeness of the flower reflect God's beauty, eternity, and wholesomeness. I, as an artist, highlighted those aspects of God's creation, thereby manifesting some of my own preferences. The rose mirrors the Creator. The rose also mirrored, to me, some aspects of my own personality, my different ethnic backgrounds. The rose also mirrored some general characteristics, beauty, maturity, eternity. The rose also had a life of its own, even as the drawing as an art piece has a life of its own. The rose grew and died. The drawing can hang on a wall and not be interpreted at all. But the drawing can not reflect the intentions of *another* artist. Yes, it can be interpreted in a variety of ways, but only one artist drew it. Also, neither the drawing nor the rose are me.

In the same way, God can teach us about God's self through God's creation, but God's creation is not god. Further, God's creation can not mirror other deities. Paul claims that creation sends out not only a visible proclamation about God, but also a self-evident and clear proclamation.

Paul does not simply say that God may be known by God's creation. He adds exactly what characteristics of God can be manifest in creation: God's unseen attributes, namely God's everlasting power and deity. Both God's "invisible qualities" (*ta aorata,* 1:20) and the verb "are being perceived thoroughly" *(kathoraō)* are formed from the same root verb "I see" *(horaō)*. Paul writes here of what "cannot be seen." Even as the God who can not be seen became visible in Jesus (Col. 1:15–16), the God who can not be seen is visibly proclaimed by what God created. Beginning with the time of the creation of the world,[6] God's unseen qualities have been demonstrated "by means of what is created." Paul specifies that God's invisible qualities can be (and are being) perceived clearly. *Kathoraō* is a verb in which "I see" *(horaō)* is intensified by the prefix *kath'* (*kata*, down). Literally, *kathoraō* signifies "look down upon," "see from above," "view from on high." Because one "sees from above," one "sees distinctly" and "sees thoroughly."[7] Paul therefore accentuates in 1:20 what he already said in Romans 1:19: "the known of God is *clear*."

He uses the present passive "are being perceived clearly" to communicate that God's invisible nature continues to be seen.

Paul therefore considers that God's invisible qualities not only can
be seen, but can be seen *clearly*. They are seen clearly "being contemplated by means of what is created." Paul modifies *kathoraō* with
a synonym *noeō*, "contemplate," which, according to Bauer's *Lexicon*, is "of rational reflection or inner contemplation."[8] In the Gospels,
Ephesians 3:4, and Hebrews 11:3, *noeō* refers to more than knowing a fact; it refers to perceiving the *significance* of the fact, as in: "Why
do you argue among yourselves, you of little faith, that you have no
bread? Do you not yet *perceive*?" (Matt. 16:8–9). The disciples did
not perceive the difference between a metaphor and a literal statement. When Jesus told them to guard against "the yeast" of the Phar-
isees and Sadducees, they thought he referred to "bread" (Matt.
16:6–7). In contrast, he was warning them about their "teaching"
(Matt. 16:12). In order to understand completely, the will must be
involved (John 12:40). In other words, when creation is contemplated with a receptive will, which looks to discern the significance
of creation, understanding creation as metaphor, then God's unseen
nature can be seen distinctly.

What are those unseen or invisible qualities? They are God's everlasting or eternal power and deity. "Power and deity" is a pleonasm,
two synonyms joined by "and" to heighten one thought.[9] What is
God's "everlasting" power? *Aïdios* is formed from the root *aei*, "ever,
always." It refers to "without beginning" or "without end." Its synonym, *aiōnios*, highlights "the *immeasurableness* of eternity" while
aeizōēs signifies "everliving."[10] God's unseen attributes have been
perceived since the creation of the world because God's power has
no beginning and it has no end. The world may have a beginning
and an end but God has no beginning or end. Peter explains that the
divine power results in life and godliness (2 Pet. 1:3–4). Only God
has a truly "everlasting" deity *(theiotēs)*, unlike the deity assigned to
Roman Emperors. For example, a certain Abinnaeus, wanting to be
appointed as tax-collector, addressed the Emperor Augustus as "our
Divine *(theiotēs)* eternal *(aiōnios)* master."[11] But Augustus died in A.D.
14. While Jesus died in A.D. 30 or 33, he resurrected from death, an
everlasting resurrection.

Paul concludes in verse 21 that humans "have known" God *(ginōskō)*, using the same word used for the intimacy of knowledge in marriage (e.g., Gen. 4:1, LXX). *Ginōskō* is similar to *noeō* in that both types

of knowledge generally have more involved in them than mere facts. *Ginōskō* is a broad word. According to Thayer *ginōskō* is "a discriminating apprehension of external impressions, a knowledge grounded in personal experience" and opposed to *eidenai,* a "mental perception,"[12] as in 1 Corinthians 14:7, 9 where understanding *(ginōskō)* comes as a result of hearing clear and audible words. *Ginōskō* can refer to personal experiential knowledge of theological truths as in knowledge of peace (Rom. 3:17), sin (Rom. 7:7; 2 Cor. 5:21), grace (2 Cor. 8:9), God's will (Rom. 2:18), God's wisdom (1 Cor. 1:21; 2:8), or it can refer to experiential knowledge of a person.[13] Paul is saying that humans can have an experiential knowledge of God by contemplating God's creation.

Humans Have Learned about God from Creation

If Paul's comments are accurate, then we should be able to find non-Christians who agree with him. And, indeed, Jews (Jews other than Paul), Greeks, and Romans have expressed similar thoughts. For example, the Jewish philosopher Philo of Alexandria wrote that superior classes of people, advancing "from down to up," see the world as a "well-ordered city."

> They have beheld the earth standing fast, highland and lowland full of sown crops and trees and fruits and all kinds of living creatures to boot; also spread over its surface, seas and lakes and rivers both spring fed and winter torrents. They have seen too the air and breezes so happily tempered, the yearly seasons changing in harmonious order, and over all the sun and moon, planets and fixed stars, the whole heaven and heaven's host, line upon line, a true universe in itself revolving within the universe. Struck with admiration and astonishment they arrived at a conception according with what they beheld, that surely all these beauties and this transcendent order has not come into being automatically but by the handiwork of an architect and world maker; also that there must be a providence, for it is a law of nature that a maker should take care of what has been made (*On Rewards and Punishments,* VII).

Creation suggests a Creator still interested in taking care of the creation. An earlier Jewish writer also wrote: "For the greatness and beauty of created things give us a corresponding idea of their Creator" (*Wisdom of Solomon,* 13:5 REB).

The Roman Orator Marcus Tullius Cicero, who was born in 106 B.C., spends page after page in *The Nature of the Gods* (II.91–168) extolling the marvel of creation, the earth, humans, sea, air, moon, plants, animals, in contrast to those who assert "the universe has been created by the blind and accidental collisions of inanimate particles." He states:

> But can there be any man worthy of the name who can consider the regular movements of the heavenly bodies, the prescribed courses of the stars, and see how all is linked and bound into a single system, and then deny that there is any conscious purpose in this and say that it is all the work of chance?
>
> The truth is that it is controlled by a power and purpose which we can never imitate. When we see some example of a mechanism, such as a globe or clock or some such device, do we doubt that it is the creation of a conscious intelligence? So when we see the movement of the heavenly bodies, the speed of their revolution, and the way in which they regularly run their annual course, so that all that depends upon them is preserved and prospers, how can we doubt that these too are not only the works of reason but of a reason which is perfect and divine? So let us put aside all casuistry of argument and simply let our eyes confess the splendour of the world, this world which we affirm to be the creation of the providence of God (II. 96–98).

Cicero sometimes writes of one God and at other times of many gods. So although he could deduce that creation reflected a Creator, he could not deny his culture's polytheism without special revelation. He needed to have heard God's direct revelation through both God's prophets and God's people (Rom. 1:2, 11–13; 3:21; 16:26).

Even today writers marvel over the way one's humanity reflects a transcendent presence. Dana Raphael exclaims about breastfeeding: "What I cannot explain is how come my body is designed to feed another. How come a day or so after childbirth my body is transformed and, as if from nowhere, fluid issues forth. And how come each time the infant sucks, within a minute my breasts swell miraculously with fluid."[14] Martin D. O'Keefe in 1987 demonstrates how philosophically a thinker can posit by natural reason "a pale reflection of the God whose existence is given in divine revelation."[15] Don Richardson has also collated numerous stories of isolated peoples who believed in "one true God."[16]

Even James Lovelock, one of the authors of the Gaia hypothesis, posits some sort of intelligence of a single organism that keeps the earth a fit place for life. He is full of awe. This intelligence is not purposeless. Why has the climate on Earth always been favorable to life, unlike Mars or Venus? Why do the oceans never get too salty? Why is pollution often removed by natural processes? Why are animate beings programmed to recognize instinctively what is good for them and others? Lovelock does not posit an all-powered loving God. Nevertheless, his scientific background leads him to posit some larger than life power.[17]

The Bible Teaches That Creation Mirrors the Creator

In Romans Paul does not cite a clear example of *how* God's everlasting power and deity may be perceived clearly in the created world. The created world probably would include the humans,[18] birds, four-footed animals, and reptiles of verse 23 because these created beings were confused by some to be gods rather than to reflect God. Jesus said that the person who gave food, gave drink, welcomed a stranger, clothed the naked, visited the sick or the inmate "did it to me," therefore showing that Christ is present in the person in need (Matt. 25:34–40). James also exhorts his readers to speak to humans with the same respect they speak to God because people "are made in the likeness of God" (James 3:9). Humans may not be murdered because we are made in God's likeness (Gen. 9:6). Similarly, since humans have been created in God's image, God's power and deity may be "perceived clearly" in them. Humans need, desire, and have the ability to interrelate with each other, reflecting the one God who is in three Persons (Gen. 1:26). The power of humans through their ability to think, to speak, to procreate, and to be moral would also reflect God's own power.

How do birds, four-footed animals, and reptiles illustrate God's power and deity? Jesus uses ravens to illustrate an apparently self-sufficient being (Luke 12:24). God tells Job about animals that reflect God's power and deity: the wild animal whose strength is great and who will not serve humans, the ostrich who knows no fear, the war horse who leaps like the locust and can not stand still at the sound of the trumpet, the hawk who soars and spreads its wings toward the south, the eagle who mounts up and makes its nest on a high rocky crag where it spies out the prey from afar, the hippopotamus (Behemoth) whose strength is in its loins and power in the muscles of its belly who neither is afraid of a turbulent river nor can be taken with a snare and, finally, Leviathan, the crocodile, whose back appears to be made of rows of shields (Job 39:9–41:34).

In several of Paul's sermons, especially when speaking to Gentiles, he uses illustrations from creation testifying of God's power and deity. For instance, at Lystra Paul speaks of "rains and fruitful seasons" as witnesses of God's goodness (Acts 14:17). Paul highlights at Athens the nascent (and customary) belief in an unknown god in order to introduce the Athenians to the God who gives "to all life and breath and all things" (Acts 17:25).

Certain psalms develop the theme to which Paul alludes, such as Psalms 19, 97, 104, and 148. In Psalm 19 David personifies creation as a human with a powerful voice or with the shofar, the ritual horn, proclaiming a wedding:

> The heavens are telling the glory of God;
> and the firmament proclaims his handiwork.
> Day to day pours forth speech,
> and night to night describes knowledge.
> There is no speech, nor are there words;
> their voice is not heard;
> yet their voice goes out through all the earth,
> and their words to the end of the world.
> In the heavens he has set a tent for the sun,
> which comes out like a bridegroom from his wedding canopy,
> and like a strong man runs its course with joy.
> Its rising is from the end of the heavens,
> and its circuit to the end of them;
> and nothing is hid from its heat (Ps. 19:1–6).

God's greatness, honor, and majesty in Psalm 104 are illustrated by the immensity of light and sea and by personifying the winds as messengers. Psalm 148 pictures the sun, moon, shining stars, and waters above the heavens as all praising the Lord; the giant sea creatures, fire and hail, snow and frost, and stormy wind as all obeying the Lord. Even

Mountains and all hills,
fruit trees and all cedars!
Wild animals and all cattle,
creeping things and flying birds

all praise the Lord together with the rulers of the earth (Ps. 148:9–11). "Everything that breathes" praises the Lord (Ps. 150:6a).

In summary, Paul teaches in Romans 1:18–20 that God may be experientially known from God's creation, not only from inanimate nature, but also animate nature, humans, birds, four-footed animals, and reptiles. Although creation is fallen, Paul still has stressed the clarity of God's self-revelation by word order (*phaneros* precedes its verb), and by the use of many synonyms for clarity (*phaneros*, "*clear*," *phaneroō*, "make clear," *gnōstos*, "known," *kathoraō*, "perceive thoroughly"). God, who "cannot be seen" (*aoratos*), is proclaimed by means of what God created. Therefore, God's "everlasting" (not temporary) power and deity can be seen thoroughly when contemplated by receptive wills (*noeō*). Nevertheless, special revelation is still indispensable. Because of the testimony of creation, humans are left with the bad news that they are accountable for their impiety to God. They have no defense. Therefore, Gentiles (and Jews alike) need to hear the good news that they may become righteous through faith in Jesus the Messiah, proclaimed by the prophets of old, and by believers in face-to-face proclamations.

All God asks is thanks. Instead of praise or thanks, Paul explains that humans instead began "worthless or futile speculation" that led to the darkening and dulling of their wills. The verb *mataioō* (Rom. 1:21) occurs only here in the New Testament. However, the related *mataios* is used by Paul in 1 Corinthians to speak of "worthless" things: if Christ is not raised, faith is worthless and the thoughts of the wise are worthless (15:17; 3:20). A *mataios* expense was a "useless" expense. A worthless speculation would be one that has no reality to it. It leads to no realistic goal. Idols are "worthless," "ineffective," in contrast to the living God who made the heaven and the earth and the sea and everything in them (Acts 14:15; 1 Pet. 1:18). Dwelling upon substitutes for the living God would certainly be an example of what Paul had in mind. These futile speculations occur in their "thoughts" or "arguments." *Dialogismos* always carries negative connotations in the New Testament. Literally it refers to a judicial argument in court.[19] By not confessing God through praise people became less like God. Their thoughts and wills were incapacitated. Unlike the God who brings light and clarity, their wills became darkened. Unlike the "only wise God" who can "put things together," who "has clear and enlightening insight and comprehension" (Rom. 1:21; 16:25–27), their hearts or wills became stupid. Why? Because they chose to worship the creation rather than the Creator.

▼ What Happens When Creation Becomes God

What is happening today is very subtle. When women or men feel bad about themselves, they in effect do not appreciate the fact that they have been created in God's image. To appreciate that humans, as created beings, mirror the Creator is one way to love ourselves more. All God created was "good." Justo González explains: "Thus the doctrine of creation is first of all an affirmation of the positive value of the world, and a rejection of any doctrine or theory that diminishes or denies that value."[20] Another way to handle a poor self-image is to see the creation reflecting oneself. Carl Jung in effect has set up a psychological-religious answer to deep hurt, setting up a movement that has developed not only outside of Christianity, but against Christianity. Christine Downing explains that we are hungry for an immanent She, transcendent to the ego, but discovered within. The gods of today are images that represent the archetype of the self. As C. Kerényi explains: "Mythology provides a foundation insofar as the teller of myths, by living out his story, finds his way back to premordial times." By identifying with a myth, someone takes a journey into one's own origin, "it is a kind of immersion in ourselves that leads to the living germ of our wholeness." "Mythology tells us of the selfsame origin and 'ground' which we once *were* and still in a sense *are*."[21] Therefore, Downing concludes that she loves the goddesses because they reflect herself in different stages of her life. Persephone is "like myself at some preschool birthday with a wreath of spring flowers in my hair." Athene is "the intelligent and athletic girl, proudly encouraged in all her activities by her devoted father." Hera is "my own youthfully blooming mother."[22]

Creation as a Mirror Accentuates Self

Can this be wrong? I do not think it is wrong to see the goddesses as reflections of human qualities. In effect, the deities are personifications of human qualities. Intelligence, a quality, is treated as having human feelings and form. Or, if nature simply mirrors the self, nature, a nonhuman entity, is personified. Paul himself uses this technique later in Romans when he dramatizes the extent of present suffering by treating creation as enslaved child-bearing women: "The creation became subject to frustration, not willingly . . . the creation itself will be set free from the destructive slavery to the glorious freedom of the children of God. For we know that all the creation groans together and suffers agony together until the present" (Rom. 8:20–22). The eager expectation of a parent is similar to the eager expectation of humans for perfection (Rom. 8:19). The danger comes when this reflection of ourself is glorified or thanked, treated "as God" (Rom. 1:21). That is the Jungian perspective. As Downing understands, "Jung affirms that images representing the archetype of the self and those embodying the archetype of the divine are functionally indistinguishable."[23] When creation is treated "as God," the mirror functions very differently. The mirror becomes the end, not the means. And when the mirror becomes the end, it no longer has the power to clarify and reflect properly.

Starhawk's shadow play exercise is an archetype, a microcosm, a synecdoche, of the key difference between humanity's relationship to nature in the neo-pagan movement and humanity's relationship to nature in Christianity. Starhawk suggests this exercise as one among many to educate people to experience a new mode of awareness that she attractively calls "starlight vision." In the exercise the participant allows the shadows of an interesting scene to fall on a blank sheet of paper. These shadows are then blocked in by pencil with patches of broad strokes. The shadows create forms. The goal is "to experience another way of seeing, in which separate objects disappear and only pattern remains." Earlier she explains that objects appear to be fixed, but in reality, they are a field of energies that congeal, temporarily, into forms: "In time, all 'fixed' things dissolve, only to coalesce again into new forms, new vehicles." In other words, the universe is a fluid, ever-changing energy pattern, not a collection of fixed and separate things. Another way she expresses this concept is through meditating on water: "You are fluid, one drop congealed out of the primal ocean that is the womb of the Great Mother."[24] She takes the idea supposedly from Anton Ehrenzweig in *The Hidden Order of Art*. He also writes of "unconscious vision," but he mentions that such a vision can treat figure *and* ground with equal impartiality. The forms do not dissolve for Ehrenzweig. Rather, more than one form can be seen at one time. The vision is "undifferentiated." For "a true artist" nothing is insignificant or accidental and every element "has to be firmly related to the total structure in a complex web of cross ties radiating across the entire picture plane." For such a vision "pattern as such" is suppressed.[25]

Behind Starhawk's attractive presentation lies the subtle truth that in witchcraft individuality is lost, control is lost, and humans, animals, nature, god/dess all become one blurred form. Life is as it were a marble cake, the chocolate and vanilla streaks change in the manner the knife is sliced through the flour. But this cake is never cooked. As in an uncooked batch, the forms can be changed whenever another knife slice moves the old patterns to form new ones.

In Christianity attention to nature accentuates individuality, it increases conscious appreciation of God as other and humans as unique and nature as unique. As an example, let us try our own "Sunlight Day Exercise." On any sunny day, look outside. In this March Massachusetts day as I look outside, I see a pastel blue sky, its blue becomes more distinct as I look up. The pine and maple trees are brown and their limbs are in clear outline in the sky. When I remind myself that all I see that is natural outside teaches me about God, I think of God's brilliance and clarity when I look up to the blue sky. God is not confused. I think of God's "homeyness" as I look at our maple tree, the thick, earthy bark reminds me that God is with me when I do the simple, mundane things of life. The tree looks so unintelligent. It is so thick and barky. Nevertheless, it can last through the cold winters and high winds. God's reign sometimes seems so flimsy, but like this tree, God's church, if even a remnant, lasts year after year after year, even in times of great troubles.

Of course, I just made up this "Sunlight Day Exercise." You can see that what I was doing was making analogies. God is the concept, nature is the image. I would no longer be making an analogy if God became nature. But, the more I make analogies, the more I appreciate the uniqueness of each part of the analogy. I am very glad that God, unlike the sky, does not have dirty or evil aspects. God, unlike the tree, does not have termites. God is not fallen. Even a clear blue sky, up high, would be cold, without air. But God is life-giving.

Jürgen Moltmann mentions in *The Spirit of Life* that the nearness of God makes life more worth living.[26] The more I learn about God from everyday images, the more life becomes for me a three-dimensional joy. But, piercing through the magical, evasive, language of the Goddess is a nightmare. We humans become lost. Rather than self-affirming, the neo-pagan Goddess is self-negating. We "merge" with time. We merge with the universal energy(ies) or force. We merge with the universe.[27] We merge with the "I" that engulfs us.

Yes, we might no longer feel alienated from nature. That is because we have become oppressed by nature, oppressed and deceived. In Aletícia Tijerina-Jim's description of the sweat lodge, the women, at some point, pierce their arms with eagle feathers and rip them out. The men pierce their chest or back and tie a rope from their back to a tree. After four days, they pull away from the tree, tearing through the skin (as in childbirth?). By blood spilling onto the Earth, people are thought to get strength.[28] If these cruel actions prove our connection with nature, then humans are now oppressed by nature. The deception is that humans are not simply nature. We are like and unlike nature.

When one rereads the early chapters of Genesis to relearn what is the relation between humans and nature, we can find many similarities, but a few key differences. Humans are one small part of all God created and we are late in that creation. Before us God creates the light, the firmament, land, vegetation, the sun and moon and stars, living creatures, birds, sea monsters, cattle, creeping things, and wild animals. And God concluded that all these creations were good long before humans ever arrived. (An early church heresy was not appreciating God's good creation [1 Tim. 4:1–5]). The animals were all blessed and given a similar command to be fruitful (Gen. 1:22, 25). When God rested from labor, that was to be a model for animals, the land, as well as for humans (Gen. 2:3; Exod. 20:10; Lev. 25:4). Humans and animals are allocated the same food (Gen. 1:29; 9:1–4). Adam *(ʾādām)*, the earthling, was formed from the earth *(ʾădāmāh)*, as were the trees, animals, and birds (Gen. 2:7, 9, 19). Adam is cursed to return to earth (Gen. 3:19).

However, humans are the first and only creations made in God's likeness and given the task of stewardship. To have dominion is defined by Gen. 2:5, 15 as tilling the ground and guarding it (Gen. 1:26–28; 2:5, 15). To "till" *(ʿābad)* the ground means not only to "work," but also to "serve" it. To "guard" *(šāmar)* the ground means to "watch" it, "protect," "preserve," "tend" it, keep any harm from coming to it, oversee it, and to "observe" it. Therefore, Ronald J. Sider concludes that Christians: "are to serve and watch lovingly over God's good garden," striding "boldly into the main stream of the green movement, showing how biblical faith offers a better foundation for environmental engagement."[29] God also expected moral responsibility from humans. We were to partake of God's gifts in appropriate ways, enjoying all the fruits except of one tree. We were created to enjoy all the animate beings God had made, but to form lifelong companionships with one human of the opposite sex (Gen. 2:16, 19, 23–24).

The fall affects all. Sin affects the relationship of Adam with his source, the ground; Eve and her source, the man; the children and their source, woman; woman and serpent, and even the self and one's own body (Gen. 3:7–18). When Abel is killed, the earth cries out to God and Cain can no longer till (Gen. 4:10–14). Because of sin, Elizabeth Achtemeier explains: "We hunger for the natural realm, but we do not know how to be reconnected with it, and that is partly the fault of the Christian church, which has not preached and taught a whole theology."[30]

Nature and humans are interconnected, they have similarities, but also differences.

Creation Is Distinct from Creator

One neo-pagan chant declares: "Woman am I, Spirit am I, I am the Infinite within my soul; I have no beginning and I have no end, all this I am."[31] Here is another deception. Neither we humans nor nature are immortal, because of who we are by creation. Solomon phrases the dilemma well. God "made all very beautiful in its time, also eternity he placed in their heart, yet humanity can not discover the doings which God does from the beginning as far as the end" (Eccles. 3:11).[32] We humans are flesh and minerals and water that breathes and yearns to live forever. The Bible teaches the resurrection of the body, not the immortality of the soul (1 Cor. 15:20; Luke 20:37–38).

As devout Jews and Christians we are on a quest to know God, know one another, know nature. That quest, if authentically followed, leads to a paradox: appreciation increases as uniqueness is learned.

When the mirror, creation, is not a means to perceiving the Creator, the distance between self and polytheistic deities is very small. For instance, Starhawk both believes that "all of us are the Goddess incarnate" *and* that "the Goddesses and Gods are real forces: if you call them, they will come and rearrange the patterns of your life. They are bigger than you, although not separate from you; be prepared to change."[33] Karen McCarthy Brown began with a desire to affirm and transform her anger. Therefore she married Ogou, a Yoruban War God. However, she has not limited herself to Ogou because "one spirit is never enough to explain any slice of life." She must serve all the human energies that "flow into war-making."[34] Many men and women seem attracted to god/dess as a psychological venture, an inward journey. But, after a while for many it becomes an outward journey, or rather, a journey of external powers moving inward.

Melissa Potter and Maria Epes explain that the Goddess they worship is "a part of" them. She is "a potent source of self-affirmation and power." They "had no one name for her." "She represents the cycles and transformations of life and nature because she is a woman, and women are the creators of life." Because she represents the cycles of nature, they made an altar to her made of rocks in the form of a circle with different items in different stages of composition or growth: a seed, a mushroom, wild berries, a broken walnut shell, a dried snakeskin.[35] Who is this Goddess they worship? We are not simply seeing here a change of title, "Goddess," rather than "God." Creation now mirrors an archetypal feminine self. (I do not think women are really limited to these qualities.) What is she like? This goddess is not "everlasting" nor powerful nor God. Potter and Epes did not even expect their altar to last a year, but to their "great surprise, the sticks we had painted, the stones we had arranged, and the strings of flowers we had hung were still there, slightly weathered, slightly rearranged, or dried in the case of the flowers." The Goddess they worshiped was "part of the transition and change that we consider a natural part of life." Rather than everlasting, this Goddess is change itself. Is she worthy of respect? Is she worth thanking? Yes, Potter and Epes were thankful to her for giving them this place. She is worthy of respect because she was part of their "cre-

168   *The Goddess Revival*

ative selves." In other words, when Potter and Epes created this altar they were also honoring their own creativity. After they made this altar, then they prayed "that the goddess grant" them "power" over their lives. Did they get that power? Because the altar was not destroyed the following year seemed to be filled with power to them.[36]

What I find confusing is how can someone worship a god who is both oneself and also external to oneself? Nevertheless, one thing is clear, the Goddess is everchanging, not everlasting, and her power, intimacy, and compassion are limited because nature is everchanging, impersonal, and limited. Creation no longer is a metaphor. It is literal. In other words, creation is now being treated as a living organism, power, or being. It is no longer a metaphor, like *and* unlike the Creator.[37] Creation has become the Creator!

When the Creator is human, the new Creator is subject to human change. Who is the Goddess? Starhawk explained to Carol P. Christ: "It all depends on how I feel. When I feel weak, she is someone who can help and protect me. When I feel strong, she is the symbol of my power. At other times I feel her as the natural energy in my body and the world."[38] The God of the Bible, in contrast, is always powerful, although we are not always worthy of thanks, but, also, always available to us for compassion, goodness, and strength.

A Divine Creation Had a Similar Appeal in Bible Times

People in Bible times were not too different from those alive today. Possibly for some people, worship of deities was an effort to acknowledge the sacred in every place.[39] By the very process of creating a physical deity one could control the deity and ultimately worship one's own creation. The Lord vividly describes the process. The carpenter

> plants a cedar and the rain nourishes it. Then it can be used as fuel. Part of it he takes and warms himself; he kindles a fire and bakes bread. Then he makes a god and worships it, makes it a carved image and bows down before it. Half of it he burns in the fire; over this half he roasts meat, eats it and is satisfied. He also warms himself and says, "Ah, I am warm, I can feel the fire!" The rest of it he makes into a god, his idol, bows down to it and worships it; he prays to it and says, "Save me, for you are my god!" (Isa. 44:14–17).

Paul wrote about a "stupid," "without understanding" heart (Rom. 1:21). In Isaiah people are described as without understanding (Isa. 44:18–19). An Old Testament counterpart is a "stubborn" heart. A "stubborn" (šĕrîrût) heart is a self-reliant heart. For instance, Moses warns the Israelites that they will not deceive God or themselves if, outwardly, they agree to God's covenant but, inwardly, they want to serve idols, because "I will be safe because I walk in the strength belonging to my heart" (Deut. 29:19). Ultimately, idolatry is relying only on one's own resources, glorifying and thanking only oneself and other humans, and not acknowledging God's provisions. George MacDonald describes the interrelationship between creating an external deity and self-worship in his fantasy *The Wise Woman*. The wise woman has her eye on Rosamond so that she not become

> one of those who kneel to their own shadows till feet grow on their knees; then go down on their hands till their hands grow into feet; then lay their faces on the ground till they grow into snouts; when at last they are a hideous sort of lizards, each of which believes himself the best, wisest, and loveliest being in the world, yea, the very centre of the universe. And so they run about forever looking for their own shadows, that they may worship them, and miserable because they cannot find them, being themselves too near the ground to have any shadows; and what becomes of them at last there is but one who knows.[40]

When the Hebrews "walked in their own counsels," they disobeyed God and they too worshiped their own creations (Jer. 7:16–24). This type of "stubbornness" is, etymologically, a strength or firmness that is twisted.[41] Idolatry is seeking what is pleasing to oneself with no regard to God. Idolatry is thanking one's own crafted calf for delivering one from oppression, rather than the powerful, forgiving, gracious, and merciful God who did do it (Neh. 9:17–18).

For some people idolatry is an act limited to objects or to the imagination. It is not an act done by *reasonable* people. They may sin, but they do not commit idolatry. Some people even hesitate to see creation as reflecting God because they fear they may commit idolatry. Idolatry, though, is *not* glorifying or thanking God for what God has made. That is why James can call "adulterers," (*moichalis*), the same term used for idolaters in Ezekiel 23:36–45, those who want something that is not theirs and are willing to fight and destroy to get it

(James 4:1–5). In Ezekiel "adultery" refers to parents who offer their children by fire to idols. Peter, as well, calls "adulterers" those who are greedy (2 Pet. 2:14). Paul specifically defines "greed" as idolatry (Col. 3:5). "Greed," in Greek *pleonexia*, literally is *echō*, "I have," and *pleon*, "more," to want more.[42] No wonder idolatry often is portrayed in the Bible as immoral and immoderate living (1 Pet. 4:3; Ezek. 23:40–42). If anything typifies our Western society it is "I Want More."

Paul J. Achtemeier has a fine discussion in his commentary on Romans on contemporary idolatry. He too observes that people become like the lord they serve. Like the ancients who worshiped statues of animals, our society today "shows signs of bestiality": "If in our desire to overcome a competitor in whatever area, whether as student or professional, whether as husband or wife, whether as business man or woman, we take as our model the rapacious drive of the beast of prey, sweeping all aside in our desire to overcome, is it any wonder that our society becomes bestial?"[43]

The point is this, creating an object is not idolatry. Appreciating people or appreciating nature is not idolatry. But thanking or praising oneself, another human, or something created when God should have been thanked or praised, that is idolatry. Idolatry is a type of greed. You are not thankful or satisfied for what God provided. Truth does make a difference. It affects who we become. If we worship the one good God of clarity and truth, we too will become more clear, wise, unique, good, secure, powerful, and free.

▼ Love and Empathy Should Guide Our Response

A shaking finger and a hissing stutter should not be the primary ways Christians should respond to Goddess worship today. Rather, we need to highlight and develop affirming places for women in the church and in all our institutions. In the next chapter I will summarize some of the reasons to do so. However, we can also take seriously the church's excessive emphasis on transcendence, and balance it by a proper perspective on knowing God through creation, a practice attractive to many women and to some men, too.

Women, as part of God's creation, should be images or reflections of God's eternal power and divine nature. I did not say women are God. Rather, they, like men, *reflect* God. Many times, often I think through sheer negligence, preachers use as positive examples only men or men's interests. Every time we balance our male examples with female examples we take one step to retain in the church a girl or a boy, a man or a woman.

One reason some secular feminists are seeking spiritual dimensions for their lives is because they are burnt-out. Jean Shinoda Bolen explains: "It is very difficult to stand on the front lines with only outrage to sustain us. In order to sustain ourselves on the front lines, I think we really have to tap into something that truly nurtures us." She also thinks that feminists seek a spiritual dimension because they believe the culture can not change without a "feminine force" to divinity.[44] Women such as Bolen are seeking to be nurtured spiritually. Here is a wonderful opportunity for Christians! In the same way as spiritually needy but socially independent women were attracted to Christianity in the first century (e.g., Acts 16:12–14; 17:12), spiritually needy but socially concerned women of the twentieth and twenty-first centuries can find their fulfillment in the God of the Bible if that God is accurately presented.

Feminists of today are of many types:

A. Secular = "equal pay for equal work, right of entry into all professions." Women should have political, economic, and social rights equal to those of men.
B. Religious = an all-encompassing perspective on the whole of reality.
   1. polytheistic / "the Goddess" may have many names.
      They reject the biblical revelation as irredeemably patriarchal and hopelessly oppressive.[45]
      "Aesthetic" feminist spirituality,[46] women's spirituality, most ecofeminism,[47] some witchcraft.[48]
      Deity reflects humans and creation. Sin and evil do not clearly exist because all parts of reality are harmonious.
      a. goddess as within
      b. goddess as other[49]
   2. monotheistic
      a. They accept a canon within the Bible. Original biblical events and texts need to be reconstructed. Goddess language may be helpful to understand the God of the Bible.[50]

"Ethical/liberation feminist spirituality." Evil is real
because original harmony is broken.

b. They accept a reliable and authoritative Bible, but it
may need to be translated and interpreted more
accurately. Neglected texts, themes, and topics need
to be highlighted.

The God of the Bible is reflected in creation.

Evil and sin permeate all institutions and people.

Among feminists who are monotheistic, some are encouraged to
seek a spirituality that arises more out of everyday experiences. Elizabeth Dodson Gray claims that women's writings on theology "are
rooted in the particular. They are clothed in the subjective. They are
luminous with the sights, sounds, and feel of a real individual
woman's life."[51] If indeed creation mirrors God, knowledge of God
through study of the Bible, through prayer,[52] and through obedience can be supplemented by learning about God from God's human
and non-human creations. In the same way that Brother Lawrence
could converse with God as he washed his dishes and peeled his
potatoes in the kitchen,[53] so too can women and men learn more
about God in their common everyday experiences if they perceive
this world differently. I call it "image theology," knowing God more
from God's images. Despite negative words about the God who creates Adam and Eve in the Bible, Gray has some inspiring words to
write about God as reflected in nature: "I have always felt connected
in some profound way with the ultimate transcendent dimension
of my life whenever I have allowed myself to experience the mystery and majesty of the created world." She takes as an example,
color: "Color is one of the largest clues I have to the nature of God."
She sees color as a sign of God's extravagance and sensuality. Color
"is not sacred in my life because it relates me to other people, but it
is sacred in my life because it relates me to the majesty of God and
the beauty of the creation."[54] Yet Carol Christ can charge Christianity
with spawning an "ascetic body-denying and life-denying culture."[55]
However, Christians worship Jesus who was accused of spending
too much time at dinner parties (Luke 7:34) and a God in whose
"right hand are pleasures forevermore" (Ps. 16:11)! Even though
Paul said he learned the secret of facing hunger and want, he also
learned the secret of facing plenty and abundance. That is what he

meant when he concluded: "All things I can handle in the One strengthening me" (Phil. 4:12–13).

However, in the process of enjoying "image theology," "woman's theology," an inductive, particular, subjective theology, a believer in the God of the Bible must always remember that God's images must reflect *God*. We need to remember the maxim that Charles Williams phrased so well: "This also is Thou; neither is this Thou."[56] Creation, animate and inanimate nature, humans, birds, four-footed animals, reptiles, all clearly, visibly, thoroughly reflect in an experiential way to receptive wills God's everlasting power and deity. But no creation should ever be glorified as Creator.

In addition, when some insight is meaningful to an individual, that insight is not necessarily true or necessarily meaningful to another person, nor does it necessarily signify God working in one's life. All these subjective and deductive insights need to be evaluated by the objective biblical revelation of God's nature and of God's desires. Sharing one's insights with other sympathetic believers is one way to receive feedback. The blessing of observing the world around us is that we learn to appreciate and thank God for the many ways, places, and people among whom God is present and active.

9

GOD OF THE LIVING WATER

*W*e all love to retell the account of Jesus and the woman of Samaria, the first recorded person to be told by Jesus that he was the Messiah. But, we also need to follow Jesus' model. Jesus' conversation with the woman of Samaria serves as a helpful construct to outline the main points of this book and to orient us as we step forward to act. Goddess spirituality has some concerns similar to Christianity's, some accurate complaints about Christianity, and, therefore, is an apt challenge to the church. Nevertheless, much of the Goddess literature fails to be completely truthful about itself and about Christianity. This chapter concludes with a summary of what Christianity has to offer Goddess worshipers.

▼ Ask for Water

Jesus did not avoid going to Samaria because a group of syncretists lived there. (The Samaritans were descendants of the Assyrian captives who worshiped the Lord and their own native gods in their new land [2 Kings 17:24–34]). When Jesus was tired out by his walking, he sat and relaxed and waited for his meal (served by men, by the way). When the woman came to draw water, Jesus did not chastise her for her heresies and her sexual promiscuity. No, he asked her: "Give me something to drink!" (John 4:7–8). One drink, that is all he wanted. No magic word here ("please"), but the woman did not take offense. She was pleased and appreciative that a Jew asked of her a drink (John 4:9). She was glad she had gifts worthy of desire: water and the strength to lift it out.

Might Christians not as well ask for a cup of water from goddess feminists? Might we not as well begin our conversation on a listening note? Indirectly the woman of Samaria had a complaint: most Jews do not ask me for water (and men do not speak with me in public) because first, I am a woman, and second, I am Samaritan (John 4:9, 27).

Goddess feminists also have many complaints about Christianity and Judaism. They have complaints about God and the church and the church's treatment of women. Nelle Morton writes: "Women had no cosmic advocate in any of the five major patriarchal religions of the world."[1] They charge that the God of the Bible is a white, male, sky god who is warlike, intolerant, and dominating. God is remote, unreal, not powerful, and impersonal.

About the church Gloria Anzaldúa writes: "Institutionalized religions impoverish all life, beauty, pleasure." They "encourage fear and distrust of life and of the body."[2] Christianity is ascetic, body-denying, life-denying. Divine experience has no sexual dimension. Carol Lee Sanchez adds: "Mainstream Jewish/Christian/Islamic thought systems are founded on the premise that a single Almighty Spirit Being authorizes and informs human thought and action, leaving the rest of 'God's Creation' to be used, abused, and destroyed according to human whim and desire."[3]

Charlene Spretnak writes: "Christianity, Judaism, Islam, and Hinduism all combine male godheads with proscriptions against women as temptress, as unclean, as evil."[4] Women are deeply hurt. They feel bad about themselves, their bodies, power, will, and heritage. They feel their creativity is not encouraged. They are blaming Judaism and Christianity and, instead, creating a goddess in their own image. Men, too, feel oppressed and they are creating gods in their own image. Naomi Goldenberg explains: "Since each woman is considered a Goddess, all of her creations are in a sense holy."[5] "Goddess is a symbol of the newfound beauty, strength, and power of women," Carol D. Christ declares.[6] Christine Downing concludes:

"To be fed only male images of the divine is to be badly malnourished. We are starved for images which recognize the sacredness of the feminine and the complexity, richness, and nurturing power of female energy."[7]

When the woman of Samaria implied a complaint against all Jews, Jesus did not get side-tracked defending his compatriots. Instead he challenged her to focus on God: "If you knew the gift of God and who is the one asking of you, give me something to drink, you would ask him and he would give you living water" (John 4:10). Since an entrance requirement for the church is to be a repentant sinner (Matt. 3:2), we can be sure, as avowed sinners, all of us Christians will offend someone sometime. Moreover, not all who call themselves "Christian" have followed Jesus' exhortations (Matt. 7:21). Some people are conservative or traditional or academic first, Christian second. Some people may forget who they were ("repentant sinners") or who they will be (like Christ). Like Jesus, we need to encourage complainers to focus on the God as revealed in the Bible. Our goal in this book has not been to defend Christians through the years, but, rather, to defend God when understood through the biblical revelation, taken to be reliable and authoritative.

▼ Everyone Drinks Water

The woman and Jesus both wanted water, literal and metaphorical—a drink for today and refreshment for eternity (John 4:10, 14–15). God/dess worshipers and Christians have similar concerns. They want to be refreshed.

Joyce Quining Erikson writes: "Both feminism and Christianity posit visions of a world that is better than the present one; both can point to reasons the present is less than perfect, and both proffer remedies for the problem."[8] Hallie Iglehart agrees: "Ultimately, the goals of spirituality and of revolutionary politics are the same: to create a world in which love, equality, freedom, and fulfillment of individual and collective potential is possible."[9] Both Christianity and Goddess spirituality favor peace, service, care (not destruction) of nature, equality, harmony, wisdom, light, vision, diversity in oneness, concern for the oppressed, power, healing, courage, right process, celebration, immediacy, truth, compassion, freedom, and the interdependence between humanity and creation.

Both movements have visions of a better world, and yet they are aware of current needs. Women who have struggled to bring about this vision are burned out and need to be nurtured spiritually. They need security and stability. Moreover, the chains of oppression are internal as well as external. Unwarranted self-criticism is destructive. Women desperately need a better self-image, a positive past with which to identify. They need an inward power that can help them act outwardly. Men, too, are concerned to grasp a more wholesome masculinity with virtues of ordering, decisiveness, knowing, compassion, being able to fight for justice, and to remain monogamous. Women might complain about a remote Father-God, men might complain about a remote father-human.

▼ You Have No Bucket

The woman of Samaria challenged Jesus, albeit politely: "Sir, you have no bucket and the well is deep; therefore, how will you have water that is living? Are you greater than our ancestor Jacob, who gave us the well and he and his children and his flocks drank out of it?" (John 4:11–12). Jesus had to confirm her desire without oppressing her nationality. The church today also needs to confirm the right desires of the goddess movement without oppressing women.

The church has a monumental task, to support women, renew its behavior and views, yet not become entranced by the god/dess movement itself. Judith Plaskow and Carol Christ highlight four key issues: "the need for a positive past with which feminists can identify, the search for new ways to image and speak about the sacred, the effort to redefine the self and to transform a patriarchal world."[10] Carol Lee Sanchez even quotes Jesus ("loving my neighbors as myself") as one of her bases for spiritual action, as does Charlene Spretnak. About the Christian Right, she writes: "Their selective religiosity allows them to piously defend ultraconservative priorities over Jesus' gospel of love: 'Love thy neighbor as thyself' becomes 'Kill a Commie for Christ.'"[11]

In Margot Adler's research she found pagans and witches were attracted by beauty, intellectual satisfaction, growth, feminism, environmental concern, and freedom. Can not we Christians even more ably appeal to these desires? Starhawk, who has a marvelous writing style, literary, creative, and thoughtful, by 1985 sold about 50,000 copies of *The Spiral Dance* after which hundreds, possibly a thousand, covens were started.[12] With God's help, can not we Christians be as, if not more, effective?

Rights Are Worth Defending

God/dess spirituality should be an impetus to the church to activate urgently its support of women. However, some Christians do not believe anyone should ever complain or talk about rights. Possibly, they might think all this wrong belief comes from some women asserting their rights rather than being satisfied with the place God has apportioned to them.

If "feminism" is the theory that women should have political, economic, and social rights equal to those of men, were the Hellenists right to complain that their widows were neglected in the daily distribution of food? Apparently the twelve decided "yes" because they picked out seven men of "good repute, full of the Spirit and of wisdom" all with Hellenist names to oversee it. Then "the word of God increased, and the number of the disciples multiplied greatly" (Acts 6:1–7). They could have said: "you are providentially blessed you are getting *anything at all* when you do not even bother to learn and keep using the sacred Hebrew language! We may consider adding *one* Hellenist to represent your interests."

Were the daughters of Zelophehad, Mahlah, Noah, Hoglah, Milcah, and Tirzah right to ask Moses, Eleazar, the leaders, and all the congregation at the door of the tabernacle "Give to us a possession"? God told Moses: "The daughters of Zelophehad are right" (Num. 27:1–4, 7). God could have said: "How dare they stand up for their own rights and in front of everyone! Have them stand outside the camp and be burned up." But God listened to them and agreed with them.

For women (or anyone else) to stand up for their own rights is acceptable and necessary in God's sight. We often misinterpret Philippians 2:4 "not to your own things let each keep looking out for, but also each to the things of others," to mean "I should not stand up for my own rights." But Paul's point here is broader—look out for *other's* rights, do not push forward your own "selfish ambition" (*eritheia*) (Phil. 2:3). Keep in mind other's interests *as much as* you keep in mind your own. If no other Christian is looking out for your interests (which they should have been), then speaking on behalf of your rights would fit under the category of speaking to a brother or sister if they "sin against you" (Matt. 18:15). They probably do not even know they have sinned against you unless you explain it to them.

Christians Have Historic Interests in Feminism

Some people might fear that Goddess worship is the real basis for feminism. In reality, Goddess worship is simply an old heresy jumping onto the feminist bandwagon, kicking out the Christian drivers.

Many contemporary historians have shown that *Christian* feminism goes back many years, way before twentieth century feminists. For example, Janette Hassey in her study of *Evangelical Women in Public Ministry Around the Turn of the Century, No Time for Silence,* notes how many fundamentalist or evangelical individuals and organizations supported women in ministry in their early years. From her many examples, A. B. Simpson, the founder of Christian and Missionary Alliance, called the Holy Spirit "our Mother God" and included women on the executive board committee, employed them as Bible professors, and supported female evangelists and branch officers (the early C and MA equivalent to a local minister). She also shows how Dwight L. Moody worked together with a number of women preachers. At the turn of the century, female graduates of Moody Bible Institute "openly served as pastors, evangelists, pulpit supply preachers, Bible teachers, and even in the ordained ministry."[13] Gordon Bible and Missionary Training School in its earliest years had an equal number of women and men professors and so many women students in its earliest years that one administrator suggested "it should be a ladies' School entirely." In 1905, 1907, and 1908 twice the number of women graduated than men.[14]

Katherine C. Bushnell had her study *God's Word to Women* published in 1919 showing that if the Bible is treated as "inspired, infallible, and inviolable" then one must conclude that "the teaching that woman must perpetually 'keep silence' in the Church, be obedient to her husband, and never presume to teach or preach, because Eve sinned, blights the doctrine of the atonement, and robs Christ of glory, in that His death atoned for all sin, including Eve's of course."[15] Five years later, Judson Press celebrated one hundred years of Bible distribution by publishing Helen Barrett Montgomery's *The New Testament in Modern English* in which she translates, as one example,

Romans 16:1–2: "our sister Phoebe, who is *a minister* of the church of Cenchreae. . . . For she herself has been made *an overseer* to many people, including myself."[16] Montgomery's translation was a natural follow-through of thoughts and examples of earlier women. Sixty years earlier Catherine Booth published her pamphlet on "Female Ministry" in 1859 on "Women's Right to Preach the Gospel."[17]

Women such as Angelina and Sarah Grimke began to speak against slavery in the early 1800s, and because they were denounced for speaking before men and women, a decade later also began a women's rights movement because women along with men have "the right and duty" "to promote every righteous cause by every righteous means, and especially in regard to the great subjects of morals and religion."[18] No wonder author and abolitionist Lydia Maria Child in 1837 explained: "The sects called evangelical were the first agitators of the woman question."[19] The historic meeting for the rights of women in the United States met at Seneca Falls, New York, in 1848 in a Methodist Church. Anne E. Carr writes: "All were inspired by fundamentally Christian notions of justice in their work for abolition, temperance, moral reform (the closing of brothels), and the rights of women."[20] Consequently, Frederick Douglass, the accomplished advisor to Abraham Lincoln, Consul General to Haiti, and a former slave, concluded: "Woman's agency, devotion, and efficiency in pleading the cause of the slave, gratitude for this high service early moved me to give favorable attention to the subject of what is called 'woman's rights' and caused me to be denominated a woman's-rights man. I am glad to say that I have never been ashamed to be thus designated."[21] Christian women and men were promoting the full use of women's gifts in the 1900s, 1800s, and even as early as the 1600s. In 1667 Margaret Fell declared that "Womens Speaking" was justified, proved, and allowed by the Scriptures because "women were the first that preached the tidings of the resurrection of Jesus, and were sent by Christ's own command, before He ascended to the Father, John 20:17."[22]

But if we were to go way back in history what would we see? What is still true today is that true freedom and misunderstood freedom in regard to women (and men) has always existed in the same way as truth has always existed near falsehood and the two must always be differentiated.

Where we have a judge and prophet like Deborah, fully commended by God, who as a "mother of Israel" gave "rest" to the land for forty years, we also have a Jezebel, a Sidonian, who worshiped Baal and encouraged the nation in Baal worship.[23]

Where we have a wise woman able to save an entire city-state, Abel of Bethmaacah, from Joab's attack (2 Sam. 20:14–22), we can also have a medium with whom Saul can consult (1 Sam. 28:7–25).

Where we have a prophetess, Anna, (Luke 2:36) or women prophets at Corinth whom Paul assumed should keep on praying and prophesying in public (1 Cor. 11:55), we also have another prophet not commended, Jezebel at Thyatira (Rev. 2:20).

And of course sometimes the same person acts wisely but at other times not, such as the prophet Miriam. Even after her sin she was still grouped with Moses and Aaron as God's appointed leader over Israel.[24] The fame of some prophets such as Philip's four daughters increased from New Testament times, when they are simply mentioned, until in later years, Eusebius, the church historian, uses them as standards by which to evaluate eminence "for a prophetic gift," those who belonged to "the first stage in the apostolic succession." The early church believed that the many women (and men) who died for their faith had a special authority. In heaven they share Christ's authority and are Christ's fellow-judges.[25]

Where we have a Perpetua, whose biographer in A.D. 2–3 saw in her life and death proof that the Holy Spirit still gives prophetic gifts and visions, we also have the prophets Maximilla and Priscilla who joined Montanus in what is usually considered to be an early church heresy.[26]

The point is this: As in all matters of life, we must be discerning. If the church, Christ's immanent presence, is not around to encourage a right view of freedom, who will do it? If we believe this world is fallen, might not some of that sin be still among us?

The Church Needs to Be "Christian"

Many of the complaints about the church by goddess feminists are simply true. African American Riua Akinshegun complains about religions in which the religious ritual is centered in a building, a one-day-a-week thing, *not* how one lives.[27] We have shown that God's sanctuary is people, not a building. Nevertheless, how many Christians still believe their "sanctuary" is a building or themselves alone?

How many people espouse a faith in God on Sunday, but live out a faith in themselves on Monday? Jesus challenged his students not to lead lives like the Gentiles' (Luke 22:25–26). Sadly, we still have many Christians eager to have or to be a "power-over" leader, one who needs to be appeased, placated, feared, and obeyed. Jesus taught us to pray, "*Our* Parent who art in heaven," yet many of us live like lone rangers (without Tonto, since we discriminate). Jesus taught us to love God with our whole being (Matt. 22:37), yet many of us still love God with mind *or* body, reason *or* experience, law *or* mystery. The Craft claims to offer diversity and flexibility.[28] With a church that is multinational, should not we too offer diversity? Instead, we are saddled with church growth experts who want individual churches to be all of one economic and social class. For witches, ritual or patterned action is a necessity. We Christians do not believe in such magic, yet we often act as if we must pray or worship only in a certain patterned action to please God.

And what we have done to God is tragic. Some men are like the other lion in *The Lion, the Witch and the Wardrobe,* the lion who is not Aslan, strutting around, "pretending to be very busy" just so they can tell everyone "Did you hear what he said? *Us lions.* That means him and me. *Us lions.*"[29] Our time is taken up arguing about whether God is more masculine or more feminine, more transcendent or more immanent, more "form"-like or more "spirit"-like. How our behavior must grieve God. We, too, like the Goddess worshipers, are treating God as Gentile idolators do: as a cosmic, transcendent, remote male. God is still oneself. If the church wants renewal, it must search for more biblical ways to understand and speak about God. We must treat metaphor as metaphor, literal as literal, and truth as truth. Who God is affects who we become. How we speak about God affects our listeners, too.

The church has a lengthy history of learning about God through nature and using masculine *and* feminine *and* nature metaphors for God, from the Psalmists, Jesus' parables, early and medieval Christians. Why now do we come to a screeching stop? The neo-pagan desire to see an aliveness in nature[30] should be redirected to a creation that mirrors its Creator.

If we trust the Bible as fully reliable, we can learn wonderful life-affirming truths from it. Many of the god/dess writers have simply appropriated a more critical use of the Bible: the nature of God in

Judaism and Christianity is evolutionary and the Bible is not historically accurate.[31] We need to be anchored firmly in a historical Bible written down by eyewitnesses willing to die for the God revealed to them.

The church has one last challenge, not to get sucked into the god/dess movement itself. Very few Christian writers note the un-Christian view of Jesus held by some of the writers in the men's movement, as Bill notes in chapter three. First is not superior. Even as some Christians have misinterpreted Paul's words, some ecofeminists have used that same reasoning to argue the earth is superior to humans.

Even as we should try not to misrepresent goddess spirituality,[32] we must also be careful not to call "evil" good and "good" evil. Witches claim Eve and the serpent were right. Much of our modern culture, and especially goddess spirituality, as did some ancient cultures, treat the female genitalia (and male phallus) as the center and creation of all life. Sexuality has become for many simply pleasure.[33]

A few people have been attempting to worship both the god/dess and the God of the Bible. Some people treat Mary as a Goddess. Some believers see the Christian God and their personal vision of God the Mother as "two movements" "not in conflict, they simply water different layers in my soul."[34] The God of the Bible, however, is unique, the only God, and all powerful to meet all needs. All can not be divine at the same time as only God is divine: "You are not able to share in the table of the Lord and the table of demons" (1 Cor. 10:21). God commands us not to make and bow down and worship anyone or anything other than "the Lord your God," a "jealous God" (Exod. 20:4–5). Therefore, we need to teach people to discern the different inner voices, the voice of their own desire, the voice of their own fears, the voice of jealousy and other sinful thoughts, the voice of the Spirit clear and strong, and the voices of the unclean spirits.

▼ You Worship What You Do Not Know

Jesus was able to evoke interest from the woman of Samaria. She no longer merely wanted the privilege to serve Jesus, a Jew, water. She now asked of Jesus, "Give me this water," just as he had asked of her "Give me to drink" (John 4:10, 15). But before Jesus explains to her how to get living water, now that he has established rapport with her, he sets out to clarify some untruths about the woman, about her faith, and about his faith. She has no committed husband, but she has had five relationships with men (John 4:17–18). She worships what she does not know. No place will be necessary as sacred space (John 4:21–23). The casual reader of the Goddess literature may as well not notice the untruths told both about goddess feminism and Christianity.

We Do Not Always Read Truths about Goddess Spirituality

Sheila D. Collins begins *A Different Heaven and Earth* with a brief idylic view of the past: "Poetry was not a mirror of life, for life *was* poetry; and ecstasy was found in the most usual of places."[35] Sadly, goddess spirituality presents an idylic view of the past and the present. Few books present a realistic view of witchcraft. On the whole, goddess spirituality is a conservative movement, with danger to oneself and others. It is not necessarily ecological, political, and not really free.

The apostle Paul writes about Jews and Gentiles, that "no one is righteous, not even one, no one understands, no one searches diligently for God" (Rom. 3:10–11). What is true of Jew and Gentile, is also true of Christian and neo-pagan, at least in terms of how they treat women. Neo-pagans as well as Christians both have problems with giving full opportunities for women.

The emphasis on Goddess, ironically, for a *feminist* movement, seems to have been started by men. Goddess spirituality owes a lot to doctor Carl Gustav Jung. His psychological perspectives undergird much of the men's movement and goddess spirituality: everyone should live a myth, ancient Greek and universal religions are resources for myths, the feminine is nature, primitive, spiritual, intuitive, and cunning, objective truth does not exist, and final authority should be the inner personality, the inner experience, never dogma. His evolutionary perspective caused him to posit the existence of a collective unconscious, a primitive, archaic remnant of the evolutionary process, with its own energy, spirit gurus, and ability even to cause parapsychological phenomena. He claimed as authoritative his dream of God where God becomes human, and therefore humans, animals, and nature became god. He concluded that God is not good, the Protestant and Jewish God is masculine, unjust, and destructive. He hated Jesus.[36]

The two numerically larger components of goddess feminism come from the ecology and witchcraft components. The Gaia theory was coauthored by the male-female research team, James Lovelock and Lynn Margulis. The writer William Golding suggested the metaphor "Gaia" for "Biocybernetic Universal System Tendency/Homoeostasis." Although Lovelock treats Gaia as having some form of intelligence, but not consciousness, the largest living creature on earth, as do Jung and goddess spiritualists, he sees human collective intelligence as simply one part of the evolved Gaia. He is almost deterministic since Gaia is an automatic operation. He hints at the metaphoric aspect of Gaia and does not so readily rebuke goddess worshipers unlike the microbiologist Margulis, who exclaimed in a 1986 interview: "The religious overtones of Gaia make me sick!" Similarly, the witchcraft movement had not been particularly popular until Gerald B. Gardner had revitalized it by emphasizing the goddess and de-emphasizing the horned god."[37]

Even though Margot Adler is herself a witch, in *Drawing Down the Moon* she has been honest in her assessment of the Craft. Goddess spirituality, on the whole, assumes the traditional male-female stereotypes. Witchcraft, like the Yang and Yin, is based on male-female, spirit-body, transcendence-immanence polarities. Traditional witchcraft is hierarchial. Adler writes: "Many men (and some women) in the more mainstream Craft groups are upset by the growth of feminist covens," and "positive reactions to feminism are not prevalent in the Craft." Witches Margo and Lee complain: "It is chiefly men who speak for the Craft; men write most of the books about the Craft, found the Witchcraft museums, and give their names to the traditions." Most of the time men also speak with authority to the public outside their Circle. As well, many traditional priestesses live unfulfilled lives outside the Craft: "Often they remain meek and silent, allowing husbands, who are often less intelligent, to hold forth. But magically, when the candles are lit and the circle is cast, these women become, for a short while, priestesses worthy of the legends of old."[38] The magic of witches depends on the differing powers of men and women, perceived stereotypically.[39] Men and women are not seen as having that higher monohumanity, unity as humans reflecting the same one God. In their attempt to address this problem the feminist covens and feminist spirituality groups have ended up, according to Adler, with a "larger percentage of lesbians" than either the neo-pagan or feminist movements.[40]

The stereotypical female may now also be found at the divine level. Self-effacement and capriciousness have been projected cosmically. As the lone ranger of the skies, humans are left to gasp, where did this masked Woman go? Nelle Morton writes: "The Goddess works herself out of business. She doesn't hang around to receive thanks. It appears to be thanks enough for her that another woman has come into her own."[41] The fictional priest Fergus explains: "The Lady is a mischief-maker, that much I know. She enjoys a good laugh at our poor mortal expense."[42] Anne E. Carr expresses the danger well: "Exclusively female images of God or Goddess worship can suggest a reversal of patterns of domination rather than genuine transformation; surely mother symbolism can quickly become as oppressive—suffocating, sentimental, possessive—as an authoritarian father symbolism. A self-critical Christian feminism is aware of the dangers of a single image, especially a parent/child image. The use of many images more clearly affirms the fully transcendent and incomprehensible reality of God."[43]

If we women are nature (an ancient stereotype), then we still are not free. Carol P. Christ's description of life, to me, sounds deterministic:

> The divine/Goddess/God/Earth/Life/It symbolizes the whole of which we are a part. . . . We come from earth and to earth we shall return. Life feeds on life. We live because others die, and we will die so that others may live. . . . We will never understand it all. We do not choose the conditions of our lives. Death may come at any time. Death is never early or late. With regard to life and death there is no ultimate justice, nor ultimate injustice, for there is no promise that life will be other than it is. . . . Knowledge that we are but a small part of life and death and transformation is the essential religious insight. The essential religious response is to rejoice and to weep, to sing and to dance, to tell stories and create rituals in praise of an existence far more complicated, more intricate, more enduring than we are.[44]

This return to the deterministic religious worldview is nowhere more evident than in Marion Zimmer Bradley's bestselling novel *The Mists of Avalon*. As Igraine, one character, explained: "She would do as they willed; it was part of her destiny." When Morgaine undergoes the great Rite of the Marriage of the Goddess and God "she went where they led her, passive, blinded, tranced, knowing only that she went to meet her destiny." What was the horrifying destiny that "the Great Mother of Love and Birth" and "Darkness and Death" had for her? The man with whom she had intercourse turned out to be her long lost brother, Arthur, whom she had "mothered" as an older sister. So Morgaine cries out: "Why did you do this to us? Great Mother, Lady, why?"[45]

And no wonder their views are fatalistic. Feminist spirituality has resurrected fatalistic, deterministic pagan religions. As Cynthia Eller's sociological study explains: "Feminist spirituality's most important base" is pagan.[46] Even Lovelock's scientific version of Gaia is also almost fatalistic. Since, he states, pollution is natural, cleaning the environment is a routine, automatic operation of homoeostasis or Gaia. Human pollution will not probably endanger the life of Gaia as a whole, even though it may destroy the human species itself.[47] Humans are simply one part of a pattern. The whole pattern has more importance than any one part. And, when in witchcraft astral powers are invited into one's life, eventually, like Faust's legend, they demand a return, as the witches say, "The energy you put into the world comes back." Possibly that is why new initiates are blindfolded and their hands or ankles tied. They are not as free as they would say.[48] In the long run, does feminist spirituality really deliver an empowerment for women?

Only a few writings hint at the danger to oneself. As well, many witches do not live by the ancient proverb: "An ye harm none, do as ye will." Starhawk felt quite right to spend all night yelling out curses at a nuclear center. Lupe's coven did not hesitate to harass her and her family and friends when she chose to leave (appendix A). Did the live fish who were thrown on the ground as fertilizer feel "love unto all beings"? Can any harm come from weapons such as "guns," "hand grenades," and "poison rings"?[49]

Despite the boasting that witches see no distinction between good and evil, they pick and choose their own sin: nuclear equipment, patriarchy, abusing women, leaving a coven (those are "sins").[50] What can *not* be sin is sexual immorality and choosing to reject the God of the Bible. The Serpent's and Eve's choice to partake of the fruit of knowledge is still acknowledged as good and right. One of the more poignant scenes in the novel *The Return of the Goddess* is

Esther's dream (while in a church service) of a snake offering her fruit. But now the serpent no longer challenges the woman, did God *really* say "You shall not eat from any tree in the garden?" Rather, it offers fruit as communion: "Take, eat. . . . This is my body, which is given for you."[51] Adler describes one amusing (or terrifying) spontaneous ritual when twenty Pagans decided to go skinny dipping in a Hyatt Hotel pool after midnight, swimming with a pet python and a boa constrictor: "It seemed right out of the Garden of Eden."[52] Some of the ancient rabbis who interpreted Eve's sin as sexual would have no disagreement here.[53] The Bible, on the other hand, never presents the fall as a sexual choice at all.

Even though Margot Adler explains witchcraft's ecological concern as one of its attractive features, toward the close of the book she quotes one coven priest: "I do not think [ecology] is a major Craft problem." Some neo-pagans are politically and ecologically concerned. Many are not. She concludes: "Quite a few spoke against any kind of militant action to save the environment."[54] Judith Antonelli begins her article: "There is a great deal of doubt expressed in various segments of the women's movement as to the relevance of feminist spirituality to politics," although she concludes that "psychic power" is political.[55]

Do we have here a movement that inherently is ecologically concerned? Not necessarily so. Not everyone who speaks ecologically necessarily acts ecologically. In the Presbyterian Church, U.S.A., in a September 1991 survey, a majority of clergy, elders, and members viewed environmental issues as among the two or three most serious problems of the day. Three-fourths of Presbyterian (USA) congregations participate in community recycling programs. Many Christians are ecologically concerned, but not everyone takes ecology as a primary mission for her or his life. However, many a church and Christian family are environmentally conscious.[56]

Even the Indians, our society's archetypal example of ecology (after our predecessors destroyed their civilization), may not be as perfect as portrayed. On the one hand, no one can underestimate the graciousness of many Indians. Squanto of the Algonkin Family welcomed the Pilgrims at Plymouth and taught them how to survive by raising corn. The Taino Indians in the West Indies were gentle, artistic, peaceful, loving, and generous. Christopher Columbus recounts: "They give all for anything that was given to them." The

Caribs, on the other hand, were cannibals, fierce and warlike, always trying to capture their peaceful neighbors. Clark Wissler, an anthropologist, relates that frequently Indians on the mainland would be at war with one another, marauding tribes would raid for blood, captives, and plunder. Some hatred was extensive. The Iroquois Five Nations ruthlessly exterminated the Huron, massacring entire towns. The Six Nations, in turn, destroyed the Iroquois Family. Most Indians would boast of killings and would torture prisoners. Probably the wild horse became extinct long before whites came to America because the early Indian hunted it. Sometimes grass would be set on fire to cause a herd of bison to fall off a cliff. Although the Teton condemned suicide and forceful sacrificial killing, they highly lauded the self-torture in the Sun Dance: thrusting a sharpened stick through the skin, the stick fastened by a cord to a post, and the individual released himself by tearing himself free. When the supplicant fainted from exhaustion and pain, he would be in "communion with the gods."

And what opportunities were there for women? Among Indians the work roles were closely tied to sex, even to this day. In general, the men hunted and women cultivated gardens.[57] Is this our ideal? Are not talent, gifts, and ability better criteria for role distribution?

I am not suggesting that Europeans are more peaceful than American Indians. By no means. Rather, I am suggesting that many of the Indians were no worse. Like all cultures, they have their assets and their debits.

We Do Not Always Read Truths about Christianity

Not only is some of the neo-pagan spirituality itself misleading, but rarely does it present Christianity fairly. Its picture of God is rarely interpreted from the Bible itself. Rather, it is an archetypal stereotype projected onto the Bible: God as impersonal, abstract, uninterested, detached, power-over. Metaphors are treated literally. Artificial divisions are made between God's immanence and transcendence. God has no paradox nor intimate concern. The patriarchal stereotype is assumed to be an accurate projection of God. Several writers have shown, in contrast, that the Old Testament prophets were against male *and* female deities, not simply against goddesses.[58] Christianity stands or falls *not* based on its Teacher and teachings but on everything and everyone who claims to be *not* neo-pagan. All of

Christian culture, it argues, must be embraced or rejected in its two extremes of liberal Christianity and cultural fundamentalism.

▼ We Have Living Water

Hopefully, after Christianity's real teachings are established, then we too will be ready to explain what Christianity has to offer those people who might be goddess feminists or who have been enticed by goddess feminism. Can we too direct them to "a spring of water gushing up to eternal life," to God the Spirit, the Messiah who speaks to us even today (John 4:14, 24–26)? We can direct them to God if we explain the nature of God, humans, and creation.

Knowing God Is Crucial

We have heard it said many times that religion offers an opiate. Rather, I have found that Christianity offers a challenge and abundancy. We do not all worship the same God.

The God we worship is unique, more powerful than any other power, yet the God of the Bible uses that power in a compassionate, socially active way. Grace and truth are balanced in the God who created and maintains the world. This God is one but multidimensional. God has one name but three distinct and equal persons.

God is also spirit. God is everywhere but especially where two or three are gathered together in Jesus' name. Because God is spirit, immanent and transcendent, God is close to all, present with us no matter where we are, ready to help us live loving and united lives. Only a transcendent God can be powerfully, immanently present. Transcendence and immanence are both categories to express power. "Transcendence" also expresses God's surpassing excellence and holiness. God exists apart from the material universe as well as in it. As Spirit, God has no form. God also is unique in that God has no evil side, but is wholly good. The unseeable God became incarnate in the human Jesus, who never uses "male" for self-description. Jesus also had a reputation for treating the poor and powerless as worthy as the rich and powerful (Matt. 22:16).

God is invisible. God has no literal "face." Therefore, God sees no "face" either. When God is described as impartial in the Bible, literally the New Testament writers are saying God "receives" no "face" (Acts 10:34). *Prosōpolēmptēs* is a Greek term coined by Christian writers.[59] When Peter learns in a vision that God does not consider people acceptable because of their nationality, he declares that respect toward God and righteousness are what counts.

The "face" is an interesting synecdoche in the Bible. It may refer to a literal "face" or visage or represent a person's will or personal attention, favor, and presence.[60] "Face" also stands for superficial characteristics such as nationality, power, wealth, and legalism.[61] None of those qualities can entice God away from justice.[62] As God told Samuel, impressed by the tall and mature Eliab, people look on the outward appearance, not the heart (1 Sam. 16:7).

No matter what so-called followers of Christ say, the church is founded on this same principle. When Jew, Gentile, slave, free, rich, poor, powerful, powerless, male, female are baptized, they rise up from the waters wearing the same regal royal robe "Christ" (Gal. 3:26–28).[63] The churches have one "face" (2 Cor. 8:24), that is Christ's face. And who is Christ? Christ is Jew, Gentile, slave, free, rich, poor, powerful, powerless, male, female. Everyone justified by Christ is needed to show Christ's full face. Therefore, at Pentecost, when the church officially begins, the Spirit is poured out upon sons and daughters, elders and youth, male and female slaves (Acts 2:17–18; Joel 2:28–29). Participation in the church should be based on God's gifts, not on external characteristics. The only way the church can become "without face," as God has no face, is by every God-created diversity being included in every aspect of leadership.[64] Then we will be prepared for the heavenly Pentecost when "a great crowd, whom no one was able to count it, from all nations and tribes and peoples and languages, [will be] standing before the throne and before the Lamb . . . crying out with a very loud voice: 'Salvation is our God's'" (Rev. 7:9–10).

Thus, God is known by the church. As well, God, although spirit, may be known by actions, adjectives, and metaphors. God is creative and personal, making good beings and allowing them freedom. Since God is love (1 John 4:8, 16), God allows us to name God—as well, God chooses attributes in self-description. God can meet all human needs. God as spirit is above gender limitations. Nevertheless, God alone is the font of whatever qualities and roles we should call feminine and masculine. The metaphor "lord" highlights that God deserves obedience. The metaphor "father" highlights God's intimacy, loving care, and power. The generic "he" expresses God's power, intimacy, unity, diversity, and action. These words were never meant to be understood literally.

Creation Is Valuable

Humans are created in the image of God. We are human first, male and female second, because God is one first. Both genders are needed to reflect a full image of God. Because God is one, God intends us as well to have one spouse. (In Genesis 2:24 the man leaves his family to cling to his wife.) Sexuality is not an end in itself, but an aspect of intimacy ("knowledge"), and sexual intercourse is the key symbol of commitment in marriage.[65] For Christians, commitment should precede sexual intimacy and pleasure.

Since God is holy, we humans also are called to be holy, like Deborah and Ruth, exemplary in our generation. Sin is a reality of the fall both within and between humans. Nevertheless, God enhances our own will. Infinite choice to do as one wants is not freedom, because love is greater than truth. God enhances our ability to be free from illusion, free from ritual, and to be free to be fulfilled, "free indeed" (John 8:36).

Only humans are made in God's trinity image and only we are morally called to be stewards of the earth, one another, and ourselves. As we reflect on creation as God's mirror, and respond in thankfulness, we can not only perceive God's power and duty but also become more like God in clarity and will. We are interconnected with the rest of nature, but God, humans, and nature are also unique. Humans should not be oppressed by nature, yet the uniqueness of everything should be appreciated more and more. Every human is important as a unique creation. We are not simply a part of a pattern. We are individually saved, but also part of a human, nonhuman, and church community. As Shannon Jung writes: "We [humans] are a significant species but we are not the sole focus of God's care."[66]

▼ Conclusion

The Goddess movement is all about inner empowerment and social change. We have proposed that that inner empowerment and social change can most wholistically, powerfully, and healthily be accomplished through the God of the Bible. I was brought up in the

Dominican Republic. In the capital, where I lived, water was stored for our home's use in a cistern. The cistern was merely a cemented "basement" under the porch. Even today you can lift up a wooden square cover and peek inside and see the water swirming around. It is not too enticing. When I was young, even so, we could drink the water pumped up through the faucet. But at this time the water is no longer drinkable. This is the cup of Goddess worship. It looks serviceable, but it quickly results in illness.

The imagery Jesus uses for God's Spirit is quite different. A few years ago we visited a geyser out in California. We waited at this nature park looking at a puddle of water. I could not imagine anything happening. But all of a sudden, hot water came gushing up higher and higher while we marveled. How I would have loved to put on a bathing suit and walk underneath! But that water was too hot. It was too dangerous. But it was pure, very, very pure. Jesus offered the Samaritan woman some of that marvelous, pure living water. If she were but willing to see her need and use Jesus as her cup, she could drink from this wholesome fountain. If the church would simply welcome women to partake of the water and to welcome others, as did the Samaritan woman ("Might not this one be the Christ?"),[67] all would enjoy the geyser gushing out into eternal life.

APPENDIX A

A PERSONAL JOURNEY

*G*uadalupe Rosalez (Lupe) has been an assembler with Parker Brothers for about five years. Reared Baptist, baptized at fifteen, since a little girl she was different from other children in that she saw things before they happened and felt people's pain. The gifts she had became distorted because her family and church would not accept them. Here is her story.

Even though I was baptized, I really did not consider myself a Christian. The word "Christian" means "Christ-like," to be like Christ. I never considered myself to be Christ-like. Christ is the Son of God. How could I even come close to being like him? How could I even come close with everything that my life had been like? How could I even come close to being anything like that? So I did not really consider myself a Christian. I knew that I believed in God, that there was a higher force, that that was what made me different from everybody else, even though I was in the craft. I know what a Christian is now. I consider myself one. I am one. And there is just so much of a difference between what I was and what I am now. And that was one of the reasons why I went into Wicca, because I did not consider myself a Christian, and I had had problems in the past where no one else considered me to be one either. So, no, I did not consider myself to be a Christian then. If I had, I would not have gone in the way I did.

▼ Witchcraft Has Personal Appeal

My involvement in witchcraft began a long time ago, but more specifically on November 17, 1989.[1] Throughout my life I had had failures, both emotional and spiritual failures. My whole life had just been a mess! I was at a point in my life where I was married and my marriage was crumbling and I needed something to hold onto. I had always been attracted to the occult. I always wanted to know what other people did not dare to find out. I always wanted to go into the why of things, and I was never afraid of things that were unknown. As a matter of fact, I was very curious about it, the unknown, the occult. Why do they call it the occult? Why are some people afraid of it? Why is it forbidden knowledge? Inside me I had a natural curiosity. As well, I felt that I was very different. I knew I was different from when I was very young. I was not afraid of the normal things people are afraid of, such as, as a child, scary movies or things that go bump in the night. I was never afraid of those things. As a matter of fact, I wanted to know what made people afraid of them and if there were such things, why were they there and how did they communicate with people? I was just full of curiosities and interest in it.

Witchcraft is called "Wicca." It comes from an ancient word meaning "Wise Ones." And my teacher was a high priest in the occult, in witchcraft, and when I went to see him, I did not know this. I went in to have a reading done, a tarot card reading, because I had looked for answers elsewhere (which I had not gotten) as to where my life was going. I spoke to my teacher then and he read the cards for me and told me what was going on in my life. I was very down and very depressed and he helped me. He told me that I was not to blame for my marriage failing and that I had a lot of good in me, that I had a good heart, that I was a very loving person, and that I was not bad. This was something I grew up thinking about myself, that I was bad. He became my friend and he did not turn me away because I had these special gifts. Unlike other people who did turn away from me before, he accepted me and became my friend and he made me feel good about myself. He lifted my self-esteem which was really on the ground when I met him. Through readings, through healings, through mixing with other people, I slowly started falling into it. I went for psychic classes and I soaked everything up like a sponge. It was like sometimes he would ask questions and I knew what he was going to ask before he even asked it. I knew the answers without even having to read any of the material or without having to be told. I knew by nature what the answers were. So, he was drawn to that. He said back then, "You're a real witch. It's inside of you. It's in your blood. It's in your soul. You know these things by nature. You are a natural-made witch, not a man-made witch." And he said that I was meant to be great in Wicca because I had the knowledge that was there by nature. "By nature," I mean, I knew what to do, how to react, and how to do things without anybody telling me.

So I kept on going to his classes and I really wound up getting wrapped up in it. I was hungering for something when I went into it and it fed me. It fed me and it brought me up from where I was. I made new friends. It took me away from everything that was real in the real world—my divorce, marriage crumbling, insecurities about myself. It lifted me up so high, I had no insecurities. And it was just the fact that they made me feel special. I learned through them, or I opened up through them, because the knowledge was already there. And I was not afraid of being who I was anymore. I was not afraid of being degraded in front of people. I was not afraid of being turned away because these people had accepted me with everything that I had come with. They accepted it *all*. They did not turn me away. They became very good friends, very close and intimate friends because we shared everything. We shared everything: food and healings. If we did not have a place to stay, they became a family and they found a place for whoever needed a place to stay. If someone was sick, we would all work together and try to make this person better, through ritual and through candle burning and through other things. If we had someone who was having a hard time in the real world, through somebody else that was bothering them, well, we would teach them and we would help them to mellow this person out or tell them how to cope with this person. It was just a family oriented thing. It gave me the family I never had. It gave me the mom and dad I never had. It gave me the love I never had. It gave me the closeness that I had never experienced in my childhood with anyone. And that's what took me in.

▼ Witchcraft Has Similar Appeal for Others

My experience was pretty much the same as others who are into Wicca because Wicca is founded on the belief from where something starts, there is where it ends. Everything is done in cycles, everything happens in cycles. And that belief is rooted into you as you are learning. You go in as a student as I was. You are taught the unity of earth, human beings, animals, trees, plants, and nature. Nature was created for you to have communion with, not just to live off of and to take and not give back. My experience was like many others that found unity not only in nature but in the people that we work with and that we live our daily lives with. Wicca showed me how to incorporate everything into a sense of oneness in the end. And, it was quite appealing to me back then because it all seemed so harmless and so beautiful. It was a beautiful experience. I had never been any place where people thought this way and it seemed to be everything I was looking for.

Witchcraft has a Goddess foundation, a guiding Goddess foundation. Witches believe in a male and female essence, with the female essence being way above that of the male essence. Women have been looked down upon for so many years as being less than men and therefore women have always had to step aside when men are around. It is a power struggle. Man has always thought that man was man and that he was above women. It is hard for a person that has fought her whole life through like I did and always been in control of myself, always having to watch out for myself, to believe that there was ever a man that could be higher than myself because the men in my life were not good examples at all. I thought that women were strong and Wicca teaches you that women are strong. The goddess is a woman and yet, yes, there is a male god but he is to bow down before the woman essence. The god bows down to the goddess essence. Through women all creation springs forth babies nurturing, loving, and chastening with love as she would her own child. That is what attracts most people. That is why there are so many women involved in Wicca. There are men, yes, but there are so many more women than there are men.

Yet Wicca does not give the authority to all women to be that way. There are some that can never have the authority to have a coven, to have other things that witches in higher degrees do. It has to be a special essence that comes within certain women that makes them stand out as leaders. This special nature does give authority but authority has to be learned and it has to be earned in Wicca. Not every woman that goes in there has the authority to do these things.

Only those that are nature born who have it almost as a second sense, like breathing is your first sense. You have a second sense without having to probe into the books or to probe into or ask teachers or others. Those are the ones that have the authority in Wicca.

Wicca teaches you how to be on your own, how to be strong, and how in rough situations not to crumble underneath them, how to rise up like a phoenix from the ashes and rebuild yourself over again. Community?—yes, Wicca builds community. It builds community because there are so many people out there seeking this oneness with the earth, this oneness with the universe, this oneness with the ultimate god and goddess aspect. Everybody wants love, everybody wants to get along, everybody wants peace, and in Wicca, when you are involved in a group, it starts off that way, and you will go to a certain level where it will just keep going that way, but then it reaches another point.

▼ How Witchcraft Lost Its Appeal

I had gone through a succession of ins and outs with the high priests and priestesses within my group because I believed, I even knew, God existed. I knew Jesus Christ was the Son of God. I knew Jehovah was God. I knew there was a Holy Spirit, but yet when I went into witchcraft I said, "Well, God is God and rules above all but he can have helpers." That is why God has spirit guides and angels, and other things. God has help. I was ignorant in God's Word and did not know God's Word very well.

But, when I started reaching my degrees in Wicca, I was being allowed to use and do things through rituals, even lead the rituals, I started incorporating Christ inside the rituals. My own group was quite different from the other groups because I taught them differently. I taught them that yes there was a Goddess but that there was also a God who was above all other gods. In paganism there are many gods: a god for everything, a god for every day of the week. I taught them that, yes, these gods existed but there was one above all others. When I reached the level to where I was able to cast a circle and cast my own rituals and cast my own spells I incorporated Christ in everything. I taught them to do the same when the circle was cast, instead of simply calling in the elemental forces as the other witches did. I would cast my circle and I would incorporate the angels. The man that taught me said that he could see so many things inside of me that were just so strong that they were just overpowering. I was a person Wicca needed. When I was brought before council because I was using Christ and the angels as my circle casting, my teacher went into the books and the laws and everything that has to do with Wicca so he could find loopholes in the laws that would allow me to keep Christ just so I would not leave. So I stayed there because they allowed me to use Christ and the angels, but the only thing that I did not realize was that I was also using the others. I also used other gods and other goddesses. I used them because to my knowledge they were God's helpers. There were other gods but God was above them all. I always had that inside of me.

That started causing problems. I met my friend at work who is a Christian and he started talking to me about Christ. Having heard about Christ when I was a child there were things that stuck to me. I was starting to get very interested in it again. By then it was causing more problems within my group, within my higher-ups in the craft because they did not like what I was doing. And I was taken to council several times, where I questioned them. I asked them: "What was wrong with one Christian God amongst all the pagan gods?" I still remember it like it was yesterday. And they just had no answers for me. They just said: "No, you are forbidden to use Christ."

By then my marriage had crumbled and divorce was taking place and everything else was falling apart and these people stuck with me through it all but there were weak links in the group. There started to be a lot of jealousy and envy within the group from the high priest and the other high priestesses that were there. I found out that the man who was my teacher loved me as a student but was also in love with me in another way. It just turned out to be a total mess. In Wicca teacher and student are never to have intimate contact. They are just teacher and student. They may be friends, but not on a romantically intimate level. It is prohibited. It is forbidden. He told me that he had feelings for me and I knew that was forbidden. Everything was falling apart. As well as my family and my marriage, also the group started going bad because there was just so much envy and so much hatred going around. It looked really ugly. A lot of back stabbing was going on by that time.

Christ reached me at that time through Peter King and I started going back to reading Christian literature. I was going back and forth for a long time. I saw it all for what it really was when I was trying to leave and separate myself from them. They made it hard for me. I had nightmares and visions that nobody else had and sicknesses that were not accounted for physically. I also realized at that point that the higher up I got in degrees, the more was required of me, not only as a person but in my use of magic. I was being pressured into going into the art of necromancy, which is raising of the dead in witchcraft. I always felt that the only one who could raise the dead was God and now it is done by others through certain rituals that are done in witchcraft that is not for humans to deal with or even think about doing. It is just too dangerous in both a spiritual sense and in a mental sense. If you are not strong enough spiritually, it will drive you crazy. But, anyway, I was being pressured by my higher ups to go deeper and deeper into the arts and when it got to that point, the necromancy, I said, "No, it is time. I can't do this anymore." God was speaking so loudly to me, I just did not feel right anymore. I felt I was wrong and I felt I was cheating God. I felt it hurt me to know that I was being dishonest with God and I just could not deal with it anymore. I had to make a choice. It was either witchcraft or God. I chose the one and only true God because I always felt that he was the one and only true God. My choice required of me to leave the craft.

To this day, almost two years later, I am still being followed. I am still being attacked on and off. I think the worst came a couple of weeks ago. I ran into this person that appeared to be demonized, on the street, and she threatened my children. She said that if I did not go back my children were going to die by the twelfth of this month, which is March. It is now after that date. I was hit pretty bad. I was sick and there was a point of stagnation where I just could not seem to move. I had no will of my own but I had much prayer through the churches and I prayed myself. My belief in God outweighed the worry that I had. Praise God my children are now fine.

▼ What the Christian Can Learn from Witchcraft

From my personal experience in witchcraft I have learned that God is always with us no matter what. The times when we feel that we are most alone, that is when God is with us. At the times when we have no will of our own, God carries us. At the time when you think that there is no forgiveness, God forgives. At the time when you think you have hit the bottom and the bottom falls out, God is there to catch you. No matter what you have done, God will forgive. God does forgive. And no matter how far you have traveled away from God, he will accept you when you come back. God does not force his will on anybody. God loves us so much that he gives us the freedom to choose. And God is there with us no matter what.

My experience has made my walk a lot stronger. It has made me cling to God's Word. I want to learn more. It has made me realize what a different world it is when we are not Christians. It has made me see how blinded we are when we are in the world. When we become Christians and walk with God, it is a totally different walk and a totally different talk. It has made me want to do something for these people that are like I once was. I want to help these people out in the name of Christ just like someone else helped me out in the name of Christ. It makes me want as a Christian to unmask everything that is not of God and show the people out there what it really is. I want to walk even closer to God daily, closer and closer. I want to seek God and seek others in his name so that God's name may be glorified.

Being a Christian and someone that was once a witch, I need to be on constant awareness of the thoughts inside my head. I need to be constantly aware of what is *God's* will and what is the *world's* will. I need constantly to be discerning and not allow myself to fall into fear as I did once before. Dangers, there are many, but through the grace of God I know I can survive them, because God has given me discernment and wisdom as to how I should watch out for things like this. I need to be aware constantly that God is my shield and my strength, and not let myself believe that I can do it alone because I do not do anything alone. We all do it through the grace of God. I can not let myself be swayed by things that are mere illusions as I allowed myself in the past.

Power, love, and healing as a Christian are all God founded. God has a selfless power, selfless love, and selfless healing. God's grace gives us the power. God's grace gives us the love. And through God's grace we do our healings. All is based on the Father, Son, and Holy Ghost. Power, love, and healing as a witch starts out as being goddess oriented. Goddess gives power, love, and the ability to heal. But as time goes on, as a witch you come to a realization that you are the god or the goddess, that you are the one that creates your own energy. You bend the will of others through your own energies. And for healing, you draw from the elemental forces, which are there for anyone who wants them, the colors, and the auric fields. And as a witch you always seem to seek the council of a spirit guide. And, so, in a sense, you build your world around a god/dess which ultimately winds up becoming you and you becoming him/her. So you no longer are indebted to the god/dess but to yourself because you have become the god or goddess in the long run.

▼ What Message Can a Christian Give to Those Considering or Currently Involved in Witchcraft or Goddess Worship?

There will come a time in your lives for all of those of you that are involved in witchcraft and goddess worship when you will come to the conclusion through the knowledge that you gained that your energies are only your own, that the god and goddess in witchcraft is only a figment of the imagination created within your own mind. Accept the fact that your mental capacities need to believe in something or someone and it is so much easier to believe in a god, a pagan god or goddess, who allows you so many things as they do. You will come to the conclusion that when you are sick, physically sick, that you do not have the energy to charge a crystal or create a shield of any kind because it all depends on your physical body and not on anyone else's. You will come to the conclusion that when you came into the craft it was because in some point in your life you had been an outcast of some kind. You were lonely, you were alone and they took you in. You will come to the conclusion that the people you thought loved you the most, that took you into the craft, your best friends, have become your worst enemies. And, you will come to the conclusion where you will feel totally worthless. You will be depressed and saddened by the fact that you have come to the realization that the goddess and the god are all in your mind. You may even come to the point of thinking of suicide which happens frequently when you come to that point.

But I have been there before and that is why I know there is a way out. There is only one God and I know you do not want to hear this but he is the Christian God. He died for many and that includes you. He forgives all and that includes you. So reach out. You have been into witchcraft and you have been with the gods and goddesses. Give the Christian God a chance. Give the Messiah a chance. God is right there. All you have to do is just say "Jesus" and you will find out that with Christ you do not have to charge a crystal or create sacred space to talk to him because he is there, anywhere. You do not have to look into a crystal ball to see him, because he is right there. You do not have to burn incense or call in the watchtowers to bring him in, because he is already there. You do not have to change your name, because he knows you by name and he loves you and he will accept you just as you are. He has so much love to give and so much forgiveness in him. God won't throw it back in your face. So, take it from someone who has been there before— you will never regret it. Whereas in witchcraft, there comes a point in your life where you will regret it. You will regret being in the craft and you will regret believing in pagan gods. Because when push comes to shove they just won't be there for you because they are only figments of the imagination. They are created inside our heads.

▼ What the Church Can Do to Prevent People from Becoming Involved in Witchcraft

The saints of God, who are the church, do not criticize, love instead. Do not be afraid and pull away from witches, but, rather, be their friends and pray for them. Be open, ask God for wisdom and discernment, and compassion above all things because these are people who are human beings. They are part of God's creation. They all have hearts and souls. These are people that just do not know what they are doing. They have been blinded. They have been lied to. And we need to have compassion for them. Let us not get angry about it. Let us not condemn. Let us not judge. We have our God, the God, who does that. Let us fight for these souls because we all belong to God. These people have been kidnapped by Satan. Their souls have been kidnapped by Satan. As saints of God, we need to go into the battle ground and retrieve them in the name of the Lord. They are not Satan's for the taking and we should not allow it to be. We need to be a little more aggressive in the fight in the battles of the Lord and for the Lord. Yes, God gives us good hearts and we are very good and very sweet people, but God also gave us a spirit of courage, and we need to stress it more within the occult community than we have been. We just can not sit back and let two or three people who are aggressive in the Lord do the job of what fourteen or fifteen others can do. We need to get more aggressive in the name of the Lord. Things are going on in the occult world and the metaphysical world. Satan has no right having these kidnapped people and we should be willing no matter what the cost to go in and retrieve them in the name of the Lord.

Eventually, I want to open a center for people who have been in the metaphysical, the occult, and the craft and have pulled away from it and are seeking God, a center where those of us who have been there can be there to talk to them and to help them out in the name of the Lord and lead them to Christ.[2] Sometimes when you are in the craft, you need a time just to get away and think, especially if you are in between witchcraft and believing in God. I want a place where there is constant prayer day and night. I also want to establish a hotline where you can call anytime during day and night. A Christian voice will always be on the other side of the line to respond to you. I would like to own and to write books directed to the witches and to those that are pulling away from it, books that will speak to them and to their souls.

I have so many things that I want to do in God's name. I would also like to work a little more with people. I want to work with people that nobody else wants to work with. I want to work with the alcoholic, I want to work with the drug addict, I want to work with people that are HIV positive, I want to work with the people that nobody else wants. These are the people that I want to work with. There has always been a special love for these people inside of me for some reason. I do not know what purpose it is for, but I know since I was a small child that I have always felt this compassion for these people, not that I do not have it for all, but these people especially, because these people do not have anybody that cares enough to be with them and to talk to them or just to let them know that someone is there. I want to be one of those persons for them. I would also like to work with those who are terminally ill. I think they should have at least one more chance to meet God before they go. I would tell them I do love them and I do care. It is not myself, but Christ in me that has this loving and caring compassion. I want them to see Christ in me. They need to know that somebody cares, I want to be the one to do that. I would like it if there were more stronger believers, but if nobody else wants to, I want to, and I am just waiting for God to come and show me the direction to go.

I want always to help in God's name. I always want to be there for somebody, because when push came to shove and I was going through these real horrible things like withdrawal from the craft, somebody was there for me. In the name of the Lord, somebody was there for me, and allowed me to know that through them Christ was there. Through them, Christ helped me and I survived.

I hope that this has helped someone and in God's name I hope that it changes their lives just like mine has been changed and transformed. God bless!

APPENDIX B

A CHRISTIAN WHO WAS THERE

eter William King has been a foam technician with Parker Brothers for about nine years. Raised Congregationalist, he was confirmed at thirteen. Throughout his life he has always experienced God's protection. At nineteen, after a life-threatening accident, he felt a resurgence to search for God's Word. Because of his own search for God in many different cults and religions, he is able to converse on many topics. He recounts:

We met at work. I operate machinery and Lupe was one of the employees who handles the products produced by it. I suspected she was involved in witchcraft when I saw her pentacle. It was worn in the open. We talked about crystals, past lives, reincarnation, auras, saints, angels, guides, channeling, and so forth.

At that time Lupe had much anger toward churches and Christians who, through the years, hung innocent people as witches.[1] She herself as a child was cast out of church due to God's gift to feel others' pain and see things before they happened. When I first met her, she was decisive, forceful, anger-motivated, but yet she had a desire to help people in need physically, mentally, emotionally, spiritually through the use of "spirit" guides. She was always consulting the tarot cards before acting. She continually read auras, colors, and horoscopes using crystals. She was also always ready to socialize and drink. All these actions she justified, while she imposed her own will on others: "I will do this," "You will do that."

Even though Lupe felt she was not doing anything wrong when she called on angels to cast circles and when she called on guides for help or information, I knew they were not from God the Father, Son, or Holy Spirit. I had read Frank Peretti's books *This Present Darkness* and *Piercing The Darkness*[2] and really felt demonic forces in use.

What approach did I use to draw her away from witchcraft? I did not judge her, but I gently led. I started with prayer, asking one church in Florida and one in New Hampshire to be my prayer warriors. I offered a book[3] for her to read that shows how the Spirit of God overcomes great adversity while it also lifted the heart and mind. I can only say that the Holy Spirit led me because I had been going through a rough separation with my wife. I had found a Spirit-filled church, but working on the off shift, I needed someone to confide in during work. I was ignorant and naive to my own dangerous situation, not knowing how pervasive witchcraft was in Salem.

Lupe had a dream that I could tell was the turning point. She stood between her teacher and myself. We were pulling her in opposite directions, one on each arm. She said she thought we would tear her in two. Darkness surrounded everything except for a light from above. She said his face was filled with anger, while mine was calm. After telling me about her dream, I knew it was the decisive moment for her. I said, "Don't go to him and don't go to me, but go to the light." I can only say the Spirit put that thought in me, because it was an answer that produced tears in my eyes and showed no personal desire to win her, but rather I gave her to God's care.

How else did I draw her away from witchcraft? When she was strongly opinionated about something, I would not refute it, but rather I might say, "I disagree," and I would show her through books or scripture. I used prayer, personal life experiences, books, friendship, compassion, whatever the Holy Spirit gave me at the time. I do not know that I consciously said I wanted to save Lupe, but I prayed over it and was led.

Her strong spirit made leaps and bounds through pain of loss. She lost her Wiccan family and her children. (Now they live with their father.) Old ways die hard. In a year and a half she had completely rid herself and her surroundings of all things having to do with witchcraft. Now she is convicted in word, deed, and even thoughts, by the Holy Spirit. Now she lives out Jesus' prayer to God in heaven: "Not my will, but thy will be done." She now has *righteous* anger and indignation over injustice, immorality, and blasphemous or ungodly actions, words, and thoughts. And she is much more compassionate.

What do I recommend to other Christians who want to help those in goddess worship and witchcraft? You must pray, pray, pray, gently lead, be patient, persevere, love the truth, and know the Bible. I never felt attracted to witchcraft myself, but felt I had to be on guard for spiritual attack against her, her children, myself, or my children. So we constantly had prayers of protection. I not only used scriptural prayers defeating Satan and his workers but also gave her copies of prayer books.[4]

Remember that the one God made and gave power to everything. Why get a distortion of his power and love by using a god or goddess that shows only a small portion of his wholeness and holiness? The one God supplies all our needs. When we are in unity with him, his grace abounds. God's love shows through as his will is active in our lives and his blessings and peace fill our beings. We need nothing but the one God.

In reality the witches and others are used by demonic forces at war even among themselves to gain control of those using the new age occult cult powers or practices. The demonic forces always start by looking beautiful and giving all good things, but eventually as the person gets more involved they are ensnared and controlled by the very forces they have expected to control. This is a truth they can not be told right off because they will either become rebellious or afraid to fight.

God worked through me by my not putting her down for being a witch and by my treating her as a person worthy of friendship. God worked through her stubbornness and strength when her teacher told her he would not allow her to read Christian books. You never could tell Lupe not to do something then, but now she gives thought before being rebellious. Her strength carried her out of their circle as God drew Lupe back.

Pilgrim Church was extremely helpful, too, by accepting openly the gifts God has given people and using them to have a whole church to do God's will more fully. Lupe felt she actually fit in this church and could use her gifts without being condemned, but rather encouraged. What a difference this view of a church allowed! A deeper, richer growth of the Word in her blossomed. Once she gains a truth it is not lost in her but becomes a part of her to use and teach.

Praise God for the victories large and small!

"FATHER" (PATĒR) IN THE BIBLE[1]

I. *Literal use: a man who can conceive children*
e.g., Herod, father of Archelaus
Matt. 2:22; 4:21–22; 8:21; 10:21, 35, 37; 15:4–5; 19:5, 19,
29; 21:31; Mark 1:20; 5:40; 9:21, 24; 13:12; 7:10–12; 10:7,
19, 29; 15:21; Luke 1:59, 62, 67; 2:33; 8:51; 9:42, 59; 12:53;
14:26; 15:6, 12, 17–18, 20–22, 27–29; 18:20; John 4:53; Acts
7:4, 14, 20; 16:1, 3; 28:8; 1 Cor. 5:1; Eph. 5:31; 6:2 (honor);
Isa. 45:10

II. *God is Father of Jesus not by physical intercourse nor creation*
Luke 1:35; 2:49; John 1:14; 2:16; 5:18; 10:33–36; Col. 1:3
(vs. Luke 2:48; 3:23; 4:22; John 6:42 son of Joseph)

III. *Synecdoche (one person who represents a larger entity)*
one person who begins something, as a nation, or who represents
someone who begins something, e.g., Abraham, father of Israel
ancestor(s)
Gen. 17:4–5; Matt. 3:9; Luke 1:32, 73; 3:8; John 8:39, 53,
56; Acts 7:2; Heb. 7:10; Mark 11:10 (David); John 4:12;
1 Chron. 29:10 (Jacob); Rom. 9:10 (Isaac); *prototype* = Isa.
43:27 (Abraham); Rom. 4:11–12, 16–18 (faith granting
righteousness); James 2:21 (faith demonstrated by action)
ancestors (pl)
Matt. 23:30, 32; Luke 1:17, 55, 72; 6:23, 26; 11:47–48; John
4:20; 6:31, 49, 58; 7:22; Acts 3:13, 25; 4:25; 5:30; 7:11–12,

15, 19, 32, 38–39, 44–45, 51–52; 13:17, 32, 36; 15:10; 22:14;
26:6; 28:25; Rom. 9:5; 11:28; 15:8; 1 Cor. 10:1; Heb. 1:1; 3:9;
8:9; 2 Pet. 3:4

IV. *Parent(s)*
singular: Luke 11:11; Heb. 12:7
plural: Luke 1:17; Eph. 6:4; Col. 3:21; Heb. 11:23 (only
mother mentioned in Exod. 2:2–3); 12:9; 1 John 2:13–14

V. *Source/Creator*
Job 38:28 (parallel to womb v. 29); 17:14

VI. *Metaphor: father, like today's everyday good father*
  A. *a human (or angel) loved and respected*
    1. *someone one imitates/obeys*
       Matt. 10:20 (devil); John 8:39–44; 1 Cor. 4:15 (Paul);
       2 Kings 2:12 (Elisha-Elijah); 13:14 (Joash-Elisha);
       Judg. 17:10
    2. *someone who exhorts*
       1 Thess. 2:11–12 (Paul, Silvanus, Timothy)
    3. *someone for whom one is genuinely concerned*
       Phil. 2:22 (Paul and Timothy)
    4. *someone who champions your cause*
       Job 29:16; Isa. 22:21–22 (ruler)
    5. *someone who adopts you and provides for you*
       Luke 16:24, 27, 30; Job 31:18–19
    6. *someone respected, elders*
       Acts 7:2 ("brothers and sisters" or "ladies and
       gentlemen"[2]); 22:1; 1 Tim. 5:1 (someone who should
       be exhorted, not rebuked)
  B. *God (has no form John 5:37; 6:46)*
    1. *forms humans*
       Deut. 32:6; Isa. 64:8; Mal. 2:10
       therefore deserves honor
       Mal. 1:6; Luke 11:2; John 4:21, 23; Rom. 15:6; Phil.
       4:20; James 3:9
       is unique (Matt. 23:9)
    2. *teaches*
       John 6:45; 8:28; Eph. 1:17
    3. *works*
       John 5:17; 15:1 (vinegrower); Matt. 15:13 (farms)
    4. *forgives*
       Ps. 103:13; Matt. 6:14–15; Mark 11:25; 2 Cor. 1:3

       5. *someone one obeys* (cf. Jer. 2:27; Ezek. 16:3, 45)
Matt. 26:39, 42; Mark 14:36; Luke 22:42; John 8:42; 14:21, 31 (obeys out of love); 15:10; 2 Cor. 6:18; 1 John 2:15–16

       6. *gets glory when children do good*
Matt. 5:16; John 14:13

       7. *loves, especially when obeyed*
John 10:17; 15:9; 2 Thess. 2:16; 1 John 3:1

       8. *disciplines*
Heb. 12:7–11 (but only for child's good); Prov. 3:12

       9. *provides and protects*
Ps. 68:5–6; Isa. 63:16; Jer. 3:4, 19; 31:9; Matt. 6:26, 32; Luke 23:46; John 6:32; 12:27; 17:11; 1 Thess. 3:11 (helps one travel); Jude 1

     10. *appreciates thanks*
Col. 1:12; 3:17; Eph. 5:20
(#5–9 also fit under VIII)

VII. *Other Metaphor for God: Idealized, exceptional, "perfect" Parent* (Matt. 5:48)

       1. *Creates—world*
Matt. 11:25; Luke 10:21; 1 Cor. 8:6; Eph. 3:14; 4:6; John 5:21, 26; Rom. 6:4; Gal. 1:1 (raises from dead); 1 John 1:2

       2. *Gives only good gifts to children*
Matt. 7:11; Luke 11:13; James 1:17

       3. *Knows what people need before they ask*
Matt. 6:8–9, 32; Luke 12:30

VIII. *Metaphor: Father-Ruler*

    A. *God as Ruler/Judge*

       1. *has a kingdom with army (of angels)*
Matt. 18:10, 14; 26:29, 53; Mark 8:38; Luke 9:26; 1 Cor. 15:24; Rev. 3:5

       2. *part of being a ruler is also being a judge with power to punish*
Matt. 18:34–35; John 5:45; 8:49–50; 2 Cor. 11:31; 1 Thess. 3:13; 1 John 2:1

       3. *gives rewards*
Matt. 6:1–6, 18; 10:32–33; 25:34–37 (acknowledges); 1 Thess. 1:3; Rev. 14:1

  4. *has a will that should be obeyed*
   Matt. 7:21; 12:50; 26:42; Mark 14:36; Luke 22:42;
   John 10:18; 37–38; 15:8; 18:11; Gal. 1:3–4; 2 John 9
  5. *gives peace*
   Rom. 1:7; 1 Cor. 1:3; 2 Cor. 1:2; Gal. 1:3; Eph. 1:2;
   2:17–18; 6:23; Phil. 1:2; Col. 1:2; (1 Thess. 1:1);
   2 Thess. 1:1–2; Philem. 3; 1 Tim. 1:2; 2 Tim. 1:2; Tit.
   1:4; 2 John 3
  6. *God is an ideal judge and king*
   a. *not limited to national interests, always merciful, not*
    wanting even one being to be lost
    Matt. 5:44–48; 10:29; 18:10, 14; 28:19; Luke
    6:32–36; 2 Cor. 1:3–4; 1 Tim. 1:2
   b. *cares for widow, impartial*
    James 1:27; 1 Pet. 1:17
   c. *all powerful*
    John 10:29; Gal. 1:1
B. *Jesus as Heir* (by nature)
  1. *The ruler appoints Jesus as heir*
   Heb. 1:5
  2. *The ruler has given all power to Jesus*
   Matt. 11:27; 16:27; Mark 8:38; Luke 9:26; 10:22;
   John 3:35; 5:27; 6:37; 10:29; 13:3; 16:15; Heb. 1:5
  3. *The ruler sends son as savior*
   1 John 4:14
  4. *The ruler reveals identity of heir*
   Matt. 16:17; John 1:18
  5. *The ruler wants heir to represent king and is sent by king*
   John 5:19, 36, 43; 6:27, 57; 8:18–19, 27–28, 38, 54;
   10:25, 30, 37; 12:28, 49–50; 10:32, 36, 38; 13:1
   (returns); 14:6, 12, 20, 24, 28; 15:23; 16:3, 10, 17,
   25–28, 32; 17:1, 5, 21, 24–26; 20:21; 1 John 2:23
  6. *The ruler wants heir to be recognized and honored*
   John 5:22–23; 6:40; 20:17; Acts 2:33; Phil. 2:11; 2 Pet.
   1:17
  7. *The ruler intimately communicates with heir*
   Matt. 11:27; Luke 10:22; John 5:20; 10:15; 11:41–42;
   14:6–7
   but some information is unique to father
   Matt. 24:36; Mark 13:32; Acts 1:7

8. *The ruler also sends Spirit as teacher*
   John 14:26; 15:26
9. *Heir also called "father" when ruler*
   Isa. 9:6

C. *Humans as heirs/members of kingdom (by adoption):*
1. *God chooses heirs to kingdom who are given power and honor*
   Matt. 13:43; 18:19; 20:23; 25:34; Luke 12:32; 22:29; 24:49 (power); John 6:44, 65; 12:26; 14:2 (mansion); 15:15–16; 16:23; Acts 1:4; Rom. 8:15–17; Gal. 3:29–4:2, 6; Eph. 1:3; 1 Pet. 1:2–4; 1 John 3:1; Rev. 1:6; 2:26–28; 3:21
2. *God chooses David as "son"*
   2 Sam. 7:13–16; 1 Chron. 17:13; 22:10; 28:6; Ps. 89:26–37
3. *Ruler intimately communicates with heirs*
   Matt. 11:25–26; 16:17; Luke 10:21; 1 John 1:3; (2:14)
4. *Heirs acknowledge, obey, and represent father*
   1 John 1:22–24; 2 John 4, 9

APPENDIX **D**

BIBLE STUDY GUIDELINES

These eight Bible studies were organized for groups or individual study. They can also be texts for sermons. They can be given by themselves as a basic class on God's nature and service to and outside the church followed by reading of this book, or each class can follow the reading of a corresponding chapter in the book. They amplify and do not simply repeat chapter content. Each participant needs a Bible. The questions can be asked by the group leader or xeroxed and given to smaller groups to answer. Each class should take about one hour. Group coordinators should feel free to adapt these studies as appropriate to each group.

▼ I. God Is Unique

(chs. 1, 2, 3, 4) (1 class)

Read 1 Kings 18:1, 17–45. One interesting way to read aloud a passage is to divide it by parts: narrator, Elijah, Ahab, God, servant, people, prophets of Baal. Three to five individuals can read aloud the individual parts. The rest of the class can be divided between "people" and "prophets."

v. 19 Who is invited to Mount Carmel? What do you know about Baal and Asherah?

["Asherim" in the plural are "groves." Asherah or Astarte was a Canaanite fertility mother-goddess, associated with the sea, trees, and wooden poles, consort of El, mother of seventy gods including Baal. "Baal" means "master." Baal is the god Hadad, god of rain and storm, another fertility-god of Canaan. Anat is his sister. He was associated with the bull and wore bull horns on his helmet. Both were worshiped in specific natural locales. See also Judg. 2:13; 3:7; 1 Sam. 7:3–4; 1 Kings 15:13; 16:30–33; 2 Kings 17:16; 21:7; 23:4; Jer. 2:8; 7:9.]

Had Elijah ever warned these false prophets that what they were doing was wrong? (v. 18)

vv. 26–38 Compare the pagan worship (vv. 26–29) to Elijah's worship (vv. 30–38).

Are Baal and Astarte worshiped today? What similarities do these deities and their worship have to ancient times?

v. 21 What is the choice Elijah has for the people? See the NRSV "go limping" or JB "hobble" translations for *pāsaḥ*. The same verb occurs in v. 26.

v. 22 Does Elijah think being outnumbered will make a difference in the final outcome?

vv. 1, 23–24 What are the two miracles Elijah will do?

v. 27 How does Elijah mock Baal? Does Baal have a form? Literally Elijah says: "Call in a great voice because he is a god who is meditating or who is temporarily withdrawn to himself or who is on a longer journey by himself, if not he is sleeping and must be awakened."

vv. 33–34 Why does Elijah have so much water placed on the altar?

vv. 36–37 To what does Elijah appeal in prayer?

vv. 38–39 How do the people respond?

v. 40 We are told that "the wages of sin" is death in Romans 6:23 and Numbers 17:12–13. That truth is vividly shown here. In the new covenant, Jesus receives the death from the sin of humankind, so that good news can be preached to all.

What are the problems with worshiping both the God of the Bible and other deities? How is the God of the Bible unlike and like Baal and Asherah?

Summary

The Bible teaches that God is unique. Choices have to be made. Only the God of the Bible is holy and all-powerful.

Application

Do you need to make a choice today? Do you honor or give thanks to anyone or anything that God made instead of honoring God? (See

Rom. 1:21). Do you need to trust God to prove God's existence in your life or in someone else's life? Or, has God already proven God's presence in your life, but you have not gone on to thank God and live in the knowledge that "the Lord is God"?

▼ II. God Has No Form

(chs. 1, 2, 5, 7) (1 class)

Read Deuteronomy 4:12–20, 23–24. See also Num. 23:19; 1 Sam. 15:29; Hos. 11:9.

vv. 12–15 Who speaks and to whom? What did the Israelites *not* see? What are the five physical senses? What sense could the Israelites use to perceive God?

vv. 16–19 What examples of "forms" does Moses list? "Form" *(tĕ-mûnāh)* occurs in Deut. 4:12, 15, 16, 23, 25. In Deut. 5:8 and Exod. 20:4 all these examples of "forms" fit under one of three categories: something in "heaven above," "on the earth beneath," or "in the water under the earth." Fit the nine items of Deut. 4:16–19 under one of these three categories and then find contemporary deities that would correspond. Chapters 1–2 may be helpful. For example, Diana would be an example of either a female or the moon, from the "heaven above" or "the earth beneath."

Does Moses think God's "form" was fire?

v. 19 Compare with Romans 1:18–23.

v. 20 How is the Lord different from these potential idols?

vv. 23–24 Why is an idol a breaking of this covenant?

By looking at the parallel verse, what is the main point the author is making with each description of God?

Summary

God is described as not in the form of human, male, female, as well as animal, bird, creeper, fish, sun, moon, or stars.

Application

How can an artist portray God? Do you pray to a certain mental image of God? If you pray to a mental image of God, do you think God approves or disapproves?

▼ III. Humans Are Created in God's Likeness

(chs. 2, 5) (1 class)
Read Genesis 1:26–27.

Are humans created in God's "form" *(tĕmûnāh)* (Deut. 4:12) or "image"? The Hebrew Bible uses *ṣelem* and *dĕmût* for "image" in Genesis 1:26–28. What clues in the context of vv. 26–27 explain what "image" means? The verb *dāmāh*, from which the noun *dĕmût* is formed, means "to be like." What comparisons are made in the following passages? *Dĕmût* occurs in Gen. 5:3; 2 Kings 16:10; (2 Chron. 4:3; Pss. 17:12; 58:4 (5); Isa. (13:4;) 40:18; Ezek. 1:5, 10, (13, 16, 22,) 26, 28; 8:2; (10:1, 10, 21–22;) 23:15; Dan. 10:16. Was this "image" lost after the fall? See Gen. 5:1–2.

Ṣelem occurs in Num. 33:52; 1 Sam. 6:5, 11; 2 Kings 11:18; (2 Chron. 23:17; Ezek. 7:20; 16:17; 23:14; Amos 5:26. In what way are humans like pagan idols? The noun *ṣelem* comes from the verb *ṣālal,* "to give shadow." In what way are we humans "shadows" of God? In what way are we not of God's same substance? How does being created in God's image affect the way we treat people? See Gen. 9:6; James 3:9; (4:14; Pss. 39:4–6; 73:18–20.)

Read Col. 3:10–11. How do the diverse people listed in v. 11 show the Creator's "image"?

Summary

Nothing on earth is God yet everything God created is *like* God. Humans in loving relationship are a living metaphor of God but they do not have God's literal form.

Application

How would you like to treat humans differently as a result of this study? Name one person to whom you want to act differently.

▼ IV. God Is Known by Metaphors

(ch. 7) (2 classes)
Read Deut. 32:18.

Find the three metaphors for God in this sentence. (A metaphor is an implied comparison between two things of unlike nature that yet have something in common, so that one or more properties of the first are attributed to the second.)

God Is a Rock

Rock is a fairly common metaphor for God. What kind of "rock" (*ṣûr*) did Moses have in mind? Look up the following passages and collate all the information you can find on the types and uses of this rock.

Exod. 33:21; 1 Chron. 11:15; Pss. 27:5; 31:3; 61:3(4); 71:3; 94:22; Isa. 2:10; Job 14:18; 24:8; Job 29:6; Ps. 81:17; Judg. 6:21; 13:19; 2 Sam. 21:10; Job 19:24; 22:24; 1 Sam. 24:3; Prov. 30:19; Plural: Josh. 5:2–3

Look at the immediate contexts of Deut. 32:4, 15, 18, 30–31, 37. When Moses uses the metaphor "rock" for God, what qualities of God is he highlighting?

An important incident in Moses' life happened around a rock. Read Exod. 17:1–7 and Num. 20:2–13. (Optional: read Deut. 8:15; Pss. 78:20; 105:41; 114:8; Isa. 48:21; 1 Cor. 10:3–4).

List in columns next to each other: the literal characteristics of *ṣûr*, characteristics of the rock at Horeb or Meribah (Exod. 17:1–7 and Num. 20:2–13), the qualities of God that came out in Deut. 32 whenever "rock" was used.

Here are my lists:

Literal char. of *ṣûr*:	Characteristics of rock at Horeb or Meribah	Qualities of God
a rock in the side of the mountain is firm, strong, and big	instead of people stoning Moses, Moses struck rock and water came out	v. 4 perfect, just, faithful, no deceit
a landmark		v. 15 made and saved Israelites
high, a refuge		v. 18 bore Israelites
it might be a mountain		v. 30 deity
a potential source of oil		v. 31 unique
it could be used as an altar or a memorial tablet		v. 37 refuge

Literal char. of *ṣûr*:	Characteristics of rock at Horeb or Meribah	Qualities of God

rocks in brooks
a place for goats or
   serpents to dwell
(in plural, flint which
   could be made into
   knives for circumcision)		

Which literal characteristics of "rocks" are images for which qualities of God?

In what way did the incident at Horeb affect Moses' use of "rock" as a metaphor?

Which literal characteristics of "rocks" are *unlike* God's qualities?

Some contemporary writers accentuate the difference between metaphor as vocative title for God, metaphor as only description of God, simile for God, and a pagan or human metaphor. Classify the following references into one of those four categories: Deut. 32:4, 15, 18, 30–31; 2 Sam. 22:32, 47; 23:3; Pss. 18:2(3), 46(47); 19:14(15); 28:1; 62:2(3), 6–7; 89:26(27); 92:15(16); 144:1; Isa. 8:14; 26:4; 51:1; Hab. 1:12.

Do you notice any difference in the use of "rock" in these different categories?

Why might "rock" have been an important metaphor for residents of Israel?

Summary

"Rock" is not a frequent metaphor for contemporary Christians in the United States, yet it is a frequently used metaphor for God in Old Testament times. God, like a massive rock, is constant, always there, protective, open (without deceit). Like only the rock at Horeb, God is also life-giving. Unlike earthly rocks, God as a rock is personal and intimate.

Application

How do you *feel* about using inanimate objects as metaphors, even titles, for God?

If you had to choose one inanimate object to describe God, what would it be? Draw it. Explain (or let others guess) what your object illustrates about God.

What danger would arise if your object were treated as God?

▼ V. God Bears Children

Moses was inspired when he sang this song. Literally, Deut. 32:18 reads: "Rock that bore you—you neglected, you forgot God bearing you as a child." Most Hebrew sentences begin with the main verb, followed by the subject, then the object. Moses begins the first clause with the object ("rock") and ends it with the main verb ("you neglected"). He has made an effort to highlight the metaphor "rock." But then, he modifies "rock" with the verb "that bore you" *(yālad)*. In what way(s) do "that bore you" modify the type of "rock" Moses describes?

Moses uses two more metaphors for God in v. 18, two synonyms for bearing children *(yālad* and *ḥûl)*.

Some people currently debate whether God is more "masculine" or "feminine." Look up *yālad* in Gen. 4:18; 5:3; 22:20; Prov. 23:22, 25. Which of these references refer to men, which to women? [See Isa. 45:10. *Yālad* is used of "father," *ḥûl* of "mother." In Job 15:7 *yālad* and *ḥûl* are used as synonyms of the creation of the first human.]

To what does *yālad* literally refer? See for example: Gen. 25:24; 38:27; Deut. 4:25; Jer. 13:21; 14:5; 17:1; 29:6; Ezek. 31:6.

To what does *ḥûl* (or *hālāh*) literally refer? It seems to refer to a strong physical feeling, especially of pain or fear. It is never explicitly used of a father siring a child. Check a few samples in each category:

a. (labor) Pss. 48:7; 51:7; 90:2 (creation); Prov. 8:24–25 (creation); Job 39:1 (goats); Isa. 13:8; 21:3; 26:17–18; 51:2; 54:1; 66:7–8; Jer. 4:31; 6:24; 22:23; 50:43; Mic. 4:9–10.
b. (trembling/pain, probably like that of a woman in labor) Exod. 15:14; Deut. 2:25; 1 Sam. 31:3 (wound); 1 Chron. 10:3; 16:30; Esther 4:4; Job 6:10; 26:5; Pss. 29:8; 55:5; 77:16(17); 96:9; 97:4; 114:7; Isa. 23:5; Jer. 4:19; 5:3, 22; 51:29 (land); Hos. 11:6; Joel 2:1; Hab. 3:10; Zech. 9:5.
c. (powerful) Jer. 23:19; 30:23 (storm).

d. (dance) Exod. 15:20; 32:19; Judg. 11:34; 21:21, 23; 1 Sam.
   18:6; 21:12; 29:5; Pss. 30:11(12); 87:7; 149:3; 150:4; Song of
   Sol. 6:13(7:1); Jer. 31:13.

Which of the preceding meanings fits the context of Deut. 32:18,
"God who gave you birth"? See 32:8–15.

To whom did God give birth? See 32:9–19.

How do "neglect" and "forgetting" contrast with birth images?
How did the Israelites "forget" God? See Deut. 31:27–29; 32:5–6,
15–17.

In what way is the strong physical pain of birth similar to *and* different from God's action toward the Israelites? Does God "give birth"
to all believers?

Summary

To reduce God to any one image is to limit God greatly. The Bible
uses inanimate and human images to help us understand God's paradoxical nature. God is as secure as a rock, as caring as a parent.

Application

Do you find these metaphors of birth helpful or not? Why? What
danger would arise if God were a literal father or mother? In what
way has God treated you like a father or mother? Do you think you
need to personalize your previous inanimate drawing or had you
done so already?

▼ VI. Ministry to the Church

(chs. 7, 10) (1 class)

List different versions of 2 Timothy 2:2 and 1 Timothy 2:5–6.
Include versions used by the group members. Eighteen versions are
listed on the next pages. Do not tell the participants which version
they are until all the following questions have been answered. Ask
the same questions of all versions:

Does Paul believe in one, two, or three Gods?

Is he highlighting Jesus' maleness or humanity? Why is the answer
important?

Did Jesus pay, by his life, to free all people or some people?

Does Paul exclude women in 2 Tim. 2:2 from among those who can teach others?

What are the main qualities Paul wants Timothy to find in the people to whom he will pass on what Timothy learned?

Which version do you prefer? Why? Which version(s) make(s) *you* feel most included in its content?

Which is the most accurate?

Versions 2, 4, 6, 8, 11 (all in italics) are revisions of 1, 3, 5, 7, and 10, respectively. How is the revised version different? Is the revised version clearer or more confusing?

Different versions of 1 Timothy 2:5–6 and 2 Timothy 2:2:

1. a. For there is one God, and one mediator between God and men, the man Christ Jesus; who gave himself a ransom for all, to be testified in due time (1 Tim. 2:5–6).
   b. And the things that thou hast heard of me among many witnesses, the same commit thou to faithful men, who shall be able to teach others also (2 Tim. 2:2).
2. a. *For there is one God and one Mediator between God and men, the Man Christ Jesus, who gave Himself a ransom for all, to be testified in due time,*
   b. *And the things that you have heard from me among many witnesses, commit these to faithful men, who will be able to teach others also.*
3. a. For there is one God, and there is one mediator between God and men, the man Christ Jesus, who gave himself as a ransom for all, the testimony to which was borne at the proper time.
   b. And what you have heard from me before many witnesses entrust to faithful men who will be able to teach others also.
4. a. *For there is one God; there is also one mediator between God and humankind, Christ Jesus, himself human, who gave himself a ransom for all this was attested at the right time.*
   b. *and what you have heard from me through many witnesses entrust to faithful people who will be able to teach others as well.*
5. a. For there is one God, and also one mediator between God and men, Christ Jesus, himself man, who sacrificed himself to win freedom for all mankind, so providing, at the fitting time, proof of the divine purpose;

b. You heard my teaching in the presence of many witnesses; put that teaching into the charge of men you can trust, such men as will be competent to teach others.

6. a. *For there is one God, and there is one mediator between God and man, Christ Jesus, himself man, who sacrificed himself to win freedom for all mankind, revealing God's purpose at God's good time;*
b. *you heard my teaching in the presence of many witnesses; hand on that teaching to reliable men who in turn will be qualified to teach others.*

7. a. For there is one God, and there is one who brings God and men together, the man Christ Jesus, who gave himself to redeem all men. That was the proof, at the right time, that God wants all men to be saved,
b. Take the words that you heard me preach in the presence of many witnesses, and give them into the keeping of men you can trust, men who will be able to teach others also.

8. a. *For there is one God, and there is one who brings God and human beings together, the man Christ Jesus, who gave himself to redeem the whole human race. That was the proof at the right time that God wants everyone to be saved,*
b. *Take the teachings that you heard me proclaim in the presence of many witnesses, and entrust them to reliable people, who will be able to teach others, also.*

9. a. There is only one God, and Christ Jesus is the only one who can bring us to God. Jesus was truly human, and he gave himself to rescue all of us. God showed us this at the right time.
b. You have often heard me teach. Now I want you to tell these same things to followers who can be trusted to tell others.

10. a. There is only one God. And there is only one way that people can reach God. That way is through Jesus Christ, who is also a man. Jesus gave himself to pay for the sins of all people. Jesus is proof that God wants all people to be saved. And that proof came at the right time.
b. You and many others have heard what I have taught. You should teach the same thing to some people you can trust. Then they will be able to teach it to others.

11. a. *There is one God and one way human beings can reach God. That way is through Jesus, who is himself human. He gave himself as a payment to free all people. He is proof that came at the right time.*

b. *You should teach people whom you can trust the things you and many others have heard me say. Then they will be able to teach others.*

12. a. For there is only one God, and there is only one mediator between God and mankind, himself a man, Christ Jesus, who sacrificed himself as a ransom for them all. He is the evidence of this, sent at the appointed time, and

b. You have heard everything that I teach in public; hand it on to reliable people so that they in turn will be able to teach others.

13. a. For there is one God and one mediator between God and men, the man Christ Jesus, who gave himself as a ransom for all men—the testimony given in its proper time.

b. And the things you have heard me say in the presence of many witnesses entrust to reliable men who will also be qualified to teach others.

14. a. That God is on one side and all the people on the other side, and Christ Jesus, himself man, is between them to bring them together, by giving his life for all mankind.

b. For you must teach others those things you and many others have heard me speak about. Teach these great truths to trustworthy men who will, in turn, pass them on to others.

15. a. That there is one God, and there is one mediator between God and mankind—the man Christ Jesus, who gave Himself as a ransom for all, a fact that was shown to be true at the proper time.

b. The things you have heard me say in the presence of many witnesses, hand on to those you can trust and who are able to teach others too.

16. a. For God is one; and one is mediator between God and man, the Man Christ Jesus, who gave himself as a ransom in behalf of all, to be attested in due time.

b. The teachings which you have heard from me, attested by many witnesses, deliver into the keeping of faithful men, who in their turn will be able to teach others also.

17. a. For God [is] one, one [is] also mediator of God and humans, human Christ Jesus, who having given himself a ransom in behalf of all, [is] the witness for [our] own times;

b. and what you heard from me through many witnesses, these things entrust to faithful people, who will be able also to teach others.

18. a. εἷς γὰρ θεός, εἷς καὶ μεσίτης θεοῦ καὶ ἀνθρώπων, ἄνθρωπος Χριστὸς Ἰησοῦς, **6** ὁ δοὺς ἑαυτὸν ἀντίλυτρον ὑπὲρ πάντων, τὸ μαρτύριον καιροῖς ἰδίοις.

b. καὶ ἃ ἤκουσας παρ᾽ ἐμοῦ διὰ πολλῶν μαρτύρων, ταῦτα παράθου πιστοῖς ἀνθρώποις, οἵτινες ἱκανοὶ ἔσονται καὶ ἑτέρους διδάξαι.

These versions have been cited:
1. King James Version, 1611; 2. NKJV, 1982; 3. Revised Standard Version, 1971; 4. NRSV, 1989; 5. New English Bible, 1970; 6. REB, 1992; 7. Today's English Version, 1966; 8. TEV, 1992; 9. Contemporary English Version, 1991; 10. New Century Version, 1988; 11. NCV, 1991; 12. Jerusalem Bible, 1966; 13. New International Version, 1984; 14. The Living Bible, 1971; 15. The New Translation, 1990; 16. The New Testament in Modern English, 1952; 17. The author's, Aída Besançon Spencer, own literal translation. 18. The Greek New Testament 3d ed. (This version is the most accurate.)
Any surprising conclusions?

Summary

Many readers of the Bible have misinterpreted 2 Timothy 2:2 by excluding women (although Paul used the generic *anthrōpos*) and misinterpreted 1 Timothy 2:5–6 by highlighting Jesus' maleness (although Paul again repeatedly used *anthrōpos,* not the male specific *anēr*). As we too apply God's good news to women, we need to be careful of our language and our actions.

Application

What one step can you take in your church to make sure women as well as men feel included? How is the best way to bring it about without inciting a lot of opposition and misunderstanding?

▼ VII. Ministry Outside the Church: Responding to Witches

(ch. 10, App. A & B) (2 classes)
King Saul and Witchcraft

A. *We Need a Proper Perspective on Witchcraft*

Background passages are Exod. 17:8–15; Deut. 25:17–19.

Read 1 Sam. 15:1–29: narrator, Samuel, Saul, God, messenger (v. 12)

vv. 1–3, 18, 21 What did God want Saul to do and why?

v. 6 How did Saul treat the Kenites? Why? How were they different from the Amalekites?

vv. 8–12, 15, 21, 24 Who or what did Saul spare? Why might Saul have spared them?

vv. 19, 22 What does God prefer: sacrifice, worship, or obedience?

v. 23 What is worse? rebellion, divination, stubbornness, sin, or idolatry? How is witchcraft like idolatry?

vv. 23, 26, 28 How did Saul's action affect his role?

v. 29 Is God human? How, then, is God different from humans? What is the main point *you* drew from this passage?

Summary

Obedience is the key quality God wants. Disobedience is as displeasing to God as witchcraft and idolatry.

B. *What Believers Should* **Not** *Do*

Background: In Old Testament times believers (and nonbelievers) seem to wait in Sheol for Jesus' resurrection:

Job 3:11–19; 26:5–6; Ps. 139:8; Num. 16:30; Isa. 14:9–11; Dan. 12:2–3; Matt. 27:51–53; 1 Pet. 3:18–20.

Read 1 Samuel 28:3–25: narrator, Saul, servants, witch, Samuel.

vv. 3–4 How had the situation changed from 1 Sam. 15? (Saul was enforcing Lev. 19:31; Deut. 18:9–14.)

vv. 3–7, 11, 15 What motivated Saul to seek out a witch (literally, "a woman owner of necromancer")?

v. 9 Did the witch at Endor want to break Saul's laws?

v. 13 What did Samuel's spirit look like?

v. 14 How did Saul respond?

v. 15 How did Samuel respond?

vv. 16–18 How did Saul's assessment of the problem (vv. 3–7, 11, 15) compare to Samuel's?

v. 19 Where will Saul go?

vv. 20–22 How does the witch treat Saul? Why?

What is the main point *you* drew from this passage?

Summary

Saul is motivated by fear, lack of response from God, and dependence on an authority figure to force Samuel's spirit back. His real need was to obey God.

Application

In what way did Saul harm the witch's spiritual development? How might believers today harm those who have stopped witchcraft?

▼ VIII. We Need to Treat Witches Differently

(The class may need to be divided into three groups, each group reporting on their findings.)

A *magos* was a neutral term. It could refer to wise persons, teachers, priests, physicians from Persia, Mesopotamia, and Arabia, or to someone who uses the arts of magic. The New Testament recounts three different "magicians" with three different spiritual states. We need, likewise, to treat people differently after we analyze their spiritual state.

A. Magi from the East

Read Matthew 2:1–12: narrator, wise people, Herod.

v. 1 What specifically are we told about the "magicians"? (*Magos* is in the plural generic form.) What additional information comes from later tradition?

vv. 1–2 Who do they seek? Who do they ask? What is their goal?

v. 3 How did Herod respond? Why?

v. 5 Do these "magicians" seem to know about the Old Testament prophecy of the place of the Messiah's birth? What information could they have gotten from Jews in exile? (Esther 1, Ezra 1)

v. 8 What is Herod's deceitful offer?

vv. 2, 7, 9 How did they find Jesus? Compare to Romans 1:19–20. (The early church thought Num. 24:17 was a prophecy of the star [Athanasius, *DeIncarnatione* 33].)

vv. 10–11 How did they respond?

v. 12 Compare the magicians' action to Romans 13:1. Why was disobedience to Herod appropriate?

v. 16 How old was Jesus at the time of this visit?

In summary, what was the Magi's spiritual condition? How would you, as a believer, treat them? How would you enable their spiritual growth?

Summary

These unnamed astrologers from the East were eager in intention and action to follow Christ.

For background on Magi see Alfred Edersheim, *The Life and Times of Jesus the Messiah* (Grand Rapids: Eerdmans, 1947) I. ch. 7; and Colin J. Humphreys, "The Star of Bethlehem, A Comet in 5 B.C. and the Date of Christ's Birth," *Tyndale Bulletin* 43(May 1992): 31–56. The Magi were thought to be "three" because three gifts were given in v. 11. Chrysostom thought twelve Magi came. Edersheim thought the Magi were from Arabia. The center of "astrolism" (study of the stars) was Mesopotamia. Those involved in astrolism would be comparable to today's nuclear physicist because of the advanced mathematics used. "Astrology" is more specifically the prediction for humans based on the effect of the heavenly bodies on human destiny.

B. Simon of Samaria

Read Acts 8:9–24: narrator, Samaritans (v. 10), Simon, Peter

vv. 9–11 What was Simon's nickname? Why? Was he influential?

v. 12 What was the core of Philip's message?

vv. 12–13 Did Simon convert to Christianity? What did Simon do after being baptized? Who was more powerful, Peter or Simon?

v. 16 Why is baptism in the name of the triune God necessary?

vv. 18–20 How did Simon interpret a symbol literally and thereby do wrong? Why was an offer of money wrong? What did Simon really want?

vv. 21–23 What was Simon's real need? Did Peter think Simon would inherit God's gifts? The words ("gall," *cholē* and "bitterness," *pikria*) Peter used to describe Simon were used in the Greek Septuagint translation of Deut. 29:17 (18). What is Peter's implied point? "Bond," *sundesmos*, of "iniquity," *adikia*, was used in Isa. 58:6. What "bonds of iniquity" did God want "loosed" in Isaiah 58:6–7? What light does that phrase shed on Simon's problem? Compare to 1 Timothy 6:6–10.

v. 22 What did Simon need to do?

v. 24 For what did Simon ask? Did he do what Peter commanded?

In summary, what was Simon Magus' spiritual condition? How would you, as a believer, treat him? How would you enable his spiritual growth?

Summary

Simon's spiritual condition is left unsure at the end of this passage. He believes in Jesus, but yet his heart was not right.

The New Testament never gives us a final account of Simon. However, Christians in the second century describe him as returning to evil arts.

Justin Martyr writes:

After Christ's ascent into heaven the demons put forward various men who said that they were gods, and you not only did not persecute them, but thought them worthy of honors. One was a certain Simon, a Samaritan from the village of Gitta, who in the time of Claudius Caesar, through the arts of the demons who worked in him, did mighty works of magic in your imperial city of Rome and was thought to be a god. He has been honored among you as a god by a statue, which was set up on the River Tiber, between the two bridges, with this inscription in Latin, SIMONI DEO SANCTO. Almost all the Samaritans, and a few in other nations, confess this man as their first god and worship him as such, and a woman named Helena, who traveled around with him in those days, and had formerly been a public prostitute, they say was the first Concept produced from him. Then we know of a certain Menander, who was also a Samaritan, from the village of Capparetaea, who had been a disciple of Simon's, and was also possessed by the demons. He deceived many at Antioch by magic arts, and even persuaded his followers that he would never die; there are still some who believe this [as they learned] from him (*First Apology*, 26, 56).

Irenaeus writes:

All those who corrupt the truth and injure the teaching of the Church are the disciples and successors of Simon Magus the Samaritan. Although, in order to deceive others, they do not confess the name of their teacher, yet they teach his views. Setting up the name of Christ Jesus as a kind of decoy, but in one way or another introducing the impiety of Simon, they bring many to destruction, spreading their evil teachings under a good name, and by the sweetness and beauty of the name [of Christ] offering them the bitter and evil poison of the serpent, the prince of the apostasy (*Against Heresies*, I.27).

C.   Elymas Bar-Jesus

Read Acts 13:1–12: narrator, Saul

vv. 1–5 Who traveled to Cyprus? Why? [Barnabas was a native of Cyprus: Acts 4:36.] Had any believers traveled to Cyprus before? To whom had they spoken? Read Acts 11:19–21.

v. 5 What is the "word of God"? Prove your definition by citing a reference in Acts 1–13:12.

vv. 6–10 How is Elymas described? ["Elymas" probably means "sage" or "interpreter of dreams."]

vv. 7–8 Was Sergius Paulus a powerful person? What was his spiritual condition?

v. 8 How did Elymas react to the message of Saul, Barnabas, and John Mark?

vv. 9–11 How did Saul respond to Elymas' interference? "Bar-Jesus" signifies "son of savior." Paul calls him instead "son of devil." A "devil" is a "slanderer." Who did Elymas slander? How?

v. 11 Why did Saul make Elymas blind? What did blindness do to Elymas?

v. 12 How did Sergius Paulus respond? Why?

In summary, what was Elymas' spiritual condition? How would you, as a believer, treat him? How would you enable his spiritual growth?

Summary

Elymas Bar-Jesus was clearly a false prophet who definitely set out to undermine Christianity.

Application

Do you know personally of someone whose spiritual state would be comparable to the witch at Endor, the Eastern Magi, Simon

Magus, or Elymas Bar-Jesus? What steps do you want to take to help them seek Christ?

Side issue: In what way are these four people different from "magicians" such as Houdini?

We can not be sure what happened to Elymas. We do know Barnabas and John Mark return to Cyprus (Acts 15:38). Possibly, the Jewish historian Josephus describes Elymas in *Antiquities,* or probably this account refers not to Elymas but it does show the importance of magi:

> Not long afterwards Drusilla's marriage to Azizus was dissolved under the impact of the following circumstances. At the time when Felix was procurator of Judaea, he beheld her; and, inasmuch as she surpassed all other women in beauty, he conceived a passion for the lady. He sent to her one of his friends, a Cyprian Jew named Atomus, who pretended to be a magician (*magos*), in an effort to persuade her to leave her husband and to marry Felix. Felix promised to make her supremely happy if she did not disdain him. She, being unhappy and wishing to escape the malice of her sister Berenice—for Drusilla was exceedingly abused by her because of her beauty—was persuaded to transgress the ancestral laws and to marry Felix. By him she gave birth to a son whom she named Agrippa (*Antiquities* 20.7.2[142]).

▼ Preface

1. Kathleen Hirsch, "Feminism's New Face," *The Boston Globe Magazine*, 25 (February, 1990): 18–36.

2. Aída Besançon Spencer, "God as Mother, Not Mother as God: A Biblical Feminist Response to the 'New Feminism,'" *Priscilla Papers* 5 (Fall 1991): 6–11.

3. A response to some of the conference ideas may be found in *Priscilla Papers* 8 (Spring 1994).

▼ Introduction

1. See also Sheila Kitzinger, *Being Born* (New York: Grosset and Dunlap, 1986), and Lennart Nilsson, *A Child Is Born,* trans. Clare James (New York: Bantam Doubleday Dell, 1990).

2. Moltmann, Jürgen, *The Spirit of Life: A Universal Affirmation* (Minneapolis: Fortress, 1992), 287; Catherine Keller, *From a Broken Web: Separation, Sexism, and Self* (Boston: Beacon, 1986), 118–19.

3. Moltmann, 157.

4. Shideler, Mary McDermott, *The Theology of Romantic Love: A Study in the Writings of Charles Williams* (Grand Rapids: Eerdmans, 1962), 25.

5. Shideler, 24–26.

6. Fowler, James W., *Stages of Faith: The Psychology of Human Development and the Quest for Meaning* (San Francisco: Harper & Row, 1981), 185.

▼ Chapter 1: *God as Female*

1. Indira A. R. Lakshmanan, "Latter-day Witches Find a Seat in Salem," *The Boston Globe*, 18 July 1993:23–4.

2. "Witches Consider Opening California Academy," *The Boston Globe*, 17 July 1993:3.

3. "Witches Gather in Ark. and March to Promote Religious Freedom for All," *The Boston Globe*, 2 August 1993:3.

4. Beth Wolfensberger, "The Return of the Pagans," *Boston Magazine*, May 1992:62.

5. Aidan A. Kelly estimated there were in 1987 several hundred thousand people in the Gardnerian witchcraft. He states there are more Gardnerian and Gardnerianistic Witches in California than in most of the rest of the United States. "Introduction," *Neo-Pagan Witchcraft I*, ed. A. Kelly (New York: Garland, 1990). Other estimates on the number of self-identified Pagans or members of Wicca run from 10,000 to more than 100,000 people in the United States. Rusty Unger, "Oh, Goddess!" *New York Magazine*, 4 June 1990:42; Margot Adler, *Drawing Down the Moon: Witches, Druids, Goddess-Worshippers, and other Pagans in America Today* (2d ed.; Boston: Beacon, 1986), 108, 455.

6. Many scholars have questioned the actual existence of a universal ancient mother religion, even neo-pagans. Adler, *Moon*, 145, 151; Patricia McGee, writing in the 12 February 1990 edition of *Maclean's Magazine*, noted, "John Hayes, curator of the Greek and Roman department at the Royal Ontario Museum in Toronto, said that the belief in an ancient culture built around goddesses is currently popular. But he said he does not agree with some of Gimbutas's interpretations of the ancient symbols she found. Said Hayes: 'She's got a fantastic wealth of knowledge in the Neolithic and Bronze ages. But we're dealing with prehistory. There are no written records, and some of her statements are quite dogmatic.' Other anthropologists and archeologists say that they question whether it is possible to interpret symbols of any prehistoric era. . . . University of Alberta anthropology professor Ruth Gruhn (said): 'Gimbutas has gone into areas where other archeologists have feared to tread, and some would say she is on thin ice. I would say what she has is a plausible interpretation.' Bruce Trigger, an anthropology professor at Montreal's McGill University, said that, although Gimbutas's theories make 'reasonably good sense,' they can really only be considered 'hunches.' Added Trigger: 'Because she isn't able to show any direct continuity to a written record, it's really hard to build up a convincing argument'" (67).

See also Sally R. Binford, "Are Goddesses and Matriarchies Merely Figments of Feminist Imagination? Myths and Matriarchies." *The Politics of Women's Spirituality: Essays on the Rise of Spiritual Power Within the Feminist Movement*, ed. C. Spretnak (Garden City: Doubleday, 1982), 541–9; Joan B.

Townsend, "The Goddess: Fact, Fallacy and Revitalization Movement," *Goddesses in Religions and Modern Debate,* ed. Larry Hurtado (Atlanta: Scholars, 1990), 179–203.

7. Marija Gimbutas, *The Language of the Goddess* (San Francisco: Harper & Row, 1989), xiv.

8. Elinor W. Gadon, *The Once and Future Goddess* (San Francisco: Harper & Row, 1989), 229–30.

9. *Woman of Power* 21 (Fall 1991): 1.

10. Z. Budapest, "A Witch's Manifesto," *Whole Earth Review,* Spring 1992: 38, 40.

11. Adler, *Moon,* xi, 4, 9.

12. Joseph Campbell, ed., *The Portable Jung* (New York: Penguin, 1976), 60.

13. Starhawk, *Dreaming the Dark: Magic, Sex and Politics* (Boston: Beacon, 1982), 9, 73.

14. Adler, *Moon,* 10–11.

15. Starhawk, *The Spiral Dance: A Rebirth of the Ancient Religion of the Great Goddess* (2d ed.; San Francisco: Harper & Row, 1989), 10–11.

16. Laurie Cabot and Tom Cowan. *Power of the Witch* (New York: Delta, 1989), 10–11, 20.

17. Rosemary Ellen Guiley, "Witchcraft as Goddess Worship," *The Feminist Companion to Mythology,* ed. Carolyne Larrington (London: Pandora, 1992), 417.

18. Lawrence E. Joseph, *Gaia: The Growth of an Idea* (New York: St. Martin's, 1990), 1.

19. Anne S. Baumgartner, *A Comprehensive Dictionary of the Gods* (New York: Carol Communications, 1984), 73.

20. Tal Brooke, "Gaia—A Religion of the Earth: An Overview," *SCP Journal* 16 (1, 1991): 6. See also Tod Connor, "Is the Earth Alive?" *Christianity Today* 37 (January 11, 1993): 25.

21. Stuart Chevre, "The Gaia Hypothesis: Science, Mythology, and the Desecration of God," *SCP Journal* 16 (1, 1991): 28.

22. David Spangler, "The Meaning of Gaia," *In Context* 24 (1990): 45.

23. The idea of the cosmos being one living creature is not new. Plato has the same thought in *Timaeus* 30, 32, 69, 92.

24. Matthew Fox, *Original Blessing: A Primer in Creation Spirituality* (Santa Fe: Bear, 1983), 29, 225–26, 235.

25. Margaret Brearley, "Matthew Fox: Creation Spirituality for the Aquarian Age," *Christian Jewish Relations* 22 (2, 1989): 45.

26. Joseph, *Gaia,* 12.

27. Unger, 46.

28. Jean Shinoda Bolen, *Goddesses in Everywoman* (New York: Harper & Row, 1984), 2, 297–300.

29. Carl Olson, ed., *The Book of the Goddess Past and Present: An Introduction to Her Religion* (New York: Crossroad, 1990), 31–3, 36, 40–2.

30. Olson, *Goddess,* 206.

31. Paula Gunn Allen, *Grandmothers of the Light: A Medicine Woman's Sourcebook* (Boston: Beacon, 1991), 27.

32. Olson, *Goddess,* 202.

33. Olson, *Goddess,* 207, 210, 212, 214–15.

34. R. J. Stewart, *Celtic Gods, Celtic Goddesses* (London: Blandford, 1990), 64. One witch who especially lauds the Celtic goddesses is Laurie Cabot, *Power of the Witch,* 41–5.

35. Kathy Jones, *The Ancient British Goddesses: Her Myths, Legends and Sacred Sites* (Glastonbury: Ariadne, 1991), 7.

36. Carolyne Larrington, "Scandinavia," *Feminist Companion to Mythology,* 160. "Many Pagans simply dismiss Norse Paganism as 'patriarchal.'" "They do not see themselves in any way as part of a universal movement." Adler, *Moon,* 277, 280.

37. Olson, *Goddess,* 244.

38. Karl Rahner and Herbert Vorgrimler, *Theological Dictionary,* ed. Cornelius Ernst, trans. Richard Strachan (New York: Herder & Herder, 1965), 15, 277, 479–80.

Norman L. Geisler notes that the dogma of Mary's bodily assumption into heaven and belief in her exaltation as "Queen of Heaven" seem little more than baptized paganism to many Protestants. Elliot Miller and Kenneth R. Samples, *The Cult of the Virgin: Catholic Mariology and the Apparitions of Mary* (Grand Rapids: Baker, 1992), 12.

39. John J. Delaney, ed., *A Woman Clothed with the Sun: Eight Great Appearances of Our Lady in Modern Times* (New York: Doubleday, 1960), 24, 26–7.

40. Delaney, *Woman,* 83.

41. Miller and Samples, *Cult,* 127. For popular examples of treating Mary as a goddess see ch. 10, David Kinsley, *The Goddesses' Mirror: Visions of the Divine from East and West* (Albany: State University of New York, 1989), 215–60.

42. Elizabeth Gould Davis, *The First Sex* (New York: G. P. Putnam's, 1971), 246. Former Roman Catholic Laurie Cabot was told by priests and nuns that Mary was not divine: "But I never really believed that. She had too much power." *Power of the Witch,* 3.

▼ Chapter 2: *God as Male*

1. Marcy Sheiner, "What Do Men Really Want . . . And Why Should We Care?," *East Bay Express* [Berkeley], 10 July 1992: 1, 10.

2. Betty Friedan, *The Second Stage* (New York: Summit, 1981), 107.

3. Robert Moore and Douglas Gillette, *King, Warrior, Magician, Lover* (San Francisco: Harper & Row, 1990), xvii–xviii.

4. Moore and Gillette, *King, Warrior, Magician, Lover,* xvii.

5. Moore and Gillette, *King, Warrior, Magician, Lover,* xvi, 6.

6. Moore and Gillette, *King, Warrior, Magician, Lover,* 6.

7. Moore and Gillette, *King, Warrior, Magician, Lover,* 135, 145.

8. Moore and Gillette, *King, Warrior, Magician, Lover,* 32.

9. Starhawk, *Dreaming the Dark: Magic, Sex, and Politics* (Boston: Beacon, 1982), 73.

For a Christian analysis (with bibliography) see, for example, Jack Balswick, *Men at the Crossroads: Beyond Traditional Roles and Modern Options* (Downers Grove: InterVarsity, 1992).

To an outside observer, the difference between Jung's and Starhawk's visions seems simply to be of degree and not of kind, whether fragmenting into four aspects working symbiotically or unified indivisibly into one psychoorganism. In reading much of the debate between men's movement writers and witches, and for that matter in Christianity itself in the debate between men and women over women's ministry, one wonders how much we are simply hearing the war of the sexes, initiated by the curse in Genesis 3:16, in action. Starhawk, a skillful writer, draws a delightful scene in *Dreaming the Dark* of fathers parenting (p. 78) that would rival the best of men's movement intentions. But beneath so many positive sentiments and desires on *all* sides lies that age-old combativeness that scars all unredeemed female/male relations, typified for us in Marcy Sheiner's article's quintessential title: "What Do Men Really Want . . . And Why Should We Care?"

Those readers interested in getting beyond the curse's scarring of familial relations are invited to consult the afterword of Aída Besançon Spencer's *Beyond the Curse* (Peabody: Hendrickson, 1985), 138–79, and its follow-up article "More Than 'Vacuum Cleaner Commandos,'" *Priscilla Papers* 5(Winter 1991): 1–3, for my fuller perspective on this issue.

10. Starhawk, *Dreaming the Dark,* 73. New books like William Anderson's *Green Man: The Archetype of Our Oneness with the Earth* (San Francisco: Harper Collins, 1990) explore these other names. Worship of the male god as "the Green Man," for example, has been observed in Great Britain by Welsh-American historian Dr. Gwenfair Walters.

11. Bill McNabb, "The Door Interview: Robert Moore," *The Door* 122(March/April 1992): 13–14.

12. Robert Moore and Douglas Gillette, *The King Within: Accessing the King in the Male Psyche* (New York: Morrow, 1992), 100–102.

13. Moore and Gillette, *King, Warrior, Magician, Lover,* 41.

14. Moore and Gillette, *King, Warrior, Magician, Lover,* 58–59.

15. "Bill and Ted's Bogus Journey" (Orion Pictures Corporation, 1991). The universe is saved in "Bill and Ted's Excellent Adventure" (Nelson Films, Inc., 1989).

16. Sam Keen, *Fire in the Belly* (New York: Bantam, 1991), 16–17.

17. Keen, *Fire in the Belly*, 21, 84.

18. Keen, *Fire in the Belly*, 92–93, 100.

19. Keen, *Fire in the Belly*, 94.

20. Keen, *Fire in the Belly*, 95–96.

21. Robert Bly, *Iron John* (Reading: Addison-Wesley, 1990), 115, 119–200.

22. Moore and Gillette, *King, Warrior, Magician, Lover*, 30–31, 127.

23. Joseph Campbell and Bill Moyers, *The Masks of Eternity* (New York: Apostrophe Productions, 1988).

24. David G. Bromley and Anson D. Shupe, Jr., *Strange Gods: The Great American Cult Scare* (Boston: Beacon, 1982), 54–55. Faith Martin has written a particularly accessible article on God's nonsexual nature, "Mystical Masculinity: The New Question Facing Women," *Priscilla Papers* 6(Fall 1992): 1–7, available from Christians for Biblical Equality, 380 Lafayette Freeway, Suite 122, St. Paul, MN 55107–1216.

25. "Enter the Dragon," (Warner Brothers–Concord Productions, Inc., 1972).

26. Nancy Gibbs, "Fire Storm in Waco," *Time* 141(May 3, 1993): 35.

27. Charles Hirshberg, ed., "The Face of God," *Life* 13(December 1990): 64.

28. "Bloodthirsty" is the term of choice for archaeologists Anne Ross and Don Robins (National Geographical Society, University of London), who have examined the sacrificial remains of Celtic and Danish ritual victims, sunk into bogs to appease the deities (see *The Life and Death of a Druid Prince* (New York: Summit, 1989), 47, and also "bogs" and "bog-burial" in Miranda J. Green, *Dictionary of Celtic Myth and Legend* (London: Thames and Hudson, 1992), 46–47, where we learn, for example, "Most of the finds are from Denmark, where a number of human sacrificial victims were dedicated to the gods during the late 1st millenium B.C."). While human sacrifice may not be required today by revitalized worship of Odin, Thor, Freya, and the Norse Pantheon, retention of the emphasis on warrior values and on racial exclusiveness has plagued current "asatru" ("belief in the gods") by attracting numerous Neo-Nazis to it.

Druidic sacrifice was noted and detailed by ancient travelers such as Caesar, Strabo, and Diodorus Siculus. Dionysion death of the male is graphically fleshed out for readers in Mary Renault's novel *The King Must Die* (New York, Pantheon, 1958), or gathered in the myriad of books on mythology like Sir James George Frazier's *The Golden Bough* (New York: MacMillan, 1951). An interesting new phenomenon is that some current scholarly studies on ancient deities like R. J. Stewart's *Celtic Gods, Celtic Goddesses* (London, Blandford, 1990) have been researched with the express purpose of worship in mind (see p. 19).

This resurrection of pagan deities for worship is one of the most disturbing aspects in neo-paganism for Christians, particularly considering their past penchant for spilling sacrificial blood. If Jesus has not died to cleanse our sin, then Deity still needs to be satisfied, whether the call for the death of the male is portrayed in poetic, highly romantic tones, see Starhawk, *Dreaming the Dark*, p. 90 for this call and p. 89 for a celebration of Christ's crucifixion and an attack on the resurrection as "Christianity cheats us with the false promise of an otherworldly resurrection," or in the graphic reportage of the bog evidence of ritual sacrifice cited earlier. A world away from European and North American ancient and contemporary neo-paganism the astute Nigerian scholar Tokunboh Adeyemo issues a similar warning against abandoning Christ's sacrifice to return to traditional religion as a "retrogression to an incomplete and inadequate system of belief," where blood would again have to be spilled since sacrifice ("an act of worship where animal life is destroyed") "is prominent in all religions. Actually it is inconceivable to have a religion without some form of sacrifice, however modified or refined it may be" *Salvation in African Religion* (Nairobi, Kenya: Evangel, 1979), 33, 36. All religions, he claims, recognize a debt for sin is owed to God. The good news of Christianity is that Christ paid that debt. That is the grace that makes it stand out.

29. Keen, *Fire in the Belly*, 202.

30. Keen, *Fire in the Belly*, 243.

31. Keen, *Fire in the Belly*, 268.

32. Bly, *Iron John*, 8.

33. Bly, *Iron John*, 110.

34. Moore and Gillette, *King, Warrior, Magician, Lover*, 34.

35. Moore and Gillette, *King, Warrior, Magician, Lover*, 152–53. While Sam Keen in such books as *Apology for Wonder* (New York: Harper, 1969) and *To a Dancing God* (New York: Harper, 1970) raises the image of Dionysus to "enliven" Christianity and Robert Bly summons up Dionysus, Hermes, and Zeus as reflective images, the therapy of Robert Moore goes a step further. Obviously, Moore himself does not believe in Eros, nor no doubt does he expect his counselees to take these deities as more than psychological archetypes, and yet all we encounter do not think so abstractly or scientifically. The Neo-Pagan Church of the Eternal Source was cofounded by one Jim Kimble, who as a teenager would invoke in reality Dionysus (Bacchus), Zeus, Poseidon, Pluto while dropping bread and wine in the ocean. Don Harrison, his cofounder, "had declared himself a priest of the Egyptian god Thoth and begun to reestablish the Thoth cult." A third cofounder polytheist, Harold Moss, championed the cult of Horus, the god

of light. "The gods," he contends "are real" (Margot Adler, *Drawing Down the Moon* [Boston: Beacon, 1986], 264, 266, 268). Witch Margot Adler describes this recommendation of serial worship of psychotherapists like Robert Moore as henotheism, worshiping one God, while recognizing the existence of others. She quotes the Sabaeon (meaning star worshiping) Odun (Frederic de) Arechaga as explaining: "For a time, one might be attuned to Venus; at another time, to Saturn . . . he never forgets that there is another imagery he can (use) if it comes to pass that he changes and no longer can identify with the image he so fondly admired" (Adler, *Drawing Down the Moon*, 258). Like the ancients, moderns can go theological temple shopping, too.

36. Hirshberg, 54. Such syncretistic chaos thrusts nonsense into the most respected and unexpected quarters when it is introduced. For example, the Masonic order is a deeply respected global fraternal society, known for its humanitarian work, the famous personages historically affiliated with the order, its ability to adapt to every culture and every religion. But, this last characteristic has caused it to posit a most nonsensical and theologically dangerous practice of referring to God as "Juh-buh-lon." As Mason Malcolm C. Duncan explains in *Duncan's Masonic Ritual and Monitor*, "JEHOVAH. Of the varieties of this sacred name in use among the different nations of the earth, three particularly merit the attention of Royal Arch Masons:

1. JAH. This name of God is found in the 68th Psalm, v. 4.
2. BAAL or BEL. This word signifies a *lord, master, or possessor*, and hence it was applied by many of the nations of the East to denote the Lord of all things, and the Master of the world.
3. ON. This was the name by which JEHOVAH was worshipped among the Egyptians.

I have made these remarks on the three names of God in Chaldaic, Syriac and Egyptian, *Baal, Jah, and On*, in the expectation that my Royal Arch Companions will readily recognize them in a corrupted form" (Malcolm C. Duncan, *Duncan's Masonic Ritual and Monitor or Guide to the Three Symbolic Degrees of the Ancient York Rite and to the Degrees of Mark Master, Past Master, Most Excellent Master, and the Royal Arch* (Chicago: Charles T. Powner Co., 1974), 226, n. 1.

John Sheville, P.G.H.P. and James L. Gould, P.G.H.P. 33° echo and expand this teaching in their chapter guide, "The true pronunciation of the great and sacred Name was preserved by the High-Priests . . . The true pronunciation, however chimerical it may appear, is said to be preserved in the ritual of Freemasonry, and, as we have before remarked, is the grand symbol of the Order. It was corrupted among all the heathen nations, in the rites of whom it yet maintained a prominent place. Thus among the

Syriac nations we find it contracted into a biliteral word JAH. Among the Chaldeans we find it changed to BEL, or *Belus,* or *Baal.* Among the Egyptians we find it changed to ON, derived, perhaps, from the Hindoo AUM or OM. Among the Latins we find *Jupiter* and *Jove"* (John Sheville and James L. Gould, *Guide to the Royal Arch Chapter: A Complete Monitor with Full Instructions in the Degrees of Mark Master, Past Master, Most Excellent Master and Royal Arch Together with the Order of High Priesthood: Historical Introduction, Explanatory Notes, Ceremonies, Installation* (Richmond: Macoy Publishing and Masonic Supply Co., 1981), 180.

And the use of "Jubulun," is affirmed in J. Blanchard, ed. *Scotch Rite Masonry Illustrated: The Complete Ritual of the Ancient and Accepted Scottish Rite, Profusely Illustrated I* (Chicago: Charles T. Powner, 1944), 452–53.

But the wars between Elijah and the priests of Baal (1 Kings 18:21–46) or Moses and the Egyptians (Exod. 5:2ff.) over whose God was supreme were not simply squabbles by ignorant ancients who really had no need to fight since they worshiped the same God under different designations. The God of Israel, both sides understood, was not the fertility gods Baal or Osiris (On) and was not worshiped through licentious fertility rites. "I know not the Lord," sneered Pharaoh to Moses in 1 Kings 5:2 (KJV), "neither will I let Israel go." To confuse these separate gods as the designations for a single deity is to misunderstand the Old Testament from the first to the last verse and to make unintended mockery of our ancestors' most poignant distinctions, an act no thinking Mason who considers himself Christian would ever want to do. This pernicious syncretistic practice should be immediately expunged from the rituals of the order.

A further by-product from Masonic ritual practice that will deeply disturb all Christians who are Masons is the fact, reported by respected occult expert Aidan Kelly, that, when Gerald Gardner and his initial coven set about recreating their expression of modern paganism, they built their rituals "within an overall Masonic framework taken from the three-degree system of the Masonic Blue Lodges." Kelly discovered: "their intellectual (Masonic) occultism was providing a framework for the spells, charms, and dances of folk magic." Gardner drew liberally from Masonic sources in constructing his *Book of Shadows,* the "bible" of contemporary witchcraft, even adopting the word "Craft," a Masonic name for Freemasonry, from Masonic sources and applying it to Wicca. Today Gardnerian Witchcraft is the chief expression of Craft neo-paganism throughout the United States. Aidan A. Kelly, ed., *Neo-Pagan Witchcraft I* (New York: Garland, 1990), introduction.

37. John Boardman, Jasper Griffin, and Oswyn Murray, eds., *The Oxford Dictionary of the Classical World* (New York: Oxford, 1986), 254.

38. Bly, *Iron John,* 25.

39. Bly, *Iron John,* 249.

▼ Chapter 3: God/dess of the Past

1. Sheila D. Collins, *A Different Heaven and Earth* (Valley Forge: Judson, 1974), 26; Laurie Cabot and Tom Cowan, *Power of the Witch* (New York: Bantam Doubleday Dell, 1989), 24, 67.

2. James B. Pritchard, ed. *Ancient Near Eastern Texts Relating to the Old Testament,* trans. W. F. Albright and others (Princeton: Princeton University, 1969), 107, 137, 152.

3. C. Mackenzie Brown, "Kali, the Mad Mother," *Book of the Goddess* III.

4. Philip E. Slater, *The Glory of Hera: Greek Mythology and the Greek Family* (Boston: Beacon, 1968), 468–69.

5. Margot Adler, *Drawing Down the Moon: Witches, Druids, Goddess-Worshippers and Other Pagans in America Today* (2d ed.; Boston: Beacon, 1986), 9. See also *Power of the Witch,* 68.

6. Pausanias 4.31.8; Artemidorus of Daldo, *Dream Book* II.36.

7. Euripides, *Iphigenia among the Taurians* 1458–60.

8. Pausanias 3.16, 7–11. See also Fritz Graf, "Das Gotterbild aus dem Tauerland" in *Antike Welt* 4, 1979, 33–41.

9. Scholion on Aristophanes, *Lysistrata* 645; Eusthathius, *Iliad* 331.

10. Herodotus IV, 103.

11. Clement of Alexandria, *Protrep.* 3.42.9. Clement also told of human sacrifice to Zeus. Aristomenes the Messenian, he reported, slew three hundred men as an offering to Ithometan Zeus; and he has read an account in Monimus' *Treatise on Marvels* of an Achaian man who was sacrificed to Peleus and Chiron at Pella in Thessaly. His reading has also included "Homeward Journeys" by Anticlides, in which he says that the Cretan Lyctii used to sacrifice men to Zeus. He recalls the mythical sacrifices made by a Greek and Roman father and cites the authors who mention them.

12. Apollonius of Rhodes, *Argonautica* IV, 479.

13. Strabo, *Geography* 5, 3, 12.

14. Perieg 861. See also Pausanias 7.19, 1–6; 8.53.

15. Tatian, *Advice to the Greeks* 29.1.

16. Strabo, *Geography* 11.7. For further information see Richard Clark Kroeger and Catherine Clark Kroeger, *I Suffer Not a Woman: Rethinking 1 Timothy 2:11–15 in Light of Ancient Evidence* (Grand Rapids: Baker, 1992), 186–87. For the association of Artemis Tauropolos and human sacrifice, see Lewis R. Farnell, *The Cults of the Greek City States,* vol. 11 (Chicago: Aegaean, 1971), 451–55. For discussions of human sacrifice see Fritz Schwenn, *Menschenopfer bei den Griechen und Romern* RGVV15 (3d ed.; Gilssen, 1915); A. C. Pearson, "Human Sacrifice (Greek)," *Encyclopedia of Religion and Ethics* VI (1914); Albert Henrichs, "Human Sacrifice in Greek Religion," *Le Sacrifice dans L'Antiquite: Entretiens sur l'Antiquite Classique* (Geneva: 1980), 194–235.

17. Herodotus IV, 117.

18. For a discussion of the Amazons of Ephesus see Tobias Dohrn, "Altes und Neues uber die Ephesischen Amazonen," *Deutsches Archaologisches Institut Jahrbuch* 94 (Berlin: 1979), 112–26.

19. Anton Bammer, *Das Heligtum des Artemis von Ephesos* (Graz, Austria: Akademischce Druck-u.Verganstalt, 1983), 159.

20. W. M. Ramsay, *Historical Geography of Asia Minor,* Royal Geographic Society, Supplementary Papers IV (London, 1890), 110.

21. Symeon Metaphrastes, *Vita Timothei,* Migne, PG, 114, 769.

22. Achilles Tatius, *Clithophon and Leucippe* VIII.2 (second century A.D.).

23. Eusebius, *Preparation for the Gospel* 40c; Dionysius of Halicanassus 1.38; Plutarch, *de Superstitione* 13. See footnote 49.

24. *Apology* 9:2; Lawrence Stager, "Carthage: A View from the Tophet," *Phonizier in Westen* (Mainz: 1982), 155–73.

25. Plutarch, *Virtues of Women* 20; *Amatorius* 22(768 B-D); W. M. Ramsay, *Historical Commentary on St. Paul's Epistle to the Galatians* (London: 1899), 88.

26. Tatian, *To the Greeks* viii.

27. Servius on Vergil's *Aeneid* 1:430.

28. Pausanias II, 2, 5–6.

29. Pausanias IV, vii.1.

30. Aelian, fragment 44. See also Marcel Detienne, "Violentes 'Eugenies' En pleines Thesmophories: des femmes couvertes de sang," Marcel Detienne and Jean-Pierre Vernant, *La Cusine de sacrifice en Pays Grec,* (Paris: Gallimard, 1972), 183–214.

31. Herodotus VI.133–5.

32. Euripides, *Ion* 436ff., (trans. Philip Vellacott). See also *Heracles* 1341–46.

33. Fragment XLVIII.11–14, Kambitsis.

34. "In the struggle of Christianity against the pagan gods, one of the most successful arguments was the accusation of immorality, for the defenders of the old order themselves could not avoid admitting its justification; most vulnerable were the unbridled love-affairs of the gods." Walter Burket, *Greek Religion,* trans. John Raffan (Cambridge: University, 1985), 246.

35. Psellus, *Quaenam sunt Graecorum opiniones de daemonibus* 3.

36. "The mysteries [memorialize] the erotic embraces of Zeus with mother Demeter and the anger of Deo." Clem. Alex., *Protr.* 2.12–13.

37. Marcel Detienne and Jean-Pierre Vernant, *Cunning Intelligence in Greek Culture and Society,* trans. Janet Lloyd (Atlantic Highlands, N.J., 1978), 21–22, 55–114, 137, 142–43, 151–59. Laurie Cabot does not deal with these negative ramifications of the "shapeshifting power" of the male gods. *Power of the Witch,* 48.

38. Socrates was likened in his external aspect to a satyr, clothed in coarse language and appearing to be a lecherous buffoon. Plato *Symposium* 215–22.

Sophist politicians also partook of the nature of satyr, being weak, shifty and given to changing shape. Plato, *Statesman* 291 A, 300. The satyr suggests bestiality, vulgarity, and degradation. He is representative of the lowest elements in human nature.

39. H. Diels, *Die Fragmente der Vorsokratiker* (6th ed. rev. by W. Kranz, 1951); Xenophanes fr. 11.

40. Isocrates, *Busiris* 38ff.

41. Plato, *Republic* 2.278. See also 3.388ff.

42. Leo C. Curran, "Rape and Rape Victims in the *Metamorphoses*," *Women in the Ancient World: The Arethusa Papers*, ed. John Peradotto and J. P. Sullivan (Albany: SUNY, 1984), 263–86.

43. Ovid, *Metamorphoses* 6.110–11.

44. Although Eusebius and Jerome maintained that a number of copies were extant in their day, no copy was known in modern times until the last century. Edgar Hennecke, *Die Apologie des Aristides, Recension und Rekonstrucktion des Textes*, (Leipzig, 1893), 44 ff. Eusebius, *Chron. Can.*, p. 166; *Ecclesiastical History* 4, 3, 1.3. Goodspeed suggests a date between the years 138 and 147 A.D. Edgar J. Goodspeed, *Kie ältesten Apologeten* (Göttingen, 1914), viii.

45. Eusebius, *Ecclesiastical History* 4.3.

46. Aristides, *Apology* ap. St. John Damascene, *Baarlam and Josaphat* xxvii (245).

47. "The Greeks have erred worse than the Chaldeans . . . calling those gods who are no gods, according to their evil lusts, in order that having these as advocates of their wickedness they may commit adultery, and plunder and kill, and do the worst of deeds." Trans. from the Syriac by J. A. Robinson, "Aristides," *Encyclopedia Britannica*, I (Eleventh Edition, New York, 1910), 496.

48. See also *The Recognition of Clement* 10.22; Pseudo-Justin, *Discourse to the Greeks* (Oratio ad Graecos), PG 6.233, 257; Ambrose, *Hypomnemata* 16; *Spic. Syr.* pp. 63–64; Arnobius, *Against the Heathen* 4:26; Firmicus Maternus 12:22; Athanasius, *Contra Gentes* 12; Nonnus, *Dionysiaca* 33.249–51, 298, 301–6.

49. Ginette Paris is more consistent than others when she says: "As Artemis might kill a wounded animal rather than allow it to live along miserably, so too a mother wishes to spare a child a painful destiny." On the basis of this "pagan morality" she encourages women to have power over life and death and decide even up to one month after birth if a child should live. Infanticide she sees as viable still today. A child should only live when it is accepted and welcomed emotionally and economically by its "collective world." Why not refrain from sexual intercourse if one knows the potential child will not be welcomed? For her that would hamper the full expression of sexual pleasure, the essence of the Aphrodite cult. Ginette Paris with James Hillman, *The Sacrament of Abortion: A Talk on the Psychological*

and Ecological Virtues of Abortion, Spring Audio, 1991. [A. B. Spencer's note]

▼ Chapter 4: *God Is Unique*

1. John C. Wister, ed., *Woman's Home Companion Garden Book* (New York: Doubleday, 1947), v–vi.

2. Carol P. Christ, "Why Women Need the Goddess: Phonomenological, Psychological, and Political Reflections," *Womanspirit Rising: A Feminist Reader in Religion*, eds. Carol P. Christ and Judith Plaskow (San Francisco: Harper & Row, 1979), 275, 279, 283, 285.

3. Margot Adler, *Drawing Down the Moon: Witches, Druids, Goddess-Worshippers, and Other Pagans in America Today* (2d ed.; Boston: Beacon, 1986), 28–29.

4. Many writers allude to Carl Jung's psychological theories, for example Naomi R. Goldenberg, *Changing of the Gods: Feminism and the End of Traditional Religions* (Boston: Beacon, 1979), 46–71; Adler, 28.

5. For instance, read the description of the "Challenging New Age Patriarchy" conference in Motvern, England in 1990. Monica Sjöö, "A Letter from Monica Sjöö," *Woman of Power* 19 (Winter 1991): 78–80.

6. Goldenberg, 22, 33, 70. Rosemary Radford Ruether writes: "As long as one has to keep knocking Moses and Jesus, one is still basically responding to them as oppressive fathers, not encountering them in the way Goldenberg encounters Freud and Jung—as human resources that might have some liberating things to say, as well as some cultural limitations." "A Religion for Women: Sources and Strategies," *Christianity and Crisis* 39 (December 10, 1979): 309.

7. Asoka Bandarage, "A Celebration of Spirit," "In Search of a New World Order," *Woman of Power* 21 (Fall 1991): 4, 9. See also Sheila D. Collins, *A Different Heaven and Earth* (Valley Forge: Judson, 1974), 51.

8. All these and other lists of quotations are from the NRSV.

9. E. G. Rosemary Radford Ruether, "Motherearth and the Megamachine: A Theology of Liberation in a Feminine, Somatic, and Ecological Perspective," *Womanspirit Rising*, 43; Carol P. Christ, "Feminist Liberation Theology and Yahweh as Holy Warrior: An Analysis of Symbol," *Women's Spirit Bonding*, eds. Janet Kalven and Mary I. Buckley (New York: Pilgrim, 1984), 205.

10. Tikva Frymer-Kensky, *In the Wake of the Goddesses: Women, Culture, and the Biblical Transformation of Pagan Myth* (New York: Free, 1992), 84.

Her proof includes Psalms 29, 82, 93, and Deuteronomy 32. In Psalm 29 David speaks of "sons" or "children" of God *(ʾĕlôhîm)*. The NRSV "heavenly beings" is very misleading. The simplest interpretation would suggest "children of God" refers to humans. Psalm 93 does not refer to any deities. Deuteronomy 32 simply refers to false deities.

Psalm 82 does seem to refer to deities. "God" *(ʾēl)* is synonymous with "God" *(ʾĕlôhîm)* in verse 1: "God stands in the congregation of God *(ʾēl)* in the midst of God *(ʾĕlôhîm)* he judges." The same point is made in Psalm 82 as is often made today. No distinction exists between god/dess and humans. So too Asaph quotes God, "You are gods" *(ʾĕlôhîm)*, or as the Jewish Publication Society renders "Ye are godlike beings, and all of you sons of the Most High" (Ps. 82:6). But what does God exhort us humans to do? "Give justice to the weak and the orphan; maintain the right of the lowly and the destitute" (82:3). False deities, like humans who do not appropriate their creation in God's image, have no "knowledge nor understanding" and "walk around in darkness" (82:5). Humans who presume to be deities will merely "die like mortals, and fall like any prince" (82:7).

11. Jean Shinoda Bolen, "Living in a Liminal Time," *Woman of Power* 21 (Fall 1991): 21.

12. Starhawk, *Truth or Dare: Encounters with Power, Authority, and Mystery* (San Francisco: Harper & Row, 1987), 4, 6, 23.

13. Andy Smith, "For All Those Who Were Indian in a Former Life," *Woman of Power* 19 (Winter 1991): 74–75.

14. Starhawk, *Truth or Dare,* 7, 15, 23, 98, 99, 136, 315.

15. See also Ps. 138:1 and 2 Chron. 2:4.

16. Feyerabend, Karl, *Langenscheidt Pocket Hebrew Dictionary to the Old Testament* (New York: McGraw-Hill, 1969), 17.

17. The authors have also divested Jesus of divinity. If Sophia is "goddess-like," *not* God, and Jesus is Sophia, then Jesus is not God incarnate, in their thinking. Their source is more the Apocrypha than the Bible. Susan Cady, Marian Ronan, Hal Taussig, *Wisdom's Feast: Sophia in Study and Celebration* (San Francisco: Harper & Row, 1989), 10, 17, 19, 28, 33, 59, 62, 66, 74, 81, 86, 102, 136, 197–98.

18. *Mishnah Berakoth* 3:3. Ironically, the rabbis made gender-specific what was not gender-specific in Moses' words. The symbols to keep on one's person, "a sign on your hand," "an emblem on your forehead," became male specific, whereas signs on "the doorposts" and the "gates" became female specific so that women could be restricted to homemaking. Nowhere was this gender-specific application commanded by Moses. See *Beyond the Curse,* 48.

19. The name was pronounced at the blessing and during the Day of Atonement service. *Mishnah Tamid* 7:2; *Sotah* 7:6; *Yoma* 6:2; 3:8.

20. The four nouns repeatedly given special treatment in the early papyri were all names of God: *theos, kurios, Iēsous,* and *Christos.* Later the scribes agreed on fifteen "sacred words": "God" *(theos),* "Lord" *(kurios),* "Jesus" *(Iēsous),* "Christ" *(Christos),* "Son" *(huios),* "Spirit" *(pneuma),* "Savior" *(sōtēr),* "heaven" *(ouranos),* and also key Jewish concepts: "David" *(Daveid),* "cross"

(stauros), "mother" *(mētēr)*, "father" *(patēr)*, "Israel" *(Israēl)*, "human" *(anthropos)*, and "Jerusalem" *(Ierousalēm)*. Bruce Metzger, *Manuscripts of the Greek Bible: An Introduction to Greek Palaeography* (New York: Oxford University, 1981), 35–37.

21. For example, Merlin Stone calls Abraham the "first prophet of the male deity Yahweh." "When God Was a Woman," *Womanspirit Rising*, 124; Emily Erwin Culpepper, "Are Women's Bodies Sacred? Listening to the Yes's and No's," *Sacred Dimensions of Women's Experience*, ed. Elizabeth Dodson Gray (Wellesley: Roundtable, 1988), 203.

22. Paul Tillich, *Systematic Theology* I (Chicago: University of Chicago, 1951), 235.

23. An excellent overview of Old Testament critical problems with solutions supporting the Bible's claims for itself may be found in Roland K. Harrison, *Introduction to the Old Testament* (Grand Rapids: Eerdmans, 1969). Pp. 568ff. deal with Moses as the author of the Pentateuch.

24. E. Kautzsch, ed., *Gesenius' Hebrew Grammar* (2d ed.; Oxford: Clarendon, 1910), 406–07.

25. *ʾĔlôhîm* is generic. It can refer to either male or female gods. For instance Ahijah uses the same word to describe the gods Astarte (female) as he does Chemosh (male) (1 Kings 11:33).

26. Francis Brown, S. R. Driver, and Charles A. Briggs, *A Hebrew and English Lexicon of the Old Testament* (Oxford: Clarendon, 1907), 43.

27. *Gesenius*, 396, 399, 428, 463.

28. Nelle Morton, "The Goddess as Metaphoric Image," *Weaving the Visions: New Patterns in Feminist Spirituality*, eds. J. Plaskow and C. P. Christ (San Francisco: Harper Collins, 1989), 111–12; Genevieve Vaughan, "Changing Values and Society through Rituals," *Woman of Power* 19 (Winter 1991): 6.

29. Joan P. Townsend, "The Goddess: Fact, Fallacy and Revitalization Movement," *Goddesses in Religions and Modern Debate* I, ed. Larry W. Hurtado (Atlanta: Scholars, 1990), 198.

30. Randall E. Otto writes: "The divine family of God the Father, Son and Spirit forms the archetype, then, for what is to be understood by the *imago Dei*. . . . It is mankind, generically understood and comprised of male and female, son and daughter, that constitutes the image of God." "The *Imago Dei* as *Familitas*," *Journal of the Evangelical Society* 35 (December 1992): 511.

31. Frymer-Kensky, *Wake of the Goddesses*, 142; Marcia Falk, "Notes on Composing New Blessings: Toward a Feminist-Jewish Reconstruction of Prayer," *Weaving*, 129.

32. See also Acts 2:21. The "name" itself is not salvific, but the Lord is.

33. For a good overview of the critical problems raised in the New

Testament with solutions that support the Bible's claims for itself see Donald Guthrie, *New Testament Introduction* (3d ed.; Downers Grove: InterVarsity, 1970).

34. A. T. Robertson, *A Grammar of the Greek New Testament in the Light of Historical Research* (Nashville: Broadman, 1934), 786, 1178. Also see Murray J. Harris, *Jesus as God: The New Testament Use of Theos in Reference to Jesus* (Grand Rapids: Baker, 1992), 307–08. See also the excellent discussion in Kermit Titrud, "The Function of *Kai* in the Greek New Testament and an Application to 2 Peter," *Linguistics and New Testament Interpretation: Essays on Discourse Analysis,* eds. D. A. Black with K. Barnwell and S. Levinsohn (Nashville: Broadman, 1992), 248–50.

35. These are only a few exemplary Bible passages that indicate both the oneness and trinity of God. Other ones are: Gal. 3:20; 1 Tim. 1:17; Isa. 44:6; James 2:19; 2 Cor. 13:14; 1 Pet. 1:1–2; 3:18; Luke 1:35; 3:22; John 3:34–35; 14:8–16, 26; 15:26; 16:13–15; Acts 2:33; Rom. 8:9–11, 26–27; 1 Cor. 12:3–6; Gal. 4:4–6; Eph. 2:18; 4:4–6; 1 Thess. 1:2–5; 2 Thess. 2:13; Heb. 9:14; 1 John 5:6–9; Isa. 48:16.

36. Frymer-Kensky, *Wake of the Goddesses,* 32, 45, 203. Even goddess-worshiping villages in India are neither particularly ecological nor feminist. Vishal Mangalwadi, *When the New Age Gets Old: Looking for a Greater Spirituality* (Downers Grove: InterVarsity, 1992), 133–34, 139.

37. Melissa Potter and Maria Epes, "The Goddess Altar in Cow Pasture Grove," *Woman of Power* 19 (Winter 1991): 22. Shakmah Winddrum, "Unveiling the Mystery of Magic," *Woman of Power* 19 (Winter 1991): 32.

38. For instance, one concept that Luke highlights in his gospel is the amazement or fear with which people respond to Jesus' teachings and practice. Aída Besançon Spencer, "'Fear' as a Witness to Jesus in Luke's Gospel, *Bulletin for Biblical Research* 2 (1992): 59–73.

39. The A.D. 357 Arian council, which concluded that the Trinity has hierarchy or "subordination," was declared "The Blasphemy of Sirnium" by Leo Bishop of Rome in 449 and reanathamatized at the Council of Chalcedon in A.D. 451. Henry Bettenson, ed., *Documents of the Christian Church* (2d ed., New York: Oxford University, 1963), 43, 51; J. N. D. Kelly, *Early Christian Doctrines* (2d ed.; New York: Harper & Row, 1960), 339. Justo L. González documents "the Trinity is the doctrine of a God whose very life is a life of sharing, its clear consequence is that those who claim belief in such a God must live a similar life" *Mañana: Christian Theology from a Hispanic Perspective* (Nashville: Abingdon, 1990), 114.

▼ Chapter 5: *God Is Invisible*

1. Carol P. Christ, "Feminist Liberation Theology and Yahweh as Holy Warrior: An Analysis of Symbol," *Women's Spirit Bonding,* eds. Janet Kalven

and Mary I. Buckley (New York: Pilgrim, 1984), 210. Not all spiritualist feminists would agree. Karen McCarthy Brown defends the Vodou male War God, Ogou, as a means "to marry one's anger." "Why Women Need the War God," *Women's Spirit Bonding*, 197–98.

2. Mary Daly, "After the Death of God the Father: Women's Liberation and the Transformation of Christian Consciousness," *Womanspirit Rising: A Feminist Reading in Religion*, eds. Carol P. Christ and Judith Plaskow (San Francisco: Harper & Row, 1979), 54; Alice Walker, *The Color Purple* (New York: Harcourt Brace Jovanovich, 1982), 166.

3. Jean Shinoda Bolen, "Living in a Liminal Time," *Woman of Power* 21(Fall 1991): 24.

4. Emily Erwin Culpepper, "Are Women's Bodies Sacred? Listening to the Yes's and No's," *Sacred Dimensions of Women's Experience*, ed. Elizabeth Dodson Gray (Wellesley: Roundtable, 1988), 203. Carol P. Christ begins *Laughter of Aphrodite: Reflections on a Journey to the Goddess* (San Francisco: Harper & Row, 1987), 3: "I left the church not only because I concluded that patriarchy was deeply rooted in Christianity's core symbolism of God the Father and Son, but also because I could no longer believe that God acts in history, nor could I affiliate myself with a religious tradition containing the seeds of anti-Judaism that resulted in the death of millions of Jews in the Nazi concentration camps."

5. Possibly these are Paul's own words or he is quoting Epimenides' poem who writes about Zeus. John B. Polhill, *The New American Commentary: Acts* (Nashville: Broadman, 1992), 375; F. F. Bruce, *The Acts of the Apostles* (2d ed.; Grand Rapids: Eerdmans, 1970), 338.

6. See also Aída Besançon Spencer and William David Spencer, *2 Corinthians*, Bible Study Commentary (Grand Rapids: Zondervan, 1989), 88–94. Christians used to meet in private homes for their own worship (Mark 14:15; Acts 1:13; 20:8). The earliest buildings built for worship were modeled on living rooms. Not until after A.D. 313, the Edict of Milan, when Christianity became legal, did Christians begin to build worship areas like other Greeks and Romans did, in basilicas, which were secular roofed meeting halls, and law courts. Jack Finegan, *Light from the Ancient Past: The Archeological Background of the Hebrew-Christian Religion* II (Princeton: Princeton University, 1946), 493–506; Robert Banks, *Paul's Idea of Community: The Early House Churches in Their Historical Setting* (Grand Rapids: Eerdmans, 1980), 41. In Eusebius' time (300s) "church" also included buildings 7.15; 8.1. Nevertheless Eusebius still speaks of the "sanctuary" as people (*The History of the Church* 10.4–5).

7. Rose Spector, "Carol Leonard: Sacred Passages of the Divine Woman," *Earth Star* 14(February/March 1993): 6; Starhawk, *Truth or Dare: Encounters with Power, Authority, and Mystery* (San Francisco: Harper & Row, 1987), 103–04. Luisah Teish, "Ancestor Reverence," *Weaving the Visions: New*

Patterns in Feminist Spirituality, eds. J. Plaskow and C. P. Christ (San Francisco: Harper Collins, 1989), 87–88.

8. God does seem to have "a presence" that all believers will "know" after death (1 Cor. 13:12). Moses was given a small perception ("back") of this presence at one point in his life (Exod. 33:22–23). Moses did not, literally, "see" *(rā'āh)* God, but he "beheld" *(nābat)* God (Num. 12:8). Jesus claims that only he has seen God's "form" *(eidos)* (John 5:27; 6:46). Recently some people are arguing that God "has form in some sense" and that men, not women, are made in God's "outer" immaterial form. Like the Goddess worshipers, the sexuality of men and women becomes more essential than their personhood. H. Wayne House, "Creation and Redemption: A Study of Kingdom Interplay," *Journal of the Evangelical Theological Society* 35 (March 1992): 7–8. In contrast, the Bible teaches that male *and* female were created in God's image. The Bible has no division between an outer bodily and an inner spiritual nature. That type of dichotomy is neo-Platonic. Even if someone were to argue that women were created only in men's image, the women too then would be created in this spiritual and bodily image. Sadly, these writers are willing to risk blasphemy in order to keep women from having full power in the church.

Ironically, Christian writers at the other extreme are developing a similar argument. For example, Sallie McFague argues that matter "perhaps ought to be, applied to God as well," because if God is not "embodied," the body is inferior. She then treats the world as God's body or "back," but not God's "face." *The Body of God: An Ecological Theology* (Minneapolis: Fortress, 1993), 19, 21, 131–32.

9. Rosemary Radford Ruether, "Feminist Theology and Spirituality," *Christian Feminism: Visions of a New Humanity*, ed. Judith L. Weidman (San Francisco: Harper & Row, 1984), 16. See also Erminie Huntress Lantero, *Feminine Aspects of Divinity*, Pendle Hill Pamphlet 191 (Wallingford: Pendle Hill, 1973), 3. John Calvin also discusses God's "infinite and spiritual essence." *Institutes of the Christian Religion* I.XIII.1. The champion of orthodoxy in the early church, Athanasius, writes, too, that the Second Person of the Trinity is bodiless: "For this reason the incorporeal and incorruptible and immaterial Word of God came to our realm; not that he was previously distant, for no part of creation is left deprived of him, but he fills the universe, being in union with his Father" (*The Incarnation of the Word of God* 8) and the Word of God "revealed himself through a body that we might receive an idea of the invisible Father" (54).

10. However, she thinks wisdom theology integrated elements of the "goddess cult," especially Isis worship, into Jewish monotheism. "Divine Sophia is Israel's God in the language and *Gestalt* of the goddess." Elisabeth Schüssler Fiorenza, *In Memory of Her: A Feminist Theological Reconstruction of Christian Origins* (New York: Crossroad, 1984), 133.

11. Joseph Henry Thayer, *Thayer's Greek-English Lexicon of the New Testament* (Marshallton: National Foundation for Christian Education, 1885), 418; J. Behm, *"Morphē, Morphoō, Morphōsis, Metamorphoō,"* Theological Dictionary of the New Testament, IV, ed. G. Kittel, trans. G. W. Bromiley (Grand Rapids: Eerdmans, 1967), 743–44.

12. Thayer, *Lexicon*, 418; J. Schneider, *"Schēma, Metaschēmatizō,"* Theologial Dictionary of the New Testament, VII, 954.

13. Examples where *anthrōpos* refers to "humans" in contrast to God include: Acts 5:4, 29; 10:26; 14:15, 17:25, 29. In Acts 22:25 Paul uses *anthrōpos* to represent his Roman citizenship. *Anēr* is used in the Book of Acts to describe Barabbas, Stephen, Cornelius, Barnabas, Sergius, Judas, Silas, Apollos, Ananias, Bar-Jesus, David, and Peter: 3:14; 6:5; 10:22, 28; 11:24; 13:7; 14:15; 15:22; 17:26, 29; 18:24; 22:12; 13:6, 22. Males are contrasted with females in Acts 5:14; 18:3, 12; 9:2; 17:12; 22:4. *Anēr* plus a clarifying pronoun or article may also refer to a husband, as in "your man" (e.g. Eph. 5:22). "The heir (or son) of humanity" is the overwhelming way Jesus speaks in self-description. Not listing references in Mark, Luke, or John, the following may be found: Matt. 8:20; 9:6; 10:23; 11:19; 12:8, 32, 40; 13:37, 41; 16:13, 27, 28; 17:9, 12, 22; 19:28; 20:18, 28; 24:27, 30, 37, 39, 44; 25:31; 26:2, 24, 45, 64. Only once did I find Jesus using simply *anthrōpos* for self-description: John 8:40. In that passage he describes the unbelieving religious leaders. They were seeking "to kill a person." Jesus also uses *anthrōpos* in parables wherein he alludes to himself or to God the Father as shepherd, ruler, landowner, master, and parent: Matt. 18:12, 23; 20:1; 21:28, 33; 22:2; 25:14, 24; Mark 12:1; Luke 12:16; 14:16; 15:11; 16:1; 19:12, 21, 22; 20:19. Other people also describe Jesus as "heir of humanity": Acts 7:56; Rev. 1:13; 14:14. *Anthrōpos* is used in several passages to highlight Jesus' humanity, which is representative of all people: Rom. 5:18; 1 Cor. 5:21, 47; Phil. 2:7; 1 Tim. 2:5; Heb. 5:1. When Jesus is described as priest in Heb. 5:1, his humanity, not his maleness is accentuated. *Anthrōpos* is also used by many people to describe Jesus. It seems to be the polite, formal, or not intimate reference, as employed by the Jewish religious leaders (Luke 7:34; John 11:47, 50; 18:14; Acts 5:28), Peter (Mark 14:71), the centurion (Mark 15:39; Luke 23:47), Pilate (Luke 23:4, 6, 14; John 18:29), the blind man (John 9:11, 16), the woman guard (John 18:17).

14. The NIV and TEV used "human" likeness for Phil. 2:7 but "a man" for 2:8, although Greek has *anthrōpos* for both phrases. The NEB has "human" for both references. Even the marvelous translator Helen Barrett Montgomery used one "men" and one "human" to render *anthrōpos* (*New Testament in Modern English*).

15. Noah Webster, *Webster's New Universal Unabridged Dictionary* (2d ed.; New York: Dorset and Baber, 1979), 883, 1092, 1328.

16. That a free man should choose to use "slavery" as his central imagery is shocking in the light that slaves were considered objects, property, with few rights. According to the Mishnah, slaves, like women, were not eligible to be witnesses and they were exempt from learning and obeying all the Torah (Ber. 3:3; Hag. 1:1; Sukk 2:8; Roš Haš 1:8). S. Scott Bartchy, *Mallon Chrēsai: First Century Slavery and the Interpretation of 1 Corinthians 7:21,* Dissertation Series II (Missoula: Scholars, 1973), 38–39; Diane Tennis, *Is God the Only Reliable Father?* (Philadelphia: Westminster, 1985), 103; Garrett Green, "The Gender of God and the Theology of Metaphor," *Speaking the Christian God: The Holy Trinity and the Challenge of Feminism,* ed. Alvin F. Kimil, Jr. (Grand Rapids: Eerdmans, 1992), 62.

17. *Beyond the Curse,* 46–51.

▼ Chapter 6: *God Is Not Male*

1. Starhawk, *Truth or Dare: Encounters with Power, Authority, and Mystery* (San Francisco: Harper & Row, 1987), 9.

2. Starhawk, *Truth or Dare,* 7.

3. Exod. 34:14; Lev. 11:44–45; Deut. 10:17–18, 21; Jer. 17:10.

4. Naomi R. Goldenberg, *Changing of the Gods: Feminism and the End of Traditional Religions* (Boston: Beacon, 1979), 112.

5. Monica Sjöö, "A Letter from Monica Sjöö," *Woman of Power* 19 (Winter 1991): 79.

6. Rosemary Radford Ruether, *Womanguides: Readings Toward a Feminist Theology* (Boston, Beacon, 1985), 82.

7. Sherry Ruth Anderson and Patricia Hopkins, *The Feminine Face of God: The Unfolding of the Sacred in Women* (New York: Bantam, 1991), 99.

8. Starhawk, *Truth or Dare,* 176.

9. Starhawk, *Truth or Dare,* 27.

10. Starhawk, *Truth or Dare,* 27.

11. Starhawk, *Truth or Dare,* 22.

12. Gen. 2:24; Matt. 19:5–6; 1 Cor. 6:16.

13. Starhawk, *Truth or Dare,* 153.

14. G. D. Searle and Co., prod., *Playing It Safe,* narr. Valerie Bertinelli, 1992; J. Isamu Yamamoto, ed., *The Crisis of Homosexuality, The Christianity Today Series* (Wheaton: Victor, 1990), 121–22; Donald M. Vickery and James F. Fries, *Take Care of Yourself: Your Personal Guide to Self-Care and Preventing Illness* (4th ed.; Reading: Addison-Wesley, 1990), 488–94. C. Everett Koop, Surgeon General of the U.S. Public Health Service, on October 22, 1986 wrote: "Couples who maintain mutually faithful monogamous relationships (only one continuing sexual partner) are protected from AIDS through sexual transmission." "The risk of infection

increases according to the number of sexual partners one has, *male or female*. The more partners you have, the greater risk of becoming infected with the AIDS virus." *Surgeon General's Report on Acquired Immune Deficiency Syndrome* (Washington: U.S. Department of Health and Human Services, 1986), 15–16.

15. See also Jer. 1:16; 2:8, 13, 20–21, 34; 3:2–3; 5:19, 28; 6:13; 7:5–9, 18, 30–31; 9:13; 10; 16:11; 17:21; 19:4–6; 22:3; 25:4; 32:23; 35; 34:11; 35:15; 36:31; 2 Kings 16:3; 2 Chron. 36:15–17; Ezek. 16:20–21; Luke 11:48–51.

16. See also Deut. 12:31; 18:10–14; 20:17–18; Lev. 18:24–28; 20:23; Num. 33:56.

17. Nah. 3:4; 2 Kings 19:11; Isa. 10:7.

18. Starhawk, *Truth or Dare*, 136.

19. Aída Besançon Spencer, *Paul's Literary Style: A Stylistic and Historical Comparison of II Corinthians 11:16–12:13, Romans 8:9–39, and Philippians 3:2–4:13*, An Evangelical Theological Society Monograph (Winona Lake: Eisenbrauns, 1984), 294, 310. Some writers have exaggerated the difference between metaphor and simile in order to conclude that "God the Father and the Son of God" as metaphors are revelations by which the divine persons are "named," whereas similes only "compare." Roland Mushat Frye, "Language For God and Feminist Language: A Literary and Rhetorical Analysis," *Interpretation* XLIII (January, 1989): 51, 55; Alvin F. Kimel, Jr., ed., *Speaking the Christian God: The Holy Trinity and the Challenge of Feminism* (Grand Rapids: Eerdmans, 1992). The difference between metaphor and simile is not a difference of identity and likeness. Rather, the difference is how the author asserts or states a comparison. Aristotle explains: "The simile also is a metaphor; for there is very little difference. . . . Similes must be used like metaphors, which only differ in the manner stated" (*The "Art" of Rhetoric,* III.4). The Bible includes many "mothering" references to God that are metaphors: Gen. 1:2 "hovers," "birth" (Deut. 32:18; Isa. 46:3–4; 45:9–11), "gather" (Luke 13:34). Often speakers will interchange simile and metaphor, as in Luke 11:34–36. Jesus begins with an extended metaphor: "The *lamp* of the body is your eye . . ." and concludes with a simile "*as* whenever the lamp with its ray gives you light." In Luke 13:34 Jesus begins with the metaphor "How often have I desired to *gather* your *children*" and develops the metaphor with a simile "*as* a hen gathers her brood under her wings." See also Luke 12:16–21, 35–40.

20. Spencer, *Paul's Literary Style*, 296.

21. See ch. 2. For a popular overview see Tod Connor, "Is the Earth Alive?" *Christianity Today* 37 (January 11, 1993): 22–25.

22. Metaphor is a type of analogy. Aristotle explains "when B is to A as D is to C, then instead of B the poet will say D and B instead of D. . . . For instance, a cup is to Dionysus what a shield is to Ares; so he will call the cup 'Dionysus's shield' and the shield 'Ares' cup'" (*Poetics,* XXI).

23. Donald Bloesch, *The Battle for the Trinity: The Debate over Inclusive God-Language* (Ann Arbor: Servant, 1985), 21, 35. For my brief review of *Battle for the Trinity* see *The Bible Newsletter* 5 (October 1985): 4.

24. Bloesch, *Battle for the Trinity*, 29, 33. He agrees God is immanent but that is derivative to an original transcendence. *Is the Bible Sexist? Beyond Feminism and Patriarchalism* (Westchester: Crossway, 1982), 57–58. See also Susan T. Foh, *Women and the Word of God: A Response to Biblical Feminism* (Grand Rapids: Baker, 1979), 163: "The Masculine Terminology [for God] has significance because God has given the man authority in the family (husband) and in the church (elder), rather than the woman." In Jann Aldredge Clanton's research of 174 men and women, approximately 91 percent of those with a concept of God as androgynous or transcendent believe churches should ordain women and give them opportunities to serve as pastors or priests and as deacons, as contrasted with 69 percent of those with a masculine concept of God. *In Whose Image? God and Gender* (New York: Crossroad, 1990), 96–98.

25. Aída Besançon Spencer, *Beyond the Curse: Women Called to Ministry* (Peabody: Hendrickson, 1985), 146. For an interesting defense of the historicity of Amazons see Phyllis Chesler, "The Amazon Legacy," *The Politics of Women's Spirituality: Essays on the Rise of Spiritual Power within the Feminist Movement*, ed. C. Spretnak (Garden City: Doubleday, 1982), 97–113.

26. Phyllis Trible, *God and the Rhetoric of Sexuality*, Overtures to Biblical Theology (Philadelphia: Fortress, 1978), 33, 45, 61.

27. Trible, *Rhetoric*, 62–63.

28. For a more detailed description read Spencer, *Beyond the Curse*, ch. 5, and Virginia Ramey Mollenkott, *The Divine Feminine: The Biblical Imagery of God as Female* (New York: Crossroad, 1983).

29. Thomas Bulfinch, *The Age of Fable or Beauties of Mythology*, ed. L. Loughran Scott (Philadelphia: David McKay, 1898), 6–12.

30. Luke 2:27, 41, 43; 8:56; John 9:2, 3, 18, 20, 22, 23.

31. Most New Testament references use *gennaō* as a more general term to refer to one's place or time of birth: Matt. 2:1, 4; 26:24; John 3:4; 9:2, 19–20, 34; Acts 2:8; 7:20; 22:3, 28; Rom. 9:11. It is also frequently used of God, but the sexuality of the image is often unspecified: John 1:13; 3:3, 7; 8:41; 18:37; 1 John 2:29; 3:9; 4:7; 5:1, 4, 18.

32. In Luke, 12 references to "father" occur in one parable (15:12–29). Figurative language in parables that clearly refer to God are included. I classified under "God" all references to God the Father, God the Trinity, and whenever the Person of the Trinity was unclear. I excluded all vocative references to "Lord" as no longer metaphorical, simply as a form of respectful address, "sir." Henry George Liddell and Robert Scott, *A Greek-English Lexicon*, eds. H. S. Jones and R. McKenzie (9th ed.; Oxford:

Clarendon, 1940), 1013. I used *The Greek New Testament,* ed. K. Aland and others (3d ed.; New York: United Bible Societies, 1983). In these two charts may be found my rough figures for figurative attributes and titles in the Greek text. I use many other categories for God not here listed. God: action toward Jesus, activity among humans, intention, presence of, means toward, teachings; and Jesus: activity among humans, allegiance to, commended, communication with Father, death, incarnation, message about, mortality, resurrection, relation to Father and words. "Kingdom" often refers to "activity among humans" or "Christian living."

33. Acts 3:13, 26; 4:27, 30, also refer to Jesus as "child."

34. Bolen, "Living in a Liminal Time," 25; Barbara Sciacca, "Honoring Our Bodies, Honoring Our Lives;" Janet L. Jacobs, "Women, Ritual, and Power," *Woman of Power* 19 (Winter 1991): 62, 64.

35. John 6:23; 11:2; 13:13, 14, 16; 15:15, 20; 20:2, 18, 20, 25, 28; 21:7, 12. *Kurios* in the vocative is not included.

36. For other false analogies see Paul R. Smith, *Is It Okay to Call God "Mother": Considering the Feminine Face of God* (Peabody: Hendrickson, 1993), 28. Brian Wren explains: "However hallowed by tradition, however enriching and suggestive, however profoundly they move us, our metaphors and names for God are not themselves God. We should no more bow down and worship mental and linguistic images of God than the graven images forbidden in the Bible, or the idols of money and success." *What Language Shall I Borrow? God-Talk in Worship: A Male Response to Feminist Theology* (New York: Crossroad, 1989), 108.

37. Matt. 2:22; 4:21; Luke 1:59; Gen. 17:4–5; Acts 7:2; James 2:21; Mark 11:10; John 4:12; Rom. 9:10. See Appendix C.

38. Matt. 6:8–9, 32; 7:11; 11:25; James 1:17.

39. 1 Macc. 2:18; 3:38–39; 6:8–15; 7:8–9; 10:19–21.

40. Rev. 1:6; Luke 11:2; Eph. 3:14; Matt. 26:53; 18:34–35.

41. John 5:22–23, 36, 43; 10:15, 30; 11:41–42; 14:6–7, 13; 15:15; 16:28; 17:25–26; Rom. 1:7; 1 John 2:23.

42. Matt. 26:39, 42; 6:1–6.

43. Matt. 5:44–48; Luke 6:32–36; 2 Cor. 1:3–4; James 1:27; 1 Pet. 1:3.

44. 2 Sam. 7:13–16; 1 Chron. 17:13; 22:10; 28:6; Ps. 89:26–37. See also Exod. 4:22–23; 6:6–8; Jer. 31:9. Being "begotten" *(gennaō)* is a synonym for the rising to power: Acts 13:33; Heb. 1:5.

45. Isa. 45:10; 50:1; 54:5–8; 37:29; 61:11; 5:1–7; 10:15, 33–34; 50:3; 28:17; 40:12, 15; 42:13–15; 29:16; 14:23; 48:10; 4:4; 63:2–6; 2:4; 30:26.

46. Isa. 8:14; 10:17; 17:13; 25:4; 27:8; 29:6; 30:27–30; 33:14; 40:24; 60:1.

47. Isa. 31:4–5; 40:22; 8:17 (face); 1:15–16 (eyes), 20 (mouth); 65:5 (nose); 37:29 (ears); 11:4 (lips); 30:27 (tongue); 1:25 (hand); 30:30 (arm); 11:5 (waist).

48. The Greek personal pronouns may be masculine or neuter (vv. 2, 3,

5, 9, 20). The Greek also has four masculine relative pronouns (vv. 5, 6, 9, 25) and nineteen masculine articles (vv. 3–5, 8–10, 19, 21, 23–26, 28, 32).

49. The numbers in parentheses are from the RSV, NEB, and TEV (1966). The Contemporary English Version (1991) has 14 masculine personal pronouns for God, and no "man" or "brothers" for the generic. The New Century Version (1991) has 14 masculine personal pronouns for God, and no "man" or "brothers" for the generic. The NCV (1988) had 12 masculine personal pronouns for God, one "brothers," and one "man," v. 25. The New Translation (1990) has 17 masculine personal pronouns for God and no "man" or "brothers" for the generic.

50. John Lyons, *Introduction to Theoretical Linguistics* (Cambridge: University, 1968), 293–384; A. T. Robertson, *A Grammar of the Greek New Testament in the Light of Historical Research* (Nashville: Broadman, 1934), 252.

51. Lyons, *Linguistics,* 284.

52. Kautzsch, E., ed., *Gesenius' Hebrew Grammar* (2d ed.; Oxford: Clarendon, 1910), 390.

53. Robertson, *Grammar,* 252.

54. Lyons, *Linguistics,* 283–84.

55. Lyons, *Linguistics,* 10–11.

56. Robertson, *Grammar,* 246–47; Lyons, *Linguistics,* 284, 293–94.

57. *Gesenius,* 390–94.

58. *Anēr* ("male") in the plural can include men and women (Dionysius and Damaris, Acts 17:34; Agrippa and Bernice, Acts 25:24). It is generic in Acts 2:14 and 14:15.

Patēr ("father") in the plural refers to "parents" in Luke 1:17, Eph. 6:4, Col. 3:21 (*patēr* is synonymous with *goneus* v. 20), Heb. 11:23; 12:9.

Adelphos in the plural ("Brothers" or "siblings") clearly include the female readers Euodia and Syntyche in Phil. 1:12; 4:1–2 and Lydia in Acts 16:40. "Brother" was a metaphor of equality (Josephus, *Antiquities,* XIX.1.1[4]).

According to Walter Bauer, *anēr* in the plural indicates national or local origin, highlighting the group is made up of individuals. *A Greek-English Lexicon of the New Testament,* trans. W. F. Arndt and F. W. Gingrich (4th ed.; Chicago: University of Chicago, 1957), 15, 66; *Gesenius,* 440, 459, 465. Robertson translates anēr *adelphos patēr* (all in the plural in Acts 7:2) "brethren and sisters," "ladies and gentlemen" *Grammar,* 419.

59. *Gesenius,* 391, 393, 440, 459. In Indo-European languages, Istvan Foder argues, the feminine is a subset not of the masculine but of the more general category *animate.* English also has examples where masculine nouns are formed from common-gender words ("widow" preceded "widower") and where masculine and feminine words have separate etymologies ("female" derives from Latin *femina,* "male" from Latin *masculus*). Dennis Baron, *Grammar and Gender* (New York: Yale University, 1986), 4, 107–08, 116–17.

60. Clement of Alexandria who lived between A.D. 150–215 used *hē diakonos*. G. W. H. Lampe, ed. *A Patristic Greek Lexicon* (Oxford: Clarendon, 1961), 352–53.

61. Robertson, *Grammar,* 253.

62. Ruether uses "God/ess" as a new written generic for the God of the Bible, for whom both male and female imagery is needed. *Womanguides,* 8.

63. Liddell and Scott, *Lexicon,* 344, 356, 1348.

64. Robertson, *Grammar,* 153.

65. Greg Boyd, "My Personal Journey," *Priscilla Papers* 6 (Spring-Summer 1992): 19–21. Ruth C. Duck has even several biblical alternatives to the trinitarian "Father, Son, and Holy Spirit": the name: one God, Mother of us all, Father, Son, and Holy Spirit. First Person: the Father, Source, Creator, Parent (my preference); Second Person: the Son, Offspring, Word, Christ, Redeemer, Servant, Heir (my preference); Third Person: the (Holy) Spirit, liberating Spirit, Guide, Companion, Sustainer, Sanctifier. *Gender and the Name of God: The Trinitarian Baptismal Formula* (New York: Pilgrim, 1991), 163, 172, 184–85. Sallie McFague suggests "the invisible face" (the mystery of God or first person), "the visible body" (the physicality of God or second person), and "the mediating spirit" (the mediation of the invisible and the visible or third person). *The Body of God: An Ecological Theology* (Minneapolis: Fortress, 1993), 193.

Some believers do not like the terms "Creator, Redeemer, and Sanctifier" because these three functions are true of all three persons of the Trinity. Ted Peters points out that "Father, Son, and Holy Spirit" are titles, not proper names. Nevertheless, he does not like substitutes. *God as Trinity: Relationality and Temporality in Divine Life* (Louisville: Westminster, 1993), 51–55. Stephen Charles Mott points out that Matt. 28:19 is not the only reference to the Trinity in the Bible. In 1 Cor. 12:4–6 Paul follows the sequence Spirit, Lord, God and in 2 Cor. 13:14 Lord Jesus Christ, God, Holy Spirit. He concludes: "To insist upon Father, Son, and Holy Spirit as the only formula is to depart from the fullness of biblical usage in favor of church tradition." "From the Word: Scriptural Faithfulness / Language for the Trinity," *Christian Social Action* (June 1992): 30.

66. Joe LaMadeleine, "Caution! Inclusive Language May Change Your Life!," *Daughters of Sarah* 18 (Summer 1992): 43.

67. Deborah L. Detering, "Beyond Fathering," *Christianity Today* 27 (January 21, 1983): 45.

68. Dennis Baron, *Grammar and Gender,* 97–98, 139–40, 192, 220. Mary Daly poignantly expresses this dissatisfaction with the generic "he": "The 'I' makes the speaker/writer deceptively feel at home in a male-controlled language. When she uses this pronoun, she may forget that "she" is buried in the false generic "he." *Gyn/Ecology: The Metaethics of Radical Feminism* (Boston: Beacon, 1978), 18–19.

69. Marchiene Vroon Rienstra, *Swallow's Nest: A Feminine Reading of the Psalms* (Grand Rapids: Eerdmans, 1992), xv.

70. As well, in the New Testament the early Christians never once used "Father" in prayer. Smith, *Is It Okay to Call God Mother?* 81–83, 213, 257–58, 269.

71. Andrew M. Greeley, *Happy Are the Meek* (New York: Warner, 1985), 203, 205. For a full discussion of Andrew M. Greeley's Blackie Ryan series see W. D. Spencer, *Mysterium and Mystery: The Clerical Crime Novel* (Carbondale: Southern Illinois University, 1989), 183–90.

72. Tikva Frymer-Kensky, *In the Wake of the Goddesses: Women, Culture, and the Biblical Transformation of Pagan Myth* (New York: Free, 1992), 87; Susanne Heine, *Matriarchs, Goddesses, and Images of God: A Critique of a Feminist Theology*, trans. J. Bowden (Minneapolis: Augsburg, 1989), 28–29, 45–46.

73. Linda A. Mercadante, *Gender, Doctrine, and God: The Shakers and Contemporary Theology* (Nashville: Abingdon, 1990), 163, 169–70. On the Community of God, see also Royce Gordon Gruenler, *The Trinity in the Gospel of John: A Thematic Commentary on the Fourth Gospel* (Grand Rapids: Baker, 1986).

▼ Chapter 7: *God Is a Paradox*

1. Judith Ochshorn, "Reclaiming Our Past," *Women's Spirit Bonding*, eds. Janet Kalven and Mary I. Buckley (New York: Pilgrim, 1984), 290–91.

2. Starhawk, "Immanence: Uniting the Spiritual and Political," *Women's Spirit Bonding*, 313; Meinrad Craighead, *The Mother's Songs: Images of God the Mother* (New York: Paulist, 1986), introduction.

3. Donald G. Bloesch, *The Battle for the Trinity: The Debate over Inclusive God-Language* (Ann Arbor: Servant, 1985), 29.

4. Noah Webster, *Webster's New Universal Unabridged Dictionary*, ed. Jean L. McKechnie (2d ed.; New York: Dorset and Baber, 1979), 1937.

5. John C. Traupman, *The New College Latin and English Dictionary* (New York: Bantam Books, 1966), 315.

6. Elizabeth Achtemeier, *Nature, God, and Pulpit* (Grand Rapids: Eerdmans, 1992), 31.

7. Webster, *Dictionary*, 908.

8. Traupman, *Dictionary*, 177.

9. H. G. Liddell and R. Scott, *A Greek-English Lexicon*, eds. H. S. Jones and R. McKenzie (9th ed.; Oxford: Clarendon, 1940), 541–42.

10. Liddell and Scott, *Lexicon*, 1108; Joseph Henry Thayer, *Thayer's Greek-English Lexicon of the New Testament* (2d ed.; Marshallton: National Foundation for Christian Education, 1889), 207, 399.

11. *Emmenō* may refer to God: Num. 23:19; Jer. 51:28; or to humans: Deut. 19:15; 27:26; Isa. 7:7; 8:10; 28:18; 30:18; Jer. 38:32; 51:25.

12. Gloria Anzaldúa, "Entering into the Serpent," *Weaving the Visions: New Patterns in Feminist Spirituality,* eds. J. Plaskow and C. P. Christ (San Francisco: Harper, 1989), 84; Alice Walker, *The Color Purple* (New York: Harcourt Brace Jovanovich, 1982), 166–67.

13. Van A. Harvey, *A Handbook of Theological Terms* (New York: Macmillan, 1964), 66, 127, 173. E.g. Sallie McFague, *The Body of God: An Ecological Theology* (Minneapolis: Fortress, 1993), 141–49.

14. Philip Edgcumbe Hughes, "Immanence," *Baker's Dictionary of Theology,* ed. E. F. Harrison (Grand Rapids: Baker, 1960), 280.

15. Millard J. Erickson, *Introducing Christian Doctrine,* ed. L. A. Hustad (Grand Rapids: Baker, 1992), 76.

16. Georgia Harkness, *Conflicts in Religious Thought* (New York: Henry Holt, 1929), 177, 262. See also Deut. 4:7.

17. Erickson, *Doctrine,* 76–77.

18. Thayer, *Lexicon,* 207.

19. Liddell and Scott, *Lexicon,* 1420.

20. T. K. Abbott, *A Critical and Exegetical Commentary on the Epistles to the Ephesians and to the Colossians,* The International Critical Commentary (Edinburgh: T. and T. Clark, 1897), 35.

21. A. T. Robertson, *A Grammar of the Greek New Testament in the Light of Historical Research* (Nashville: Broadman, 1934), 600–03.

22. Erickson, *Doctrine,* 77.

23. Robertson, *Grammar,* 580–82.

24. Eph. 1:13; Acts 28:16. J. B. Lightfoot, *St. Paul's Epistle to the Philippians* (Grand Rapids: Zondervan, 1913), 8–9.

25. Robertson, *Grammar,* 586.

26. G. Frederick Owen and Steven Barabas, "Dress," *Zondervan Pictorial Bible Dictionary* (1967): 225–26.

27. Starhawk, *Truth or Dare: Encounters with Power, Authority, and Mystery* (San Francisco: Harper & Row, 1987), 310–11.

28. Robertson, *Grammar,* 584, 591, 594.

29. Tikva Frymer-Kensky, *In the Wake of the Goddesses: Women, Culture, and the Biblical Transformation of Pagan Myth* (New York: Free, 1992), 154.

30. Naomi R. Goldenberg, *Changing of the Gods: Feminism and the End of Traditional Religions* (Boston: Beacon, 1979), 89.

31. Nelle Morton, "The Goddess as Metaphoric Image," *Weaving,* 111–12; Starhawk, *Truth or Dare,* 118.

32. Rose Spector, "Carol Leonard: Sacred Passages of the Divine Woman," *Earth Star* 14 (February/March 1993): 7.

33. Starhawk, *Truth or Dare,* 104; Christina Springer, "Child-Spirit," *Woman of Power* 19 (Winter 1991): 10; Shakmah Winddrum, "Unveiling the Mystery of Magic," *Woman of Power* 19 (Winter 1991): 33; Ed McGaa, Eagle Man, *Mother Earth Spirituality: Native American Paths to Healing Ourselves*

and Our World (San Francisco: Harper, 1990), 66. Karen McCarthy Brown adds: "Vodou technicians of the sacred" must "learn how to manage this perilous ego-exchange." "Women's Leadership in Haitian Vodou," *Weaving,* 227.

34. Mayumi Oda, "Creativity and Spirituality," *Woman of Power* 21 (Fall 1991): 18–19.

35. Rosemary Radford Ruether, *Womanguides: Readings Toward a Feminist Theology* (Boston: Beacon, 1985), 6.

36. Monica Sjöö, "A Letter from Monica Sjöö," *Woman of Power* 19 (Winter 1991): 79.

37. See also Deut. 32:17 and Rev. 9:20.

38. Birgit Meyer, "'If You Are a Devil, You Are a Witch and, If You Are a Witch, You Are a Devil.' The Integration of 'Pagan' Ideas into the Conceptual Universe of Ewe Christians in Southeastern Ghana," *Journal of Religion in Africa* XXII (May 1992): 110, 122.

39. John L. Nevius, *Demon Possession and Allied Themes: Being an Inductive Study of Phenomena of Our Own Times* (New York: Fleming H. Revell, 1894), 9, 22–27.

40. Sheila S. Walker, "Witchcraft and Healing in an African Christian Church," *Journal of Religion in Africa* X (May 1979): 131. The apostle Paul also uses the metaphor of "consumption" for the results of the work of the false superapostles (2 Cor. 11:20). Maya Deren documents the loss of freedom in Voudoun: "The possessed benefits least of all men from his own possession. He may even suffer for it in material loss, in the sometimes painful, always exhausted physical aftermath. . . . The serviteur must be induced to surrender his ego, that the archetype become manifest. . . . the structure has evolved . . . which, in even the most dedicated, must triumph against that final terror which attends the loss of self, . . . Now there is only terror. 'This is it!' Resting upon that leg I feel a strange numbness enter it from the earth itself and mount, within the very marrow of the bone, as slowly and richly as sap might mount the trunk of a tree." *Divine Horsemen: The Living Gods of Haiti* (New York: McPherson, 1953), 249–50, 259.

For helpful books on demon possession see Rodger K. Bufford, *Counseling and the Demonic,* Resources for Christian Counseling 17 (Dallas: Word, 1988); Michael Green, *Exposing the Prince of Darkness* (Ann Arbor: Servant, 1981), a reprint of *I Believe in Satan's Downfall* (Grand Rapids: Eerdmans, 1981). "White" witches have always claimed to help people. The traditional witch Sybil Leek even used the term "white witch" for herself. *The Complete Art of Witchcraft* (New York: Thomas Y. Crowell, 1971), 75, 80. However Kurt E. Koch documents the residue harm caused even by "white witch" healings. *Christian Counseling and Occultism,* trans. A. Petter (Grand Rapids: Kregel, 1965).

41. C. S. Lewis, *The Screwtape Letters and Screwtape Proposes a Toast* (New York: Macmillan, 1961), xi–xii.

42. E.g., Margot Adler, *Drawing Down the Moon: Witches, Druids, Goddess-Worshippers, and Other Pagans in America Today* (2d ed.; Boston: Beacon, 1986), xi, 54, 69, 99, 416.

43. Luke 10:18; Rev. 20:10.

44. Luke 10:17–18; 11:14–23; Rev. 16:13–14; Thayer, *Lexicon*, 124. Other passages on demons mention: deception of sorcery (Rev. 18:23; Nah. 3:4), their recognition of God (James 2:19), and that some teach asceticism (1 Tim. 4:1–5). In the ancient secular Greek society *daimōn* may refer to "god, goddess" or spiritual being inferior to the Gods. *Daimonion* refers to "divine Power" or "evil spirit." Liddell and Scott, *Lexicon*, 365–66.

45. Liddell and Scott, *Lexicon*, 1917.

46. The witch trials at Salem beginning in 1692 erred in not always being biblical. "Witches" who "confessed" were allowed to live. The young girls Ann Putnam, Elizabeth Parris, Abigail Williams, Mary Walcott, and others who appeared to be demon possessed were not delivered during the trial process from their evil spirits. A number of ministers repeatedly stated that the criteria for finding witches, such as spectral evidence, having devils' marks on their skin, causing the girls to fall, were not at all biblical ones. Marion L. Starkey, *The Devil in Massachusetts: A Modern Enquiry into the Salem Witch Trials* (Garden City: Doubleday, 1949), 39, 53, 157, 188, 213–14, 227. See also Chadwick Hansen, *Witchcraft at Salem* (New York: George Braziller, 1969), 123–25.

47. 1 Sam. 28:3, 9, 13. Other passages mention the relationship of divination to human sacrifice (2 Chron. 33:6) and how God wanted divination terminated (2 Kings 23:24; Mic. 5:12; 2 Kings 9:22; Isa. 8:19–22). As terrifying as this condemnation is, no one should be too self-righteous, because the prophet Samuel teaches that rebellion and stubbornness are no less sins than divination and idolatry. Obedience is what God seeks (1 Sam. 15:22–23).

48. Meyer, 117. Women have also been very attracted to Christianity. Jesus had women disciples who were very supportive (Luke 8:2–3; 23:27, 49; 24:1–10). Even today the churches have many active women. For example, in the four states of Maine, Vermont, New Hampshire, and northern Massachusetts, where I am an active ordained minister, in 1988, 60% of Presbyterian Church (USA) members were female, 40% male; in 1990, 48% of Presbyterian Church (USA) members were female, 52% male; in 1990, 56% of the elders were female, 44% male. *Presbyterian Church (USA) 1988, 1990 Minutes, Part II, Statistics* (Louisville: Office of the General Assembly, 1988, 1990).

49. See Aída Besançon Spencer, *Beyond the Curse: Women Called to Ministry* (Peabody: Hendrickson, 1985), 47–57, 81–86.

50. Ruether, "Motherearth and the Megamachine: A Theology of Liberation in a Feminine, Somatic and Ecological Perspective," *Womanspirit*

Rising: A Feminist Reader in Religion, eds. Carol P. Christ and Judith Plaskow (San Francisco: Harper & Row, 1979), 44. E. Dodson Gray, "General Introduction," *Sacred Dimensions of Women's Experience,* ed. E. D. Gray (Wellesley: Roundtable, 1988), 2.

51. Starhawk, *Truth or Dare,* 118.

52. For a further study on this issue from a psychological perspective, see Mary Stewart Van Leeuwen, *Gender and Grace: Love, Work, and Parenting in a Changing World* (Downers Grove: InterVarsity, 1990). For example, she concludes: "The complexity of human functioning eludes simple stereotypes about what men and women 'are' or 'should be' like" (p. 105). Elizabeth A. Johnson agrees that to assign greater value to the "feminine" polarity "is to keep women, earth, and Spirit in their pre-assigned box, which is a cramped, subordinate place. . . . In truth, women are not any closer to nature than men are; this is a cultural construct." Elizabeth A. Johnson, *Women, Earth, and Creator Spirit* (New York: Paulist, 1993), 21.

53. Johnson, *Women, Earth, and Creator Spirit,* 19, 30–31, 59. In reaction to ecofeminist critique of Judaeo-Christianity many new books on the care of the earth are now being published such as: Richard D. Land and Louis A. Moore, eds. *The Earth Is the Lord's: Christians and the Environment* (Nashville: Broadman, 1992); Shannon Jung, *We Are Home: A Spirituality of the Environment* (New York: Paulist, 1993); Berit Kjos suggests many ecological family projects in *Under the Spell of Mother Earth* (Wheaton: Victor, 1992), 170–75; John Hart reminds the reader of three basic biblical principles that encourage good stewardship of the earth: the land is God's, the land is entrusted to humanity (Lev. 25:2–7, 20–28), and the land is to be shared equitably through the ages (Num. 33:53–54; 35:8); *The Spirit of the Earth* (New York: Paulist, 1984), 2, 68–71, 77–81, 122, 154; Achtemeier, *Nature, God, and Pulpit.* Carolyn Merchant blames poor ecology on a mechanistic view of nature, developed by seventeenth century natural philosophers and based on a Western mathematical tradition going back to Plato. *The Death of Nature: Women, Ecology and the Scientific Revolution* (2d ed.; San Francisco: Harper, 1990), 290; Janice E. Kirk and Donald R. Kirk, *Cherish the Earth: The Environment and Scripture* (Scottdale, Pa.: Herald, 1993).

▼ Chapter 8: *God Is Reflected*

1. Thomas Bulfinch, *The Age of Fable or Beauties of Mythology,* ed. J. Loughran Scott (Philadelphia: David McKay, 1898), 1, 18.

2. See my arguments in *Paul's Literary Style: A Stylistic and Historical Comparison of II Corinthians 11:16–12:13, Romans 8:9–39, and Philippians 3:2–4:13,* Evangelical Theological Society Monograph (Winona Lake: Eisenbrauns, 1984), 108–11. The information on Romans 1 has been

adapted from my previous essay "Romans 1: Finding God in Creation" in *Through No Fault of Their Own? The Fate of Those Who Have Never Heard*, eds. W. V. Crockett and J. G. Sigountos (Grand Rapids: Baker, 1991), 125–35.

3. Henry George Liddell and Robert Scott, *A Greek-English Lexicon*, eds. H. S. Jones and R. McKenzie (9th ed.; Oxford: Clarendon, 1940), 255, 1588; Joseph Henry Thayer, *Thayer's Greek-English Lexicon of the New Testament* (2d ed.; Marshallton: National Foundation for Christian Education, 1889), 79, 572.

4. A. T. Robertson, *A Grammar of the Greek New Testament in the Light of Historical Research* (Nashville: Broadman, 1934), 606; James Hope Moulton and George Milligan, *The Vocabulary of the Greek Testament: Illustrated from the Papyri and Other Non-Literary Sources* (Grand Rapids: Eerdmans, 1930), 336–37.

5. Moulton and Milligan, *Vocabulary*, 663; Liddell and Scott, *Lexicon*, 355, 1915.

6. The preposition "from" (*apo*) usually suggests the general starting point (Robertson, *Grammar*, 577).

7. Liddell and Scott, *Lexicon*, 856; Thayer, *Lexicon*, 314, 451–52.

8. Walter Bauer, *A Greek-English Lexicon of the New Testament*, trans. William F. Arndt and F. Wilbur Gingrich (4th ed.; Chicago: University of Chicago, 1957), 542.

9. A. T. Robertson adds that when one article is used for two distinct groups, they are treated as one for the purpose in hand. *Te* and *kai* also have a closer unity than *kai . . . kai*. *Grammar*, 787, 1178.

10. Thayer, *Lexicon*, 13–14, 21; Liddell and Scott, *Lexicon*, 26, 36.

11. Moulton and Milligan, *Vocabulary*, 286.

12. Thayer, *Lexicon*, 118.

13. God: Gal. 4:9; God's mind: Rom. 11:34; Christ: 2 Cor. 5:16; Spirit: 1 Cor. 2:11; a human: 1 Cor. 8:3; a person's power: 1 Cor. 4:19.

14. Dana Raphael, "The Tender Gift of Breastfeeding." *Sacred Dimensions of Women's Experience*, ed. E. D. Gray (Wellesley: Roundtable, 1988), 181.

15. Martin D. O'Keefe, *Known from the Things That Are: Fundamental Theory of the Moral Life* (Houston: Center for Thomistic Studies, 1987), 101, 317–24.

16. Don Richardson, *Eternity in Their Hearts* (2d ed.; Ventura: Regal, 1981).

17. J. E. Lovelock, *Gaia: A New Look at Life on Earth* (2d ed.; Oxford: Oxford University, 1987), x, 12, 19, 27, 92, 108–15, 142–43.

18. In Col. 1:23 and Mark 10:6 "creation" (*ktisis*) refers to humans.

19. Moulton and Milligan, *Vocabulary*, 151, 391. For example, James 2:4; Luke 5:21–22; 6:8.

20. Justo L. González, *Mañana: Christian Theology from a Hispanic Perspective* (Nashville: Abingdon, 1990), 117.

21. C. G. Jung and C. Kerényi, *Essays on a Science of Mythology: The Myths of the Divine Child and the Divine Maiden*, trans. R. F. C. Hull (2d ed.; New York: Harper & Row, 1963), 8, 17.

22. Christine Downing, *The Goddess: Mythological Images of the Feminine* (New York: Crossroad, 1981), 6, 221, 223; Margot Adler notes: "Most Pagan goddess-oriented groups are growing more and more polytheistic." *Drawing Down the Moon: Witches, Druids, Goddess-Worshippers, and Other Pagans in America Today* (2d ed.; Boston: Beacon, 1986), 174.

23. Downing, *Goddess*, 221.

24. Starhawk, *The Spiral Dance: A Rebirth of the Ancient Religion of the Great Goddess* (2d ed.; San Francisco: Harper & Row, 1989), 32, 34, 78.

25. Anton Ehrenzweig, *The Hidden Order of Art: A Study in the Psychology of Artistic Imagination* (Berkeley: University of California, 1967), 14, 21.

26. Jürgen Moltmann, *The Spirit of Life: A Universal Affirmation* (Minneapolis: Fortress, 1992), 84.

Someone like Matthew Fox is difficult to understand. Although he claims to be pan*en*theistic ("God is *in* everything and everything is in God") not pantheistic ("everything is God and God is everything"), I think, in reality he is pantheistic. He moves from creation being "God's shadow," to worshiping the shadow (creation), rather than the One who makes the shadow. Creation is God: the "sacredness of creation" is the "first article of faith." "Creation is the source of all worship." He begins *Creation Spirituality* paraphrasing John 1: "the gift was with God and the gift was God." But who or what is the "gift"? It is "a fire ball," the earth. He claims to be a "trinitarian Christian," but nowhere is the triune God separate from creation. He writes with awe and joy of the universe, which is wonderful. However, because God is limited to creation, everything that happens, glory *and* pain, comes from God. Therefore, all religions, including pagan religions, must be true. Matthew Fox, *Original Blessing: A Primer in Creation Spirituality* (Santa Fe: Bear, 1983), 90; *Creation Spirituality: Liberating Gifts for the Peoples of the Earth* (San Francisco: Harper, 1991), 1–2, 9–10, 41, 55, 100–01.

27. Geraldine Hatch Hanon, "Astrology and the Ritual of Midlife," Shakmah Winddrum, "Unveiling the Mystery of Magic," *Woman of Power* 19 (Winter 1991): 24, 32.

28. Aletícia Tijerina-Jim, "The Sweat Lodge—A Source of Power," *Woman of Power* 19 (Winter 1991): 41.

29. Brown, Francis, S. R. Driver, and Charles A. Briggs, *A Hebrew and English Lexicon of the Old Testament* (Oxford: Clarendon, 1907), 712, 1036–37. Ronald J. Sider, "Redeeming the Environmentalists," *Christianity Today* 37 (June 21, 1993): 28. Even Lynn White, Jr., whose essay "The Historical Roots of Our Ecologic Crisis" is renowned for blaming the ecologic crisis on the so-called "Christian axiom that nature has no reason for existence save to serve man" (which we saw contradicts Genesis 2:15), concludes by positing an alternative *Christian* view: "I propose Francis as a patron saint for ecologists." *The Environmental Handbook: Prepared for the First National*

Environmental Teach-In, ed. Garrett DeBell (New York: Ballantine, 1970), 25–26.

30. Elizabeth Achtemeier, *Nature, God, and Pulpit* (Grand Rapids: Eerdmans, 1992), 4.

31. Janet L. Jacobs, "Women, Ritual, and Power," *Woman of Power* 19 (Winter 1991): 64.

32. For a further discussion of recognizing one's mortality see ch. 2 of A. Besançon Spencer and W. D. Spencer, *Joy through the Night: Biblical Resources for Suffering People* (Downers Grove: InterVarsity, 1994).

33. Starhawk, *Truth or Dare: Encounters with Power, Authority, and Mystery* (San Francisco: Harper & Row, 1987), 106, 315.

34. Karen McCarthy Brown, "Why Women Need the War God," *Women's Spirit Bonding,* eds. Janet Kalven and Mary I. Buckley (New York: Pilgrim, 1984), 197, 199.

35. Melissa Potter and Maria Epes, "The Goddess Altar in Cow Pasture Grove: A Ritual Creation," *Woman of Power* 19 (Winter 1991): 22–23.

36. Potter and Epes: 22–23.

37. Ruth C. Duck explains: "Metaphorical language, however, keeps alive the tension between likeness and unlikeness, and between the possibility and limits of all human language about God." *Gender and the Name of God: The Trinitarian Baptismal Formula* (New York: Pilgrim, 1991), 22.

38. Carol P. Christ, "Why Women Need the Goddess: Phenomenological, Psychological, and Political Reflections," *Womanspirit Rising: A Feminist Reader in Religion,* eds. C. P. Christ and J. Plaskow (San Francisco: Harper & Row, 1979), 278–79.

39. John Ferguson, *The Religions of the Roman Empire,* Aspects of Greek and Roman Life (Ithaca: Cornell University, 1970), 65–66.

40. George MacDonald, *The Wise Woman, or the Lost Princess* (Grand Rapids: Eerdmans, 1980), 43.

41. Aída Besançon Spencer, "*Sĕrîrût* as Self-Reliance," *Journal of Biblical Literature* 100 (June 1981): 247–48.

42. Thayer, *Lexicon,* 516.

43. Paul J. Achtemeier, *Romans,* Interpretation: A Bible Commentary for Teaching and Preaching (Atlanta: John Knox, 1985), 38. Tragically when women come to glorify *only* their own feminine reflections, sometimes they may end up not appreciating that which is "other" than themselves, men. For example, Nelle Morton writes: "This sense of oneness within and with one another has brought us into more erotic relationship with one another as women." "The Goddess as Metaphoric Image," *Weaving the Visions: New Patterns in Feminist Spirituality,* eds. Judith Plaskow and Carol P. Christ (San Francisco: Harper, 1989), 116. Mary Daly also writes: "Female-identified erotic love is not dichotomized from radical female friendships, but rather

is one important expression/manifestation of friendship. Women loving women do not seek to lose our identity, but to express it, dis-cover it, create it." *Gyn/Ecology: The Metaethics of Radical Feminism* (Boston: Beacon, 1978), 373. Sally Gearhart urges "re-sourcement" for the women's movement. Going to "a new place for our energy" "has a strong and unashamed lesbian component." "Womanpower: Energy Re-Sourcement," Gina Foglia and Dorit Wolffberg, "Spiritual Dimensions of Feminist Anti-Nuclear Activism," *The Politics of Women's Spirituality: Essays on the Rise of Spiritual Power within the Feminist Movement,* ed. C. Spretnak (Garden City: Doubleday, 1982), 195, 203, 450, 454. The apostle Paul, too, notes that not thanking God for creation results in giving oneself sexually to those of one's own sex (Rom. 1:24–27). According to psychologist Ruth Tiffany Barnhouse, homosexuality is an immaturity that can not experience "otherness" ("Homosexuality," *Anglican Theological Review* 6[June 1976]:130). Even Plato describes homosexual men (for him a positive attribute) as those who "embrace that which is like them" (Rosemary Radford Ruether, *Womanguides: Readings Toward a Feminist Theology* [Boston: Beacon, 1985], 78).

44. Gail Hanlon, "Living in a Liminal Time: An Interview with Jean Shinoda Bolen," *Woman of Power* 21 (Fall 1991): 23, 25; Jade, "To Know Our Goddess-Selves," *Woman of Power* 19 (Winter 1991): 15.

45. Although the Goddess movement overwhelmingly is anti-Christian, some authors espouse Goddess worship at the same time they espouse Christianity. As any Goddess feminist, Meinrad Craighead has the usual beliefs in ritual, invoking spirits and ancestors, all being divine, form being fluid, the great mother bringing death and life, and emphasis on birth and the uterus. In reality, one can not be both polytheistic and monotheistic at the same time. (See ch. 5 "God Is Unique.") *The Litany of the Great River* (New York: Paulist, 1991), 8–10, 27–29, 68–69; *The Mother's Songs: Images of God the Mother* (New York: Paulist, 1986), introduction, 1, 34–35, 65.

46. "Aesthetic" and "ethical/liberation" feminist spirituality are categories suggested by Rosemary Radford Ruether, "Feminist Theology and Spirituality," *Christian Feminism: Visions of a New Humanity,* ed. J. L. Weidman (San Francisco: Harper & Row, 1984), 13–15. Anne E. Carr explains that "women's spirituality" is "the distinctive female relationship to the divine in contrast to the male." In contrast to male spirituality, women's spirituality has been described as more related to nature and to the home. "Feminist spirituality" is "that mode of relating to God" "that has integrated into itself the central elements of feminist criticism of the patriarchal tradition." It could refer to women *and* men who promote "genuine mutuality, reciprocity, and equality." A "Christian feminist spirituality" integrates feminist spirituality within a framework of Christian response to God. *Transforming Grace: Christian Tradition and Women's Experience* (San Francisco:

Harper & Row, 1988), 206–07. Charlene Spretnak prefers "Goddess spirituality." On the other hand, some practitioners of "women's spirituality" are "uncomfortable with any anthropomorphizing of the One." *Politics*, xvii.

47. The term "Ecofeminism," or *l'écoféminisme*, is credited to Françoise d'Eaubonne, *Le Féminisme ou la mort* (Paris: Pierre Horay, 1974), 216. She cites Shulamith Firestone as founding an Ecological Feminist Center in 1973.

48. Not every coven calls itself feminist. Naomi R. Goldenberg, *Changing of the Gods: Feminism and the End of Traditional Religions* (Boston: Beacon, 1979), 91. Margot Adler is more specific. The School of Wicca has been charged with sexism by many people such that some witches began feminist covens. Many witches lately highlight the Goddess but in practice they believe in a Goddess (in three aspects of Maiden, Mother, and Crone) *and* a God, the horned lord. Duality is crucial to witchcraft in practice. *Moon*, 86, 102, 112, 121, 128, 149, 178, 187, 208, 211–16, 226, 228, 250.

49. See also Carol P. Christ, "Why Women Need the Goddess," *Womanspirit*, 278.

50. Rosemary Radford Ruether and Elisabeth Schüssler Fiorenza are examples of two scholars I have quoted who would fit this category. Ruether explains her use of nonbiblical religions as positive resources for Judaeo-Christianity while she rejects the "romantic feminism" of Goddess feminism in *Sexism and God-Talk: Toward a Feminist Theology* (Boston: Beacon, 1983), 39–41, 44, 46, 104–05.

51. Elizabeth Dodson Gray, "General Introduction," *Sacred Dimensions*, 1.

52. For further information on prayer see William David Spencer and Aída Besançon Spencer, *The Prayer Life of Jesus: Shout of Agony, Revelation of Love, A Commentary* (Lanham: University Press of America, 1990).

53. Brother Lawrence, *The Practice of the Presence of God: Being Conversations and Letters of Nicholas Herman of Lorraine* (Old Tappan: Fleming H. Revell, 1958), 8, 16, 27–28. Brother Lawrence became a believer from observing nature: "That in the winter, seeing a tree stripped of its leaves, and considering that within a little time the leaves would be renewed, and after that the flowers and fruit appear, he received a high view of the providence and power of God" (p. 11). Brother Lawrence also does not refrain from using feminine imagery for God. He felt more "sweetness and delight" than "an infant at the mother's breast" when at "the bosom of God" (p. 37).

54. Gray, "Introduction," "Women as Creators of Sacred Order," *Sacred Dimensions*, 48–49, 97–98.

55. Carol P. Christ, "In Praise of Aphrodite: Sexuality as Sacred," *Sacred Dimensions*, 224.

56. Mary McDermott Shideler, *The Theology of Romantic Love: A Study in the Writings of Charles Williams* (Grand Rapids: Eerdmans, 1962), 21.

▼ Chapter 9: *God of the Living Water*

1. Nelle Morton, "The Goddess as Metaphoric Image," *Weaving the Visions: New Patterns in Feminist Spirituality*, eds. J. Plaskow and C. P. Christ (San Francisco: Harper, 1989), 112.

2. Gloria Anzaldúa, "Entering into the Serpent," *Weaving*, 85; Meinrad Craighead, *The Mother's Songs: Images of God the Mother* (New York: Paulist, 1986), introduction.

3. Carol Lee Sanchez, "New World Tribal Communities: An Alternative Approach for Recreating Egalitarian Societies," *Weaving*, 346.

4. Charlene Spretnak, "The Politics of Women's Spirituality," *The Politics of Women's Spirituality: Essays on the Rise of Spiritual Power within the Feminist Movement*, ed. C. Spretnak (Garden City: Doubleday, 1982), 394.

5. Naomi Goldenberg, *Changing of the Gods: Feminism and the End of Traditional Religions* (Boston: Beacon, 1979), 93. She also notes that the first national all-women conference on women's spirituality was held in Boston in April, 1976 (92). See also Margot Adler, *Drawing Down the Moon: Witches, Druids, Goddess-Worshippers, and Other Pagans in America Today* (2d ed.; Boston: Beacon, 1986), 222.

6. Carol P. Christ, "Why Women Need the Goddess: Phenomenological, Psychological, and Political Reflections," *Womanspirit Rising: A Feminist Reader in Religion*, eds. C. P. Christ and J. Plaskow (San Francisco: Harper & Row, 1979), 286.

7. Christine Downing, *The Goddess: Mythological Images of the Feminine* (New York: Crossroad, 1981), 4; William D. Hendricks, *Exit Interviews* (Chicago: Moody, 1993), 21, 261.

8. Joyce Quiring Erickson, "What Difference? The Theory and Practice of Feminist Criticism," *Christianity and Literature* 33 (Fall 1983): 71.

9. Hallie Iglehart, "The Unnatural Divorce of Spirituality and Politics," *Politics*, 413.

10. Judith Plaskow and Carol P. Christ, "Introduction," *Weaving*, 9.

11. Sanchez, "Tribal Communities," *Weaving*, 347; Charlene Spretnak, "The Christian Right's 'Holy War' Against Feminism," *Politics*, 487.

12. Adler, *Moon*, 22–23; 418–19. In a letter to me dated June 10, 1993, Harper San Francisco's Erich Van Rijn documents 185,145 copies sold of *The Spiral Dance!* 1.9 million copies of Frank E. Peretti's antiwitchcraft novel *This Present Darkness* (Westchester: Crossway, 1986) have been sold as of July 1993.

13. Janette Hassey, *No Time for Silence: Evangelical Women in Public Ministry Around the Turn of the Century* (Grand Rapids: Zondervan, 1986), 16, 31.

14. Nathan R. Wood, *A School of Christ* (Boston: Halliday, 1953), 25–27, 34–35. In 1895 at A. J. Gordon's death the teachers and administrators were: Dr. James Gray, Dr. Julia Morton Plummer, Dr. John McElwain, Mrs. Gordon,

Professor Cole, Dr. F. Chapell, and Mrs. Chapell. In 1901: Dr. Emory W. Hunt, Dr. John McElwain, Dr. J. D. Herr, Mrs. Gordon, Mrs. Alice B. Coleman (sec.), Rev. Arthur Gordon (treas.), Dr. James Gray, Mrs. Gray, Dr. Julia Morton Plummer, Miss Blanche Tilton.

15. Katherine C. Bushnell, *God's Word to Women: One Hundred Bible Studies on Woman's Place in the Divine Economy* (Ray B. Munson, Box 52, North Collins, NY 14111), paragraphs 2, 830, lessons 1, 100.

16. Helen Barrett Montgomery, trans. *The New Testament in Modern English* (2d ed.; Valley Forge, Judson, 1952).

17. Catherine Booth, *Female Ministry; or, Woman's Right to Preach the Gospel* (London, 1859). Reprinted by New York: The Salvation Army.

18. Douglas W. Carlson, "Discovering their Heritage: Women and the American Past," *Gender Matters: Women's Studies for the Christian Community,* ed. June Steffenson Hagen (Grand Rapids: Zondervan, 1990), 100–01.

19. Dorothy C. Bass, "Their Prodigious Influence: Women, Religion and Reform in Antebellum America," *Women of Spirit: Female Leadership in the Jewish and Christian Traditions,* eds. Rosemary Ruether and Eleanor McLaughlin (New York: Simon & Schuster, 1979), 280.

20. Anne E. Carr, *Transforming Grace: Christian Tradition and Women's Experience* (San Francisco: Harper & Row, 1988), 10–11.

21. Frederick Douglass, *The Life and Times of Frederick Douglass* (2d ed.; New York: Collier, 1892), 472.

22. Ruth A. Tucker and Walter L. Liefeld, *Daughters of the Church: Women and Ministry From New Testament Times to the Present* (Grand Rapids: Zondervan, 1987), 231.

23. Judg. 4:4; 5:7, 31; 1 Kings 16:31–33.

24. Mic. 6:4; Exod. 15:20–21; Num. 12:1–16.

25. *History of the Church* III.37; VI.42; Acts 21:8–9. See A. Besançon Spencer, "Early-Church Heroines: Rulers, Prophets and Martyrs," *Christian History* 7 (1988): 12–16, and *Priscilla Papers* 7 (Winter 1993): 4–6.

26. Eusebius, *History of the Church* V.16–19. Patricia Wilson-Kastner, *A Lost Tradition: Women Writers of the Early Church* (Lanham: University Press of America, 1981), 1, 19. Compare Ronald A. N. Kydd, *Charismatic Gifts in the Early Church* (Peabody: Hendrickson, 1984), 31–36.

27. Gail Hanlon, "Homegrown Juju Dolls: An Interview with Artist Riua Akinshegun," *Woman of Power* 21 (Fall 1991):31.

28. Judith Antonelli, "Feminist Spirituality: The Politics of the Psyche," Gina Foglia and Dorit Wolffberg, "Spiritual Dimensions of Feminist Anti-Nuclear Activism," *Politics,* 401, 454; Adler, *Moon,* 225.

29. C. S. Lewis, *The Lion, the Witch and the Wardrobe: A Story for Children* (New York: Collier, 1950), 171–72.

30. Adler, *Moon,* 4.

31. E.g., Sheila D. Collins, *A Different Heaven and Earth* (Valley Forge: Judson, 1974), 59, 63, 101; Downing, *Goddess*, 14; Carol P. Christ, "Feminist Liberation Theology and Yahweh as Holy Warrior: An Analysis of Symbol," *Women's Spirit Bonding*, eds. Janet Kalven and Mary I. Buckley (New York: Pilgrim, 1984), 205, 207.

32. "Introduction," *Weaving*, 8.

33. Cathleen Rountree, "The Vulva Dance: Notes from an Interview with Arisika Razak," *Woman of Power* 19 (Winter 1991): 49; Adler, *Moon*, 102. The goddess for many is a sexual presence. In the novel *The Return of the Goddess: A Divine Comedy* by Elizabeth Cunningham, the hero Marvin Greene has a sexual response to the earth of a sacred grove. He becomes Pan reincarnated, a "sexton." (Barrytown: Station Hill, 1992), 30–31, 327, 375, 382.

34. Craighead, *The Mother's Songs*, introduction. Aidan A. Kelly suggests that in reality the gentle, loving Goddess of today is a new creation from investing Mary with some of the divine attributes of Jesus. Adler, *Moon*, 174. Moreover, his research shows that the earliest Gardnerian circle rituals were "all adapted from the Kabalistic procedures of *The Greater Key of Solomon*." None of them were based on a "pagan" theology. *Crafting the Art of Magic, Book 1: A History of Modern Witchcraft 1939–1964*, Llewellyn's Modern Witchcraft Series (St. Paul: Llewellyn, 1991), 49, 101.

35. Collins, *A Different Heaven and Earth*, 26.

36. C. G. Jung, *Memories, Dreams, Reflections,* ed. Aniela Jaffé, trans. Richard and Clara Winston (2d ed.; New York: Vintage, 1965), 3–4, 9, 12, 23, 27, 36–42, 44–46, 50–51, 56, 58–59, 66–70, 74, 89–94, 98, 134, 138–39, 141, 171, 177, 184–87, 190–91, 195, 200–02, 205, 216, 225, 300, 314, 338, 340–41, 358, 363; *Aion: Researches into the Phenomenology of the Self,* trans. R. F. C. Hull, Bollingen Series XX (2d ed.; Princeton: Princeton University, 1968), 47, 55; *Man and His Symbols* (New York: Doubleday, 1964), 45, 52, 55, 57, 67, 79, 82, 85, 101. Janet and Stewart Farrar write: "Jung's ideas strike an immediate chord with almost every witch who turns serious attention to them." They also like Jung's male-female polarity. *The Witches' Way: Principles, Rituals and Beliefs of Modern Witchcraft* (London: Robert Hale, 1984), 147. The value of Jung's perspective is his insistence that dreams are helpful for understanding a person's subliminal thoughts, no one method is good for every patient, patients can help in the interpretation of their dreams, and religion is helpful for psychological health. *Memories,* 170–71.

37. J. E. Lovelock, *Gaia: A New Look at Life on Earth* (2d ed.; Oxford University, 1987), xii, 1, 10, 13, 27, 34, 107–08, 127, 140, 145–47. Lawrence E. Joseph, *Gaia: The Growth of an Idea* (New York: St. Martin's, 1990), 1, 15, 29–30, 70. Aidan Kelly, a former witch, credits Gardner with reforming witchcraft by highlighting the Goddess: "It is the Goddess who captures the

imagination, or hearts, or souls, or whatever else they are caught by, of those who enter into this movement." He writes that Gardner's group focused on a male god and the male high priest until 1957. Adler, *Moon,* 83; Gerald B. Gardner, *Witchcraft Today* (New York: Citadel, 1955), 40–42, 145; Kelly, *Crafting the Art of Magic, Book 1,* 34.

38. Adler, *Moon,* 86, 100, 102, 112, 178, 187, 206, 211, 214, 216–17; Edward C. Whitmont, *Return of the Goddess* (New York: Crossroad, 1982), x; Gloria Z. Greenfield, "Does Hierarchy Have a Place in Women's Spirituality? Spiritual Hierarchies: The Empress' New Clothes?" *Politics,* 533; Starhawk, *Truth or Dare: Encounters with Power, Authority, and Mystery* (San Francisco: Harper & Row, 1987), 10; Jade, *To Know: A Guide to Women's Magic and Spirituality* (Oak Park: Delphi, 1991), 63, 66, 72, 96, 112, 138. Emily Erwin Culpepper builds a case against using only the Mother Goddess partly because of the conservative Jungian polarity. "Contemporary Goddess Theology: A Sympathetic Critique," *Shaping New Vision: Gender and Values in American Culture,* eds. Clarissa W. Atkinson, Constance H. Buchanan, and Margaret R. Miles, The Harvard Women's Studies in Religion Series, 5 (Ann Arbor: U. M. I. Research, 1987), 60–62. Diane Tennis and Baba Copper also speak to the danger of male-female polarity. Diane Tennis, *Is God the Only Reliable Father?* (Philadelphia: Westminster, 1985), 29, 98. Baba Copper, "The Voice of Women's Spirituality in Futurism," *Politics,* 499, "Women should not identify themselves with those repressed parts of the male psyche that males have projected upon them as 'feminine.'" Rosemary Radford Ruether, *Sexism and God-Talk: Toward a Feminist Theology* (Boston: Beacon, 1983), 111–13.

39. For Stewart Farrar, the divine Male is active, fertilizing, energetic, pursuing while the divine Female is passive, fertile, gestating, nourishing. *What Witches Do: A Modern Coven Revealed* (Custer: Phoenix, 1983), 22.

40. Adler, *Moon,* 184.

41. Morton, "Goddess," *Weaving,* 113, 116.

42. Cunningham, *Return,* 286.

43. Carr, *Transforming Grace,* 142–43.

44. Carol P. Christ, "Rethinking Theology and Nature," *Weaving,* 316, 320–21.

45. Marion Zimmer Bradley, *The Mists of Avalon* (New York: Knopf, 1982), 59, 136, 172, 181.

46. Cynthia Eller, *Living in the Lap of the Goddess: The Feminist Spirituality Movement in America* (New York: Crossroad, 1993), 49.

47. Lovelock, *Gaia,* 27, 107–08, 146.

48. Adler, *Moon,* ix, 96, 112–13. The "three-fold law" states that "the energy one sends out is returned to the sender three-fold." Jade, *To Know,* 47. Farrar, *Witches,* 15, 78.

49. Adler, *Moon,* 7, 101, 105, 147; Starhawk, "Ritual as Bonding: Action as Ritual," *Weaving,* 333–34; Carolyn R. Shaffer, "Spiritual Techniques for

Re-Powering Survivors of Sexual Assault," *Politics*, 465–67; "WITCH: Spooking the Patriarchy during the Late Sixties," *Politics*, 429; Starhawk, "Witchcraft and Women's Culture," *Womanspirit*, 264.

50. Spretnak, "Christian Right," *Politics*, 475.

51. Cunningham, *Return*, 302.

52. Adler, *Moon*, 200, 422–23.

53. Rabbi Johanan (probably second century) stated: "When the serpent copulated with Eve, he infused her with lust." *Babylonian Talmud Yebamoth* 103b, *'Abodah Zarah* 22b, *Shabbath* 146a.

54. Adler, *Moon*, 17–19, 22–23, 147, 400–01.

55. Judith Antonelli, "Feminist Spirituality: The Politics of the Psyche," *Politics*, 399, 403.

56. "Presbyterian Panel Summary" (September 1991): 1–2. For example, the First Presbyterian Church of Urbana published its own guidelines for "The Environmentally Conscious Church" with suggestions on recycling and ecology education. *Monday Morning* 58 (April 5, 1993): 14–15. See also "eco-justice" in *Restoring Creation for Ecology and Justice: A Report Adopted by the 202nd General Asssembly (1990) Presbyterian Church (U.S.A.)* (Louisville: Distribution Management Service, 1990). Berit Kjos concludes her study with ten family ecological projects, as well as several pages of resources. *Under the Spell of Mother Earth* (Wheaton: Victor, 1992), 170–82.

57. Clark Wissler, *Indians of the United States* (2d. ed.; New York: Doubleday, 1966), 8, 63, 71, 131–32, 145, 181, 261, 266, 270, 272, 274, 287; Kjos, *Spell*, 60–61; *The Journal of Christopher Columbus*, trans. Cecil Jane (London: Anthony Blond, 1968), 23–28, 49, 57–58, 86, 102, 124–25, 147–48, 152, 194, 200.

58. Tikva Frymer-Kensky writes that the prophets mainly fought Ba'al and El and we have no clear proof that Goddess was treated as a consort of the God of the Bible. *In the Wake of the Goddesses: Women, Culture, and the Biblical Transformation of Pagan Myth* (New York: Free, 1992), 157–58; Rosemary Radford Ruether, "Sexism and God-Language," *Weaving*, 153.

59. *Prosōpolēmptēs, prosōpolēmpteō, and prosōpolēmpsia* are found only in Christian writers. Walter Bauer, *A Greek-English Lexicon of the New Testament and other Early Christian Literature*, trans. W. F. Arndt and F. W. Gingrich (4th ed.; Chicago: University of Chicago, 1957), 728. *Prosōpon*, "face," and *lambanō*, "I take," are joined into one word to signify "show partiality."

60. Visage: Acts 6:15; Rev. 10:1; 2 Cor. 3:18; James 1:23; will of person or group: Luke 9:51; 2 Cor. 1:11; Acts 5:41; personal attention, favor, or presence: 1 Cor. 13:12; Col. 2:1; 1 Thess. 2:17; 3:10; 1 Pet. 3:12; Jude 16; Rev. 22:4; Matt. 18:10; 2 Cor. 2:10; 4:6; 2 Thess. 1:9; Heb. 9:24; "face" is also used in personification: James 1:11; Matt. 16:3; Luke 21:35.

61. Acts 10:34; 2 Cor. 5:12; Rom. 2:11; Matt. 22:16; Gal. 2:6; 6:3; Eph. 6:9; John 7:24.

62. Deut. 10:17; Col. 3:25; 1 Pet. 1:17.

63. A. Besançon Spencer, *Beyond the Curse: Women Called to Ministry* (Peabody: Hendrickson, 1985), 65–71.

64. The disciples looked on the "outward appearance" when they received the resurrection announcement of Mary Magdalene, Joanna, Mary—mother of James, and the other women as "idle tales" (Luke 24:10–11). Yet the women were the first commissioned apostles and evangelists (Mark 16:7; Matt. 28:7, 10).

65. Gen. 2:23–5; 4:1; 1 Cor. 6:16; Matt. 19:5; Eph. 5:31; Exod. 22:16; Deut. 22:28–29.

66. Shannon Jung, *We Are Home: A Spirituality of the Environment* (New York: Paulist, 1993), 85.

67. John 4:14, 29; A. T. Robertson notes that the woman uses the negative *mē,* not *ou.* "*Ou* would have challenged the opposition of the neighbors by taking sides on the question whether Jesus was the Messiah. The woman does not mean to imply flatly that Jesus is not the Messiah by using *mē ti,* but she raises the question and throws a cloud of uncertainty and curiosity over it with a woman's keen instinct." *A Grammar of the Greek New Testament in the Light of Historical Research* (Nashville: Broadman, 1934), 1167.

▼ Appendix A: *A Personal Journey*

1. This appendix was dictated onto a cassette, taped between March and May 1993, typed by Heidi Hudson, and edited by Aída Besançon Spencer.

2. In 1994 an interchurch organization, "The Way Out Ministries," was begun with these goals:

> 1. *To reach out to people who are pulling or have pulled away from or are attracted to the Craft/Occult/New Age.*
> *How?*
> A. *Model of a Christian*—They need to know and understand someone who has been in the craft before, that you can leave and be victorious through God's grace and the Christian community.
> B. *Model of Christ*—They have a positive view of Christ (cf. people).
> C. *Support*—Support needs to be physical, emotional, mental, and spiritual.
> > 1. people need a *place* to get away and think, where Christ is the foundation, including at times a place to sleep. Different families are needed and a flexible retreat center.
> > 2. *prayer*
> > 3. *hotline*, especially at night (12–3)
> > 4. *support group meeting* (Occult Survivors Anonymous—

people need to be allowed to express feelings, but including Bible Study component) participants must be interviewed first

5. *Written and audio material*—Spiritual Warfare, Bible Promises, tapes, etc.

6. *Various churches* who are willing and prepared (at least two from every church) to help "lambs." Churches' strengths and resource people need to be listed.

7. *diaconal resources* in the area

D. *Training* the Christian participants (and later the larger church) how to minister. Bible Study will be part of this training

2. *To protect all the participants, their families, and the churches from attack*
   A. prayer, communication
   B. interview of new interested people
   C. interchurch ministry, use of different facilities

3. *To support all the Christians participating in this ministry*
   A. clear leadership, resource core group
   B. prayer, protection, education (see "Support")
   C. resource people who can help on what to do in different situations and on different biblical questions

▼ Appendix B: *A Christian Who Was There*

1. See Laurie Cabot, and Tom Cowan, *Power of the Witch* (New York: Delta, 1989), 68–79. The study of the killing of witches could be a multivolume series in itself. However, the simple position that churches and Christians persecuted many innocent people is very distorted. For instance, at the 1692 Salem witch trials, one of the great ironies of history is that Christians were accused, Christians died, Christians tried to stop the trials, and still Christianity gets the blame. Devout lay Christians, such as Martha Cory and Rebecca Nurse were accused, as well as devout ministers George Burroughs and Samuel Willard. The slaves Tituba and John Indian (Carib Indians) teaching the girls Voodoo magic certainly had a hand in bringing in the hosts of the Accuser, the Devil. Boredom, lust for power, money, and property were also crucial factors. Once people were *convicted* of witchcraft, their property was forfeit. Yet Sheriff Corwin and Chief Judge Stoughton took possessions as soon as people were *accused* and only a few people ever got any possessions returned.

Jesus exhibited grace and truth. Neither of those qualities was present at that time. They had no truth because biblical ways to recognize and deal with demonic possession were not used. They had no mercy to the innocent until the criteria for recognizing witchcraft were changed.

Some people who claimed to be Christians were involved in this affair. As Cotton Mather preached: "Tis our Worldliness, our Formality, our Sensuality and our Iniquity that has helped this letting of the Devils in." Fortune-telling and healing by witchcraft was very common in New England as well as Europe during the seventeenth century. Moreover, Salem Village had the reputation of being one of the most contentious communities in the Massachusetts Bay Colony before any witch trials began. The minister Samuel Parris was very judgmental with others. By enslaving two people of Barbados, Tituba and John Indian, Parris was ultimately responsible for the witchcraft they brought with them. The young girls who came to learn Voodoo from Tituba were bored. One accusing adolescent even admitted they were lying "for sport." What opportunities for travel and acknowledgment did a woman, especially a teenager, have in Puritan society anyway?

In contrast to some popular opinion, Marion L. Starkey proves: "Far more ministers were making a stand against prosecution than were lending themselves to it." Almost everyone agreed at the end: "Not God but the devil had been in command here. Their leaders had suffered the devil to guide them." Marion L. Starkey, *The Devil in Massachusetts: A Modern Enquiry into the Salem Witch Trials* (Garden City: Doubleday, 1949), 24–30, 37, 40, 53–55, 67, 77–78, 86, 93, 96, 120–25, 147, 157, 159–60, 176, 180, 191–92, 213, 225–29, 237, 249, 256, 263.

Chadwick Hansen is even stronger: "The popular elements in society (the jury, and the people's representatives in the General Court) were far more ready to believe in witchcraft than the leaders of society (the magistrates and ministers)." "In fact the clergy were, from beginning to end, the chief opponents to the events at Salem." Cotton Mather warned his congregation in "A Discourse on Witchcraft":

> Take heed that you do not wrongfully accuse any other person, of this horrid and monstrous evil. . . . What more dirty Reproach than that of Witchcraft can there be? Yet it is most readily cast upon worthy persons, when there is hardly a shadow of any reason for it. An Ill-look, or a cross word will make a Witch with many people, who may on more ground be counted so themselves. There has been a fearful deal of Injury done in this way in this Town (in *Memorable Providences, Relating to Witchcrafts and Possessions*).

Hansen concludes in *Witchcraft at Salem* that "there was witchcraft at Salem," the majority who were executed were innocent but a few were guilty of witchcraft, and rather than the clergy arousing accusations of witchcraft, they typically tried to keep in check the endemic accusations of witchcraft among the common people: "A witch hunt can occur only when the majority of a community feels itself so beset by malice—real or imagined—that it loses the capacity to distinguish between the innocent and the guilty" (New York: George Braziller, 1969), x, 13, 27–28, 219, 226–27.

Wallace Notestein even writes that "good" witches would even accuse one another so as to ruin a rival's "business." *A History of Witchcraft in England from 1558 to 1718* (New York: Russell and Russell, 1965), 22–23.

2. Frank E. Peretti, *This Present Darkness* (Westchester: Crossway, 1986); *Piercing the Darkness* (Westchester: Crossway, 1989).

3. Benny Hinn, *Good Morning, Holy Spirit* (Nashville: Thomas Nelson, 1990). This book describes the revitalization of Hinn's faith. Unfortunately he also treats metaphorical language literally. God has "mysterious form" with human features. He accentuates the distinctiveness of the Trinity, not God's oneness, 82–83, 139.

4. David Wilkerson, ed., *The Jesus Person Pocket Promise Book* (Ventura: Regal, 1972). Peter himself used *The NIV Bible Promise Book* (Westwood: Barbour Books, 1990); *Precious Bible Promises from the NKJV* (Nashville: Thomas Nelson, 1983); Word Ministries Inc., *Prayers that Avail Much* (Tulsa: Harrison House, 1980).

▼ Appendix C: *"Father" (Patēr) in the Bible*

1. God as *patēr* complete in Old Testament. All New Testament references to *patēr* are included. Other references in Old Testament are samples only.

2. A.T. Robertson, *A Grammar of the Greek New Testament in the Light of Historical Research* (Nashville: Broadman, 1934), 419.

BIBLIOGRAPHY

▼ **Critiques of Goddess Spirituality**

Achtemeier, Elizabeth. *Nature, God, and Pulpit*. Grand Rapids: Eerdmans, 1992.

Achtemeier sees goddess feminism as one way to fill human hunger for reconnection to the natural realm. Her response: God owns the world and we are only stewards of it. Biblical expositions are followed by sample sermons on the chapter topic. Basically a sound approach hampered at times by a neo-orthodox view of the Bible and a Barthian view of nature. In and of itself, nature gives no true knowledge of God. God's revelation in history is essential before nature can reveal the deity.

Balswick, Jack. *Men at Crossroads: Beyond Traditional Roles and Modern Options*. Downers Grove: InterVarsity, 1992.

Binford, Sally R. "Are Goddesses and Matriarchies Merely Figments of Feminist Imagination? Myths and Matriarchies." *The Politics of Women's Spirituality: Essays on the Rise of Spiritual Power Within the Feminist Movement*. Ed. Charlene Spretnak. Garden City: Doubleday, 1982.

Brief essay by secular anthropologist and prehistoric archeologist debunking an early matriarchal period.

Black, Veronica. *A Vow of Silence* (a mystery). New York: St. Martin's, 1990.

Veneration of Mary turns to Goddess worship.

Bloesch, Donald G. *The Battle for the Trinity: The Debate over Inclusive God-Language*. Ann Arbor: Servant, 1985.

Bloesch responds by highlighting God's transcendence and masculinity.

Brooke, Tal. "Gaia—A Religion of the Earth: An Overview." *SCP Journal* 16(1, 1991):4–7.

Chevre, Stuart. "The Gaia Hypothesis: Science, Mythology, and the Desecration of God." *SCP Journal* 16(1, 1991):23–30.

Connor, Tod. "Is the Earth Alive?" *Christianity Today* 37 (January 11, 1993): 22–25.

Culpepper, Emily Erwin. "Contemporary Goddess Theology: A Sympathetic Critique." *Shaping New Vision: Gender and Values in American Culture.* Eds. Clarissa W. Atkinson, Constance H. Buchanan, Margaret R. Miles. The Harvard Women's Studies in Religion Series. Ann Arbor: U.M.I. Research, 1987, 51–71.

She argues against the Mother Goddess as the primary symbol for feminism because Jungian base is too conservative, all women are not mothers, and it is too much like One God/Father. She prefers more pluralistic symbols and placing real, living women ahead of any imagery.

Falk, Marcia. "Notes on Composing New Blessings." McFague, Sallie. "God as Mother." Ruether, Rosemary Radford. "Sexism and God-Language." *Weaving the Visions: New Patterns in Feminist Spirituality.* Eds. Judith Plaskow and Carol P. Christ. San Francisco: Harper, 1989.

Frymer-Kensky, Tikva. *In the Wake of the Goddesses: Women, Culture, and the Biblical Transformation of Pagan Myth.* New York: Free, 1992.

Jewish and evolutionary view of God, yet excellent defense of biblical monotheism.

Gore, Al. *Earth in the Balance: Ecology and the Human Spirit.* Boston: Houghton Mifflin, 1992.

Gore supports the interconnectedness of all humans and nature. Chapters 12 and 13 develop a biblical dominion (not domination) as care and stewardship of God's earth. Ecological problems come from Platonic and scientific thought. Deep ecologists and pantheists are mistaken.

Heine, Susanne. *Matriarchs, Goddesses, and Images of God: A Critique of a Feminist Theology.* Trans. John Bowden. Minneapolis: Augsburg, 1989.

Higher critical German theologian who believes in the evolutionary development of monotheism, argues that in its final form the Bible holds to God the parent, "all in all." "Any name of God which is not understood as an analogy makes God an idol, and that means a tangible or imagined object." She shows that the original matriarchal goddesses were secondary or violent (ch. 2), and the mother-cult reduces women once again to nature, pleasure, and childbearing (ch. 3).

Johnson, Elizabeth A. *Women, Earth, and Creator Spirit.* New York: Paulist, 1993.

She argues with ecofeminists that the exploitation of the earth is linked to the sexist definition and treatment of women. When the relationships of humans with nature, among themselves, and with God are shaped by hierarchical dualism, then disaster occurs. She suggests that humans take on a "kinship" model toward nature and highlight the Spirit as life-giver. It is well written, empathetic, limited by an evolutionary/big bang theory of creation.

————. *She Who Is: The Mystery of God in Feminist Theological Discourse*. New York: Crossroad, 1992.

Catholic panentheistic theologian ably defends the use of female images to disclose Christian truth about God acting in the world, "the creative, relational power of being who enlivens, suffers with, sustains, and enfolds the universe." Instead of "I A.M.," "She Who Is."

Jung, Shannon. *We Are Home: A Spirituality of the Environment*. New York: Paulist, 1993.

A popular positive response to ecofeminism. Advocates appropriating many of their views while still maintaining some uniqueness to the human species.

Kjos, Berit. *Under the Spell of Mother Earth*. Wheaton: Victor, 1992.

A popular book addressed to families who have to deal with ecological emphasis on Gaia. It has good resources and includes chapters on ecofeminism, goddess, and witchcraft and a good appendix on family projects to take care of environment. It is written in a sensationalistic manner to get reader worried, fearful, and upset. She has no empathy for opponents.

Leazer, Gary H. "The New Age Movement and the Environment." *The Earth Is the Lord's: Christians and the Environment*. Eds. R. D. Land and L. A. Moore. Nashville: Broadman, 1992.

Mangalwodi, Vishal. *When the New Age Gets Old: Looking for a Greater Spirituality*. Downers Grove: InterVarsity, 1992.

Chapter 6, "Doing Ecology Is Being Human," critiques goddess spirituality as it affects ecology. Indian Christian brings perspective of a country with traditional Goddess cults.

McFague, Sallie. *The Body of God: An Ecological Theology*. Minneapolis: Fortress, 1993.

McFague has a subtle critique of the deep ecology or creation spirituality that glosses over evil, has an undeveloped sense of the differences in nature, and limits God to the world (pp. 72, 128, 134). She takes as her guiding model the big bang evolutionary theory ("the common creation story") instead of Genesis 1. The world is God's "body," but not God's "face."

————. *Metaphorical Theology: Models of God in Religious Language*. Philadelphia: Fortress, 1982. Pp. 152–64 criticize "revolutionary feminist theology" as promoting stereotypical feminine virtues and uncritically elevating women as savior of self and world.

Moltmann, Jürgen. *The Spirit of Life: A Universal Affirmation*. Trans. M. Kohl. Minneapolis: Fortress, 1992.

He answers the theological quest of the goddess movement to be sensitive to "God's life-giving and life-affirming Spirit." It is excellent, sensitive, and orthodox.

Rose, Ellen Cronan. "The Good Mother." *Ecofeminism and the Sacred.* Ed. Carol J. Adams. New York: Continuum, 1993.
Goddess spirituality invites misogynist rhetoric and is "wholesale regression to infancy, when mother seemed omnipotent."

Ruether, Rosemary Radford. "Feminist Theology and Spirituality." *Christian Feminism: Visions of a New Humanity.* Ed. J. L. Weidman. San Francisco: Harper & Row, 1984.

———. *Gaia and God: An Ecofeminist Theology of Earth Healing.* San Francisco: Harper, 1992.
From a Christian liberal perspective she aims to evaluate objectively strengths and weaknesses of different religions and scientific perspectives on ecology. In ch. 6 she critiques the ecofeminist movement's view that nature originally was paradisaical. Early life was not so egalitarian, peaceful, nor monotheistic as pictured. Moreover, the matricentric pattern is the breeding ground of male resentment as violence. In ch. 8 she presents a positive biblical view of God and nature.

———. "Goddesses and Witches: Liberation and Countercultural Feminism." *The Christian Century* 97 (September 10–17, 1980): 842–47.

———. "Motherearth and the Megamachine." *Womanspirit Rising: A Feminist Reader in Religion.* Eds. C. P. Christ and J. Plaskow. San Francisco: Harper & Row, 1979.

———. "A Religion for Women: Sources and Strategies." *Christianity and Crisis* 39 (December 10, 1979): 307–11.

———. *Sexism and God-Talk: Toward a Feminist Theology.* Boston: Beacon, 1983.
She discredits "Romantic feminism" as unhistoric and sexist. Yet, she believes biblical religion incorporated helpful elements of nonbiblical religion into monotheism.

Sider, Ronald J. "Redeeming the Environmentalists." *Christianity Today* 37 (June 21, 1993): 26–29.
This is a well-balanced essay encouraging environmental concern.

Spencer, Aída Besançon. "Avoiding the 'Either-Or' Trap." *Priscilla Papers* 8 (Spring 1994): 4–5.
The entire issue addresses a November 1993 Christian conference which was affected by goddess spirituality.

———. "God as Mother, not Mother as God: A Biblical Feminist Response to the 'New Feminism.'" *Priscilla Papers* 5 (Fall 1991): 6–11.

Tennis, Diane. *Is God the Only Reliable Father?* Philadelphia: Westminster, 1985.
This is a popular book from a neo-orthodox perspective.

Townsend, Joan B. "The Goddess: Fact, Fallacy and Revitalization." *Goddesses in Religions and Modern Debate.* Ed. Larry Hurtado. Atlanta: Scholars, 1990.
She proves that there was no universal European Goddess religion.

Tucker, Ruth. *Looking for God in All the Wrong Places: Goddess Worship.* Albuquerque, NM: Manna Conference Taping, 1704 Valencia NE, 1993. Cassette.

Weidman, Judith L., ed. *Christian Feminism: Visions of a New Humanity.* San Francisco: Harper & Row. 1984.

▼ Other Works Cited

Abbott, T. K. *A Critical and Exegetical Commentary on the Epistles to the Ephesians and to the Colossians.* The International Critical Commentary. Edinburgh: T. & T. Clark, 1897.

Achtemeier, Paul J. *Romans.* Interpretation: A Bible Commentary for Teaching and Preaching. Atlanta: John Knox, 1985.

Adeyemo, Tokunboh. *Salvation in African Tradition.* Nairobi: Evangel, 1979.

Adler, Margot. *Drawing Down the Moon: Witches, Druids, Goddess-Worshippers, and Other Pagans in America Today.* 2d ed. Boston: Beacon, 1986.

Allen, Paula Gunn. *Grandmothers of the Light: A Medicine Woman's Sourcebook.* Boston: Beacon, 1991.

Anderson, Sherry Ruth, and Patricia Hopkins. *The Feminine Face of God: The Unfolding of the Sacred in Women.* New York: Bantam, 1991.

Anderson, William. *Green Man: The Archetype of Our Oneness with the Earth.* San Francisco: Harper Collins, 1990.

Atkinson, Clarissa W., Constance H. Buchanan, and Margaret R. Miles. *Shaping New Vision: Gender and Values in American Culture.* The Harvard Women's Studies in Religion Series 5. Ann Arbor: U. M. I. Research, 1987.

Bandarage, Asoka. "A Celebration of Spirit." "In Search of a New World Order." *Woman of Power* 21 (Fall 1991): 4, 9–16.

Banks, Robert. *Paul's Idea of Community: The Early House Churches in Their Historical Setting.* Grand Rapids: Eerdmans, 1980.

Barnhouse, Ruth Tiffany. "Homosexuality." *Anglican Theological Review* 6 (June 1976): 107–34.

Baron, Dennis. *Grammar and Gender.* New Haven: Yale University, 1986.

Bartchy, S. Scott. *Mallon Chrēsai: First Century Slavery and the Interpretation of 1 Corinthians 7:21.* Dissertation Series II. Missoula: Scholars, 1973.

Bauer, Walter. *A Greek-English Lexicon of the New Testament and Other Early Christian Literature.* Trans. William F. Arndt and F. Wilbur Gingrich. 4th ed. Chicago: University of Chicago, 1957.

Baumgartner, Anne S. *A Comprehensive Dictionary of the Gods.* New York: Carol Communications, 1984.

Bettenson, Henry, ed. *Documents of the Christian Church.* 2d ed. New York: Oxford University, 1963.

Black, David Alan, Katharine Barnwell, and Stephen Levinsohn, eds.

Linguistics and New Testament Interpretation: Essays on Discourse Analysis.
Nashville: Broadman, 1992.

Blanchard, J. ed. *Scotch Rite Masonry Illustrated. The Complete Ritual of the Ancient and Accepted Scottish Rite, Profusely Illustrated.* Chicago: Charles T. Powner, 1944.

Bloesch, Donald. *Is the Bible Sexist? Beyond Feminism and Patriarchalism.* Westchester: Crossway, 1982.

Bly, Robert. *Iron John.* Reading: Addison-Wesley, 1990.

Boardman, John, Jasper Griffin, and Oswyn Murray, eds. *The Oxford Dictionary of the Classical World.* New York: Oxford, 1986.

Booth, Catherine. *Female Ministry; or, Woman's Right to Preach the Gospel.* London: The Salvation Army, 1859 [1975].

Boyd, Greg. "My Personal Journey." *Priscilla Papers* 6 (Spring-Summer 1992): 19–21.

Bradley, Marion Zimmer. *The Mists of Avalon.* New York: Alfred A. Knopf, 1982.

Brearley, Margaret. "Matthew Fox: Creation Spirituality for the Aquarian Age." *Christian Jewish Relations* 22 (2, 1989): 45.

Bromley, David G., and Anson G. Strupe, Jr. *Strange Gods: The Great American Cult Scare.* Boston: Beacon, 1982.

Brown, Francis, S. R. Driver, and Charles A. Briggs. *A Hebrew and English Lexicon of the Old Testament.* Oxford: Clarendon, 1907.

Bruce, F. F. *The Acts of the Apostles.* 2d ed. Grand Rapids: Eerdmans, 1970.

Bufford, Rodger K. *Counseling and the Demonic.* Resources for Christian Counseling 17. Dallas: Word, 1988.

Bulfinch, Thomas. *The Age of Fable or Beauties of Mythology.* Ed. J. Loughran Scott. Philadelphia: David McKay, 1898.

Bury, R. G., trans. *Plato.* The Loeb Classical Library. 12 vols. Cambridge: Harvard University, 1929.

Bushnell, Katharine C. *God's Word to Women: One Hundred Bible Studies on Woman's Place in the Divine Economy.* New York: Ray B. Munson, [n. d.].

Cabot, Laurie, and Tom Cowan. *Power of the Witch.* New York: Delta, 1989.

Cady, Susan, Marian Ronan, Hal Taussig. *Wisdom's Feast: Sophia in Study and Celebration.* San Francisco: Harper & Row, 1989.

Campbell, Joseph, and Bill Moyers. *The Masks of Eternity.* New York: Apostrophe, 1988.

Carr, Anne E. *Transforming Grace: Christian Tradition and Women's Experience.* San Francisco: Harper & Row, 1988.

Christ, Carol P. *Laughter of Aphrodite: Reflections on a Journey to the Goddess.* San Francisco: Harper & Row, 1987.

————, and Judith Plaskow, eds. *Womanspirit Rising: A Feminist Reader in Religion.* San Francisco: Harper & Row, 1979.

Clanton, Jann Aldredge. *In Whose Image? God and Gender.* New York: Crossroad, 1990.

Collins, Sheila D. *A Different Heaven and Earth*. Valley Forge: Judson, 1974.

Colson, F. H., and G. H. Whitaker, trans. *Philo I*. The Loeb Classical Library. Cambridge: Harvard University, 1929.

Craighead, Meinrad. *The Litany of the Great River*. New York: Paulist, 1991.

————. *The Mother's Songs: Images of God the Mother*. New York: Paulist, 1986.

Crockett, William V., and James G. Sigountos, eds. *Through No Fault of Their Own? The Fate of Those Who Have Never Heard*. Grand Rapids: Baker, 1991.

Cunningham, Elizabeth. *The Return of the Goddess: A Divine Comedy*. Barrytown: Station Hill, 1992.

Daly, Mary. *Gyn/Ecology: The Metaethics of Radical Feminism*. Boston: Beacon, 1978.

Danby, Herbert, trans. *The Mishnah*. Oxford: Oxford University, 1933.

D'Eaubonne, Françoise. *Le Féminisme ou la mort*. Paris: Pierre Horay, 1974.

DeBell, Garrett, ed. *The Environmental Handbook: Prepared for the First National Environmental Teach-In*. New York: Ballantine, 1970.

Delaney, John J., ed. *A Woman Clothed with the Sun: Eight Great Appearances of Our Lady in Modern Times*. New York: Doubleday, 1960.

Deren, Maya. *Divine Horsemen: The Living Gods of Haiti*. New York: McPherson, 1953.

Detering, Deborah L. "Beyond Fathering." *Christianity Today* 27 (January 21, 1983): 45.

Detienne, Marcel, and Jean-Pierre Vernant. *Cunning Intelligence in Greek Culture and Society*. Trans. Janet Lloyd. European Philosophy and the Human Sciences. Atlantic Highlands: Humanities, 1978.

Douglass, Frederick. *Life and Times of Frederick Douglass*. 2d ed. New York: Collier, 1892.

Downing, Christine. *The Goddess: Mythological Images of the Feminine*. New York: Crossroad, 1981.

Duck, Ruth C. *Gender and the Name of God: The Trinitarian Baptismal Formula*. New York: Pilgrim, 1991.

Duncan, Malcolm C. *Duncan's Masonic Ritual and Monitor or Guide to the Three Symbolic Degrees of the Ancient York Rite and to the Degrees of Mark Master, Past Master, Most Excellent Master, and the Royal Arch*. 2d ed. Chicago: Charles T. Powner, 1974.

Edersheim, Alfred. *The Life and Times of Jesus the Messiah*. Grand Rapids: Eerdmans, 1947.

Ehrenzweig, Anton. *The Hidden Order of Art: A Study in the Psychology of Artistic Imagination*. Berkeley: University of California, 1967.

Eller, Cynthia. *Living in the Lap of the Goddess: The Feminist Spirituality Movement in America*. New York: Crossroad, 1993.

Epstein, I., ed. *The Babylonian Talmud*. 36 vols. London: Soncino, 1948.

Erickson, Joyce Quiring. "What Difference? The Theory and Practice of Feminist Criticism." *Christianity and Literature* 33 (Fall 1983): 65–74.

Erickson, Millard J. *Introducing Christian Doctrine*. Ed. L. Arnold Hustad. Grand Rapids: Baker, 1992.

Farrar, Janet and Stewart. *The Witches' Way: Principles, Rituals and Beliefs of Modern Witchcraft*. London: Robert Hale, 1984.

Farrar, Stewart. *What Witches Do: A Modern Coven Revealed*. Custer: Phoenix, 1983.

Ferguson, John. *The Religions of the Roman Empire*. Aspects of Greek and Roman Life. Ithaca: Cornell University, 1970.

Feyerabend, Karl. *Langenscheidt Pocket Hebrew Dictionary to the Old Testament*. New York: McGraw-Hill, 1969.

Finegan, Jack. *Light from the Ancient Past: The Archeological Background of the Hebrew-Christian Religion II*. Princeton: Princeton University, 1946.

Fiorenza, Elisabeth Schüssler. *In Memory of Her: A Feminist Theological Reconstruction of Christian Origins*. New York: Crossroad, 1984.

Foh, Susan T. *Women and the Word of God: A Response to Biblical Feminism*. Grand Rapids: Baker, 1979.

Fowler, James W. *Stages of Faith: The Psychology of Human Development and the Quest for Meaning*. San Francisco: Harper & Row, 1981.

Fox, Matthew. *Creation Spirituality: Liberating Gifts for the Peoples of the Earth*. San Francisco: Harper, 1991.

———. *Original Blessing: A Primer in Creation Spirituality*. Santa Fe: Bear, 1983.

Frazier, James George. *The Golden Bough*. New York: MacMillan, 1951.

Freese, John Henry, trans. *Aristotle XXII: The 'Art' of Rhetoric*. The Loeb Classical Library. Cambridge: Harvard University, 1926.

Frieden, Betty. *The Second Stage*. New York: Summit, 1981.

Frye, Roland Mushat. "Language for God and Feminist Language: A Literary and Rhetorical Analysis." *Interpretation* XLIII (January 1989): 45–57.

Fyfe, W. Hamilton. *Aristotle XXIII: The Poetics*. The Loeb Classical Library. 2d ed. Cambridge: Harvard University, 1932.

Gadon, Elinor W. *The Once and Future Goddess*. San Francisco: Harper & Row, 1989.

Gardner, Gerald B. *Witchcraft Today*. New York: Citadel, 1955.

Gibbs, Nancy. "Fire Storm in Waco." *Time* 141 (May 3, 1993): 26–43.

Gimbutas, Marija. *The Language of the Goddess*. San Francisco: Harper & Row, 1989.

Goldenberg, Naomi R. *Changing of the Gods: Feminism and the End of Traditional Religions*. Boston: Beacon, 1979.

González, Justo L. *Mañana: Christian Theology from a Hispanic Perspective*. Nashville: Abingdon, 1990.

Gray, Elizabeth Dodson, ed. *Sacred Dimensions of Women's Experience*. Wellesley: Roundtable, 1988.

Greeley, Andrew M. *Happy Are the Meek*. New York: Warner, 1985.

Green, Michael. *I Believe in Satan's Downfall*. Grand Rapids: Eerdmans, 1981, or *Exposing the Prince of Darkness*. Ann Arbor: Servant, 1981.

Green, Miranda J. *Dictionary of Celtic Myth and Legend*. London: Thames and Hudson, 1992.

Gruenler, Royce Gordon. *The Trinity in the Gospel of John: A Thematic Commentary on the Fourth Gospel*. Grand Rapids: Baker, 1986.

Guthrie, Donald. *New Testament Introduction*. 3d ed. Downers Grove: InterVarsity, 1970.

Hagen, June Steffensen, ed. *Gender Matters: Women's Studies for the Christian Community*. Grand Rapids: Zondervan, 1990.

Hanlon, Gail. "Creativity and Spirituality: Notes from an Interview with Mayumi Oda." "Homegrown Juju Dolls: An Interview with Artist Riua Akinshegun." "Living in a Liminal Time: An Interview with Jean Shinoda Bolen." *Woman of Power* 21 (Fall 1991): 17–25, 31–35.

Hanon, Geraldine Hatch. "Astrology and the Ritual of Midlife." *Woman of Power* 19 (Winter 1991): 24–27.

Hansen, Chadwick. *Witchcraft at Salem*. New York: George Braziller, 1969.

Harkness, Georgia. *Conflicts in Religious Thought*. New York: Henry Holt, 1929.

Harris, Murray J. *Jesus as God: The New Testament Use of Theos in Reference to Jesus*. Grand Rapids: Baker, 1992.

Harrison, Everett F., ed. *Baker's Dictionary of Theology*. Grand Rapids: Baker, 1960.

Harrison, Roland K. *Introduction to the Old Testament*. Grand Rapids: Eerdmans, 1969.

Hart, John. *The Spirit of the Earth*. New York: Paulist, 1984.

Harvey, Van A. *A Handbook of Theological Terms*. New York: Macmillan, 1964.

Hassey, Janette. *No Time for Silence: Evangelical Women in Public Ministry Around the Turn of the Century*. Grand Rapids: Zondervan, 1986.

Hendricks, William D. *Exit Interviews*. Chicago: Moody, 1993.

Hirsch, Kathleen. "Feminism's New Face." *The Boston Globe Magazine*, 25 February 1990: 18–36.

Hirshberg, Charles, ed. "The Face of God." *Life* 13 (December 1990): 47–78.

House, H. Wayne. "Creation and Redemption: A Study of Kingdom Interplay." *Journal of the Evangelical Theological Society* 35 (March 1992): 3–17.

Humphreys, Colin J. "The Star of Bethlehem, A Comet in 5 B.C. and the Date of Christ's Birth." *Tyndale Bulletin* 43 (May 1992): 31–56.

Hurtado, Larry W., ed. *Goddesses in Religions and Modern Debate*. University of Manitoba Studies in Religion I. Atlanta: Scholars, 1990.

Jackson, Dixie. "The Environmentally Conscious Church." *Monday Morning* 58 (April 5, 1993): 14–15.

Jacobs, Janet L. "Women, Ritual, and Power." *Woman of Power* 19 (Winter 1991): 64–69.

Jade. *To Know: A Guide to Women's Magic and Spirituality.* Oak Park: Delphi, 1991.

———. "To Know Our Goddess-Selves: An Interview." *Woman of Power* 19 (Winter 1991): 14–18.

Jane, Cecil, trans. *The Journal of Christopher Columbus.* London: Anthony Blond, 1968.

Joseph, Lawrence E. *Gaia: The Growth of an Idea.* New York: St. Martin's, 1990.

Jung, Carl G. *Aion: Researches into the Phenomenology of the Self.* Trans. R. F. C. Hull. Bollingen Series XX. 2d ed. Princeton: Princeton University, 1968.

———. *Memories, Dreams, Reflections.* Ed. Aniela Jaffé. Trans. Richard and Clara Winston. 2d ed. New York: Vintage, 1965.

———, and others. *Man and His Symbols.* New York: Doubleday, 1964.

———, and C. Kerényi. *Essays on a Science of Mythology: The Myths of the Divine Child and the Divine Maiden.* Trans. R. F. C. Hull. New York: Harper & Row, 1963.

Kalven, Janet, and Mary I. Buckley, eds. *Women's Spirit Bonding.* New York: Pilgrim, 1984.

Kautzsch, E., ed. *Gesenius' Hebrew Grammar.* 2d ed. Oxford: Clarendon, 1910.

Keen, Sam. *Apology for Wonder.* New York: Harper, 1969.

———. *Fire in the Belly.* New York: Bantam, 1991.

———. *To a Dancing God.* New York: Harper, 1970.

Keller, Catherine. *From a Broken Web: Separation, Sexism, and Self.* Boston: Beacon, 1986.

Kelly, Aidan A. *Crafting the Art of Magic, Book 1: A History of Modern Witchcraft, 1939–1964.* Llewellyn's Modern Witchcraft Series. St Paul: Llewellyn, 1991.

———, ed. *Neo-Pagan Witchcraft I.* New York: Garland, 1990.

Kelly, J. N. D. *Early Christian Doctrines.* 2d ed. New York: Harper & Row, 1960.

Kimel, Alvin F., Jr. *Speaking the Christian God: The Holy Trinity and the Challenge of Feminism.* Grand Rapids: Eerdmans, 1992.

Kinsley, David. *The Goddesses' Mirror: Visions of the Divine from East and West.* Albany: State University of New York, 1989.

Kirk, Janice E., and Donald R. Kirk. *Cherish the Earth: The Environment and Scripture.* Scottsdale, Pa.: Herald, 1993.

Kittel, Gerhard, ed. *Theological Dictionary of the New Testament.* 10 vols. Trans., ed. Geoffrey W. Bromiley. Grand Rapids: Eerdmans, 1964.

Kitzinger, Sheila. *Being Born.* New York: Grosset and Dunlop, 1986.

Koch, Kurt E. *Christian Counseling and Occultism.* Trans. Andrew Petter. Grand Rapids: Kregel, 1965.

Kroeger, Richard Clark, and Catherine Clark Kroeger. *I Suffer Not a Woman: Rethinking 1 Timothy 2:11–15 in Light of Ancient Evidence.* Grand Rapids: Baker, 1992.

Kydd, Ronald A. N. *Charismatic Gifts in the Early Church.* Peabody: Hendrickson, 1984.

Lakshmanan, Indira A. R. "Latter-day Witches Find a Seat in Salem." *The Boston Sunday Globe,* 18 July, 1993: 23, 27.

LaMadeleine, Joe. "Caution! Inclusive Language May Change Your Life!" *Daughters of Sarah* 18 (Summer 1992): 42–43.

Lampe, G. W. H., ed. *A Patristic Greek Lexicon.* Oxford: Clarendon, 1961.

Land, Richard D., and Louis A. Moore, eds. *The Earth Is the Lord's: Christians and the Environment.* Nashville: Broadman, 1992.

Lantero, Erminie Huntress. *Feminine Aspects of Divinity.* Pendle Hill Pamphlet 191. Wallingford: Pendle Hill, 1973.

Larrington, Carolyne, ed. *The Feminist Companion to Mythology.* London: Pandora, 1992.

Lash, John. *The Seekers' Handbook: The Complete Guide to Spiritual Pathfinding.* New York: Harmony, 1990.

Lawrence, Brother. *The Practice of the Presence of God: Being Conversations and Letters of Nicholas Herman of Lorraine.* Trans. Old Tappan: Fleming H. Revell, 1958.

Leek, Sybil. *The Complete Art of Witchcraft.* New York: Thomas Y. Crowell, 1971.

Lewis, C. S. *The Lion, The Witch, and the Wardrobe: A Story for Children.* New York: Collier, 1950.

————. *The Screwtape Letters and Screwtape Proposes a Toast.* New York: Macmillan, 1961.

Liddell, Henry George, and Robert Scott. *A Greek-English Lexicon.* Eds. Henry Stewart Jones and Roderick McKenzie. 9th ed. Oxford: Clarendon, 1940.

Lightfoot, J. B. *St. Paul's Epistle to the Philippians.* Grand Rapids: Zondervan, 1913.

Lovelock, J. E. *Gaia: A New Look at Life on Earth.* 2d ed. Oxford: Oxford University, 1987.

Lyons, John. *Introduction to Theoretical Linguistics.* Cambridge: University, 1968.

MacDonald, George. *The Wise Woman, or the Lost Princess.* Grand Rapids: Eerdmans, 1980.

McGaa, Ed, Eagle Man. *Mother Earth Spirituality: Native American Paths to Healing Ourselves and Our World.* San Francisco: Harper, 1990.

McGregor, Horace C. P., trans. *Cicero: The Nature of the Gods.* The Penguin Classics. Baltimore: Penguin, 1972.

McNabb, Bill. "The Door Interview: Robert Moore." *The Door* 122 (March/April 1992): 10–14.

McNeil, John T., ed. *Calvin: Institutes of the Christian Religion.* 2 vols. Trans. Ford Lewis Battles. The Library of Christian Classics XX. Philadelphia: Westminster, 1960.

Marchant, E. C., trans. *Xenophon: Memorabilia and Oeconomicus*. The Loeb Classical Library. Cambridge: Harvard University, 1923.

Martin, Faith. "Mystical Masculinity: The New Question Facing Women." *Priscilla Papers* 6 (Fall 1992): 1–7.

Mercadante, Linda A. *Gender, Doctrine, and God: The Shakers and Contemporary Theology*. Nashville: Abingdon, 1990.

Merchant, Carolyn. *The Death of Nature: Women, Ecology, and the Scientific Revolution*. San Francisco: Harper, 1989.

Metzger, Bruce M. *Manuscripts of the Greek Bible: An Introduction to Greek Palaeography*. New York: Oxford University, 1981.

Meyer, Birgit. "'If You Are a Devil, You Are a Witch and, If You Are a Witch, You Are a Devil,' The Integration of 'Pagan' Ideas into the Conceptual Universe of Ewe Christians in Southeastern Ghana." *Journal of Religion in Africa* XXII (May 1992): 98–132.

Miller, Elliot, and Kenneth R. Samples. *The Cult of the Virgin: Catholic Mariology and the Apparitions of Mary*. Grand Rapids: Baker, 1992.

Mollenkott, Virginia Ramey. *The Divine Feminine: The Biblical Imagery of God as Female*. New York: Crossroad, 1983.

Montgomery, Helen Barrett, trans. *The New Testament in Modern English*. 2d ed. Valley Forge: Judson, 1952.

Moore, Robert, and Douglas Gillette. *King, Warrior, Magician, Lover*. San Francisco: Harper & Row, 1990.

———. *The King Within: Accessing the King in the Male Psyche*. New York: Morrow, 1992.

Mott, Stephen Charles. "From the Word: Scriptural Faithfulness / Language for the Trinity." *Christian Social Action* (June 1992): 30.

Moulton, James Hope, and George Milligan. *The Vocabulary of the Greek Testament: Illustrated from the Papyri and Other Non-Literary Sources*. Grand Rapids: Eerdmans, 1930.

Nevius, John L. *Demon Possession and Allied Themes: Being an Inductive Study of Phenomena of Our Own Times*. New York: Fleming H. Revell, 1894.

Nilsson, Lennart. *A Child Is Born*. Trans. Clare James. New York: Bantam Doubleday Dell, 1990.

Notestein, Wallace. *A History of Witchcraft in England from 1558 to 1718*. New York: Russell and Russell, 1965.

O'Keefe, Martin D. *Known from the Things That Are: Fundamental Theory of the Moral Life*. Houston: Center for Thomistic Studies, 1987.

Oldfather, C. H., trans. *Diodorus of Sicily*. Loeb Classical Library. 10 Vols. Cambridge: Harvard University, 1935.

Olson, Carl, ed. *The Book of the Goddess Past and Present: An Introduction to Her Religion*. New York: Crossroad, 1990.

Otto, Randall E. "The *Imago Dei* as *Familitas*." *Journal of the Evangelical Theological Society* 35 (December 1992): 503–13.

Peretti, Frank E. *This Present Darkness*. Westchester: Crossway, 1986.

Peters, Ted. *God as Trinity: Relationality and Temporality in Divine Life.* Louisville: Westminster/John Knox, 1993.

Plaskow, Judith, and Carol P. Christ, eds. *Weaving the Visions: New Patterns in Feminist Spirituality.* San Francisco: Harper, 1989.

Polhill, John B. *The New American Commentary: Acts.* Nashville: Broadman, 1992.

Potter, Melissa, and Maria Epes. "The Goddess Altar in Cow Pasture Grove: A Ritual Creation." *Woman of Power* 19 (Winter 1991): 22–23.

Rahner, Karl, and Herbert Vorgrimler. *Theological Dictionary.* Ed. Cornelius Ernst. Trans. Richard Strachan. New York: Herder & Herder, 1965.

Renault, Mary. *The King Must Die.* New York: Pantheon, 1958.

Restoring Creation for Ecology and Justice: A Report Adopted by the 202nd General Assembly (1990) Presbyterian Church (U.S.A.). Louisville: Distribution Management Service, 1990.

Richardson, Cyril C., and others, trans., ed. *Early Christian Fathers.* New York: Macmillan, 1970.

Richardson, Don. *Eternity in Their Hearts.* 2d ed. Ventura: Regal, 1981.

Rienstra, Marchiene Vroon. *Swallow's Nest: A Feminine Reading of the Psalms.* Grand Rapids: Eerdmans, 1992.

Robertson, A. T. *A Grammar of the Greek New Testament in the Light of Historical Research.* Nashville: Broadman, 1934.

Ross, Anne, and Don Robins. *The Life and Death of a Druid Prince.* New York: Summit, 1989.

Rountree, Cathleen. "The Vulva Dance: Notes from an Interview with Arisika Razak." *Woman of Power* 19 (Winter 1991): 48–51.

Ruether, Rosemary Radford. *Womanguides: Readings Toward a Feminist Theology.* Boston: Beacon, 1985.

———, and Eleanor McLaughlin, eds. *Woman of Spirit: Female Leadership in the Jewish and Christian Traditions.* New York: Simon & Schuster, 1979.

Sanford, Agnes. *The Healing Gifts of the Spirit.* Philadelphia: J. B. Lippincott, 1966.

Sciacca, Barbara. "Honoring Our Bodies, Honoring Our Lives." *Woman of Power* 19 (Winter 1991): 62–63.

Sheiner, Marcy. "What Do Men Really Want . . . And Why Should We Care?" [Berkeley] *East Bay Express,* 10 July 1992: 1–15.

Sheville, John, and James L. Gould. *Guide to the Royal Arch Chapter: A Complete Monitor with Full Instructions in the Degrees of Mark Master, Past Master, Most Excellent Master and Royal Arch Together with the Order of High Priesthood.* Richmond: Macoy, 1981.

Shideler, Mary McDermott. *The Theology of Romantic Love: A Study in the Writings of Charles Williams.* Grand Rapids: Eerdmans, 1962.

Sjöö, Monica. "A Letter from Monica Sjöö." *Woman of Power* 19 (Winter 1991): 78–80.

Slater, Philip E. *The Glory of Hera: Greek Mythology and the Greek Family.* Boston: Beacon, 1968.

Smith, Andy. "For All Those Who Were Indian in a Former Life." *Woman of Power* 19 (Winter 1991): 74–75.

Smith, Paul R. *Is It Okay to Call God "Mother": Considering the Feminine Face of God.* Peabody: Hendrickson, 1993.

Spangler, David. "The Meaning of Gaia." *In Context* 24 (1990): 45.

Spector, Rose. "Carol Leonard: Sacred Passages of the Divine Woman." *Earth Star* 14 (February/March 1993): 6–7.

Spencer, Aída Besançon. *Beyond the Curse: Women Called to Ministry.* Peabody: Hendrickson, 1985.

———. "Early-Church Heroines: Rulers, Prophets and Martyrs." *Christian History* 7 (1988): 12–16, and *Priscilla Papers* 7 (Winter 1993): 4–6.

———. "'Fear' as a Witness to Jesus in Luke's Gospel." *Bulletin for Biblical Research* 2 (1992): 59–73.

———. *Paul's Literary Style: A Stylistic and Historical Comparison of II Corinthians 11:16–12:13, Romans 8:9–39, and Philippians 3:2–4:13.* An Evangelical Theological Society Monograph. Winona Lake: Eisenbrauns, 1984.

———. "*Šerîrût* as Self-Reliance." *Journal of Biblical Literature* 100 (June 1981): 247–48.

———, and William David Spencer. *Joy through the Night: Biblical Resources for Suffering People.* Downers Grove: InterVarsity, 1994.

———. *The Prayer Life of Jesus: Shout of Agony, Revelation of Love, A Commentary.* Lanham: University Press of America, 1990.

———. *2 Corinthians.* Bible Study Commentary. Grand Rapids: Zondervan, 1989.

Spencer, William D. "More Than 'Vacuum Cleaner Commandos.'" *Priscilla Papers* 5 (Winter 1991): 1–3.

———. *Mysterium and Mystery: The Clerical Crime Novel.* Carbondale: Southern Illinois University, 1989.

Spretnak, Charlene, ed. *The Politics of Women's Spirituality: Essays on the Rise of Spiritual Power within the Feminist Movement.* Garden City: Doubleday, 1982.

Springer, Christina. "Child-Spirit." *Woman of Power* 19 (Winter 1991): 8–10.

Starhawk. *Dreaming the Dark: Magic, Sex, and Politics.* Boston: Beacon, 1982.

———. *The Spiral Dance: A Rebirth of the Ancient Religion of the Great Goddess.* 2d ed. San Francisco: Harper & Row, 1989.

———. *Truth or Dare: Encounters with Power, Authority, and Mystery.* San Francisco: Harper & Row, 1987.

Starkey, Marion L. *The Devil in Massachusetts: A Modern Enquiry into the Salem Witch Trials.* Garden City: Doubleday, 1949.

Stewart, R. J. *Celtic Gods, Celtic Goddesses.* London: Blandford, 1990.

Thayer, Joseph Henry. *Thayer's Greek-English Lexicon of the New Testament.* 2d ed. Marshallton: National Foundation for Christian Education, 1889.

Thomson, Robert W., ed. *Athanasius: Contra Gentes and De Incarnatione.* Oxford Early Christian Texts. Oxford: Clarendon, 1971.

Tijerina-Jim, Aletícia. "The Sweat Lodge—A Source of Power." *Woman of Power* 19 (Winter 1991): 40–41.

Tillich, Paul. *Systematic Theology I.* Chicago: University of Chicago, 1951.

Traupman, John C. *The New College Latin and English Dictionary.* New York: Bantam, 1966.

Trible, Phyllis. *God and the Rhetoric of Sexuality.* Overtures to Biblical Theology. Philadelphia: Fortress, 1978.

Tucker, Ruth A., and Walter L. Liefeld. *Daughters of the Church: Women and Ministry from New Testament Times to the Present.* Grand Rapids: Zondervan, 1987.

Van Leeuwen, Mary Stewart. *Gender and Grace: Love, Work, and Parenting in a Changing World.* Downers Grove: InterVarsity, 1990.

Vaughan, Genevieve. "Changing Values and Society through Rituals." *Woman of Power* 19 (Winter 1991): 6.

Vickery, Donald M., and James F. Fries. *Take Care of Yourself: Your Personal Guide to Self-Care and Preventing Illness.* 4th ed. Reading: Addison-Wesley, 1990.

Walker, Alice. *The Color Purple.* New York: Harcourt Brace Jovanovich, 1982.

Walker, Sheila S. "Witchcraft and Healing in an African Christian Church." *Journal of Religion in Africa* X (May 1979): 127–38.

Webster, Noah. *Webster's New Universal Unabridged Dictionary.* Ed. Jean L. McKechnie. 2d ed. New York: Dorset & Baker, 1979.

Whitmont, Edward C. *Return of the Goddess.* New York: Crossroad, 1982.

Williamson, G. A., trans. *Eusebius: The History of the Church from Christ to Constantine.* Minneapolis: Augsburg, 1965.

Wilson-Kastner, Patricia, and others. *A Lost Tradition: Women Writers of the Early Church.* Lanham: University Press of America, 1981.

Winddrum, Shakmah. "Unveiling the Mystery of Magic." *Woman of Power* 19 (Winter 1991): 32–33.

Wissler, Clark. *Indians of the United States.* 2d ed. New York: Doubleday, 1966.

Wister, John C., ed. *Woman's Home Companion Garden Book.* New York: Doubleday, 1947.

Wood, Nathan R. *A School of Christ.* Boston: Halliday, 1953.

Wren, Brian. *What Language Shall I Borrow? God-Talk in Worship: A Male Response to Feminist Theology.* New York: Crossroad, 1989.

Yamamoto, J. Isamu, ed. *The Crisis of Homosexuality.* The *Christianity Today* Series. Wheaton: Victor, 1990.

SUBJECT INDEX

SCRIPTURE INDEX